Out of the Closets and into the Courts

OUT OF THE CLOSETS
& into the Courts

Legal Opportunity Structure and Gay Rights Litigation

ELLEN ANN ANDERSEN

THE UNIVERSITY OF MICHIGAN PRESS   ANN ARBOR

Copyright © by the University of Michigan 2005

Published in the United States of America by
The University of Michigan Press
Manufactured in the United States of America
⊚ Printed on acid-free paper

2008   2007   2006   2005   4   3   2   1

A CIP catalog record for this book is available from
the British Library.

Library of Congress Cataloging-in-Publication Data

Andersen, Ellen Ann.
    Out of the closets and into the courts : legal opportunity
structure and gay rights litigation / Ellen Ann Andersen.
        p. cm.
    Includes bibliographical references and index.
    ISBN 0-472-11397-6 (cloth : alk. paper)
    1. Gays—Legal status, laws, etc.—United States.   I. Title.

KF4754.5.A963   2004
342.7308'7—dc22   2004014190

TO MY PARTNER,

Susanmarie Harrington,

AND OUR DAUGHTER,

Sofia Ksenia Andersen Harrington

Contents

Figures

Tables

Acknowledgments

This book was years in the making, and I've accrued many debts in the course of its production. It was both inspired and informed by the ongoing efforts of legal activists to secure basic civil rights for lesbian, gay, bisexual, and transgendered people. My thanks go first to the good people at the Lambda Legal Defense and Education Fund, who allowed me to set up camp in their New York office and plow through thirty years of their organizational records and case files. I am indebted in particular to Executive Director Kevin Cathcart, who gave me the initial permission to examine Lambda's records and whose generosity of spirit revealed itself in the many hours of conversation he spent with me. I am also indebted to Louanne Marchand, Fran Goldstein, Gillian Chi, and Marisol Velazquez, who moved mountains to accommodate both my practical needs (*Is there a desk I can use?*) and my scholarly interests (*Is there any way I can track down this decades-old case?*).

I benefited enormously from the insights of Lambda's litigators, both past and present, who provided me with a wealth of information about specific cases and patiently instructed me in the finer aspects of legal argument. Their voices are heard throughout this book, although in the interests of confidentiality they are rarely identified specifically.

Three women who served as Lambda's legal directors over the years must receive special mention because they each provided invaluable assistance to me. Abby Rubenfeld (director from 1983 to 1988) spent hours on the phone with me filling in the missing pieces of Lambda's legal and organizational history. Paula Ettelbrick (director from 1989 to 1993) did the same for later years. In addition, she planted the seed that germinated into a dissertation, and eventually this book, in the autumn of 1994 when she taught a seminar on sexual orientation and the law at the University of Michigan School of Law. My conversations with her and with my classmates convinced me that the progress of gay rights litigation offered an excellent lens through which to examine the subject of legal change. Beatrice Dohrn (director from 1993 to 2000), likewise filled in missing pieces for me. More than that, however, she pushed me to examine the set of assumptions about the law and legal change I carried with me as a social scientist, which in some cases can be very different from the assumptions held by a practicing movement litigator. My conversations with her helped me to bridge the gap between the two worlds, or at least to recognize where such gaps existed.

Although my focus in this book is on Lambda and its litigation, I did not confine my inquiries to Lambda's litigators. I have benefited greatly from conversations held with others involved in litigation on behalf of gay rights. I am particularly grateful to Kathy Wilde, Michael Hardwick's lead counsel through much of the litigation over the constitutionality of Georgia's sodomy law. Her conversations with me helped me understand the early phase of the case. Beth Robinson was also a treasure. One of the three lead attorneys in the litigation over the constitutionality of Vermont's ban on same-sex marriage, Beth gave me great insight into the behind-the-scenes workings of activists trying to secure the right to same-sex marriage.

I owe myriad intellectual and personal debts to the members of my dissertation committee at the University of Michigan. Kent Jennings, Kim Lane Scheppele, Mayer Zald, and Mark Brandon all "own" a piece of this project. They worked with me for three years to complete the dissertation from which the book emerged, helping me to perform the intricate juggling act of interdisciplinary research. My gratitude is immeasurable.

Many other people also took a hand in this project. David Meyer, Catherine West-Newman, and Jeffrey Bernstein all helped me to engineer my theoretical approach to the subject of movements and legal change. Ken Sherrill read several parts of this manuscript; his insights as both a political scientist and an expert witness in gay rights cases helped me to hone my arguments considerably. Evan Gerstmann lent his ear and his perspective on more than one occasion. Bill Blomquist, Paisley Currah, Paula Denney, Margie Ferguson, Jyl Josephson, Julie Novkov, Liz Shapiro, Joan Sitomer, and Beth Windisch read and commented on chapters along the way, cheered me on, and otherwise pushed and pulled me through the process of writing. Panel members and discussants at various Law and Society meetings and American Political Science Association conferences offered helpful comments on individual chapters; here I'd like to extend special thanks to Scott Barclay, Bradley Canon, Lief Carter, and Michael McCann. Two anonymous reviewers read this manuscript closely and provided cogent critiques; I am very grateful for their time and careful attention to my work. I also need to thank the marvelous editors at the University of Michigan Press for their patience, support, and unwavering faith in this project.

The best parts of this book are the product of the conversations I had with the members of my dissertation committee, Lambda's litigators, and the myriad other people mentioned. They will recognize many of their suggestions in this project. They will also see some of what they warned me against. Any errors or oversights in the following pages are strictly my own.

Institutional support for the development and preparation of the manuscript came from an IUPUI School of Liberal Arts Summer Research Grant as well as a University of Michigan Gerald R. Ford Dissertation Fellowship. The marvelous Kinsey Institute at Indiana University, Bloomington, possessed a nearly complete collection of Lambda's early newsletters, and I am immensely grateful that an institution devoted to preserving historical documents pertaining to sex and sexuality exists.

Finally, Susanmarie Harrington has given me more than I could even begin to catalogue. I married her in 1995, just before I began the research for this project. How the world has changed since then. The concept of same-sex marriage was only beginning to seep into the public consciousness in 1995. As I write these acknowledgments, Vermont recognizes civil unions and Massachusetts issues marriage licenses to same-sex couples. Both of these changes occurred in large part thanks to the efforts of gay rights litigators. And, thanks again to gay rights litigators, Susan and I are both legally recognized as parents to our daughter. What this means is that my partner and I have acquired at least a few of the legal tools we need to protect and care for our family, tools that have long been denied to people in same-sex relationships. Lambda and other gay rights litigators are working hard to ensure that my family gets all the legal protection it needs, and for that I salute them.

ONE

The Puzzle of Gay Rights Litigation

ttorney Bill Thom came across a request for a gay lawyer as he was reading a magazine one day in 1972. Although he was closeted at his midtown Manhattan law firm, Thom was active in the Gay Activists Alliance, one of several gay liberation groups formed in the immediate aftermath of the Stonewall Riot.[1] He decided to reply to the request and discovered that he was the *only* person willing to come forward. As Thom later recalled, the event brought home to him the need for lesbians and gay men to have legal representation. He envisioned an organization that would work to advance gay civil rights just as the National Association for the Advancement of Colored People (NAACP) Legal Defense and Educational Fund had advanced the civil rights of African Americans. Marshaling a small group of gay lawyers, he filed papers in 1972 to create the nation's first public interest law firm dedicated to the advancement of gay rights: the Lambda Legal Defense and Education Fund.[2]

In New York, voluntary associations can only practice law if they are "organized for benevolent or charitable purposes, or for the purpose of assisting persons without means in the pursuit of any civil remedy."[3] To ensure that Lambda's petition for incorporation as a nonprofit law firm met these guidelines, Thom copied verbatim from the application of the Puerto Rican Legal Defense and Education Fund—a group that had been granted approval by the New York courts only a few months earlier. Where the latter application said *Puerto Ricans,* Thom simply altered the text to say *homosexuals.* The completed petition stated that Lambda would engage in a number of activities designed to protect the civil rights of lesbians and gay men, including

> providing without charge legal services in those situations which give rise to legal issues having a substantial effect on the legal rights of homosexuals [Puerto Ricans]; to promote the availability of legal services to homosexuals [Puerto Ricans] by encouraging and attracting homosexuals into the legal profession; to disseminate to homosexuals [Puerto Ricans] general information concern-

ing their legal rights and obligation, and to render technical assistance to any legal services corporation or agency in regard to legal issues affecting homosexuals [Puerto Ricans]. (Quoted in *In re Thom*, 1972, 589)

The application was denied.

According to the three-judge panel assigned to review it, Lambda's purpose was neither benevolent nor charitable. No parallel existed, they wrote, between Lambda and the Puerto Rican Legal Defense and Education Fund. Puerto Ricans needed a legal defense fund because widespread indigence effectively deprived them of legal representation. Homosexuals were in a different situation. While they too faced widespread discrimination, the difficulties they had in securing legal representation merely reflected "a matter of taste" on the part of individual lawyers. In response to this decision, Lambda became its own first client, suing to establish its very right to exist. Thom made two major claims in his appeal to New York's highest court (which is incongruously called the Court of Appeals). Drawing on U.S. Supreme Court precedent holding "collective activity undertaken to obtain meaningful access to the courts [to be] a fundamental right within the meaning of the First Amendment,"[4] he argued that the lower court's decision infringed impermissibly on the speech and association rights of homosexuals. He also argued that the lower court's denial of Lambda's application after approving the virtually identical application of a similarly situated group raised serious equal protection considerations under the Fourteenth Amendment.

Persuaded by Thom's argument, the Court of Appeals reversed the lower court's decision and remanded the case to the lower court for a reevaluation of Lambda's incorporation papers. With little option to do otherwise, the lower court reluctantly granted the application—with one modification. Refusing to lend their approval to the purpose of encouraging homosexuals to enter the legal profession, the three judges used their discretion to strike that clause from Lambda's charter.

The Lambda Legal Defense and Education Fund was officially authorized to practice law on October 18, 1973, nearly eighteen months after the organization was first conceived. Thom deposited twenty-five dollars into a bank account, installed a second phone line in his Manhattan apartment, and added Lambda's name to his mailbox. Lesbians and gay men requesting legal assistance began phoning almost at once.

Lambda's struggle to incorporate speaks volumes about the sociolegal position of lesbian, gay, and bisexual (lgb) people in the 1970s. The notion that homosexuals had the "right" to be free from discrimination based on their sexuality seemed absurd to many. The notion is still a contested one today, but in the intervening years the issue has moved from the fringes of American social consciousness to a central position. The issues in contention have been myriad. The question of gay rights has entered areas as diverse as the bedroom, boardroom, and battlefield. The possibility of same-sex marriage, the creation of civil unions in Vermont, the "Don't Ask; Don't Tell" compromise over military service by lgb people, the referenda on antigay initiatives in several states (most notably Colorado and Oregon), and the criminal regulation of same-sex sexual conduct are among the most visible and fractious of the disputes over the extent and propriety of gay rights.

Yet they are only the tip of the figurative iceberg. The movement has also encompassed a host of other concerns, including AIDS (mandatory testing, patient confidentiality, and employment and housing discrimination); employment (hiring and firing, provision of benefits, and sexual harassment); family (custody, adoption, guardianship, inheritance, and housing); schools (teachers, curricula, library offerings, student groups, and peer harassment); immigration; prison; and even parades.

Lambda has played an important role in all of these issues. Like the civil rights and women's movements before it, the modern gay rights movement has been transformational in nature, in that it has engaged a broad range of issues that deeply affect individual living experiences. It has differed from its predecessors, however, in that the courts have been the primary locus of movement activity. In the years since Lambda's incorporation, virtually every gay rights concern has been the subject of sustained litigation, either by Lambda itself or by the handful of other gay rights law firms that have emerged.

This book is about the role of litigation in the movement for gay rights. More specifically, it seeks to answer two questions. First, under what circumstances are gay rights claims more or less likely to prevail in court? Second, what impact does winning—or losing—in court have on the real lives of lgb people? That is, does litigation matter? Both of these questions tie into large and contentious bodies of scholarly inquiry. I address the first now but hold off on discussing the second until later in the chapter.

Gay Rights in Court

Courts have varied enormously in their treatment of gay rights claims. Two Supreme Court cases dealing with the same subject—the constitutionality of sodomy laws—vividly illustrate this phenomenon.

In *Bowers v. Hardwick* (1986), gay rights litigators attempted to use the courts to overturn a Georgia law that prohibited oral and anal sex, even when performed by consenting adults in private. Such laws were widely considered by activists as the bedrock of discrimination against lgb people because they were invoked to justify discrimination in multiple domains, including employment, military service, housing, public accommodations, immigration, speech and association, custody, adoption, marriage, and the provision of government benefits.[5]

Bowers was a carefully selected test case designed to build on a decade of legal and political mobilization—a decade in which seventeen states had eliminated their sodomy provisions. Lambda, the American Civil Liberties Union (ACLU), and other gay rights activists hoped *Bowers* would serve as the mechanism for voiding sodomy laws in the remaining states. The strategy backfired, however, when the Supreme Court upheld the constitutionality of Georgia's sodomy law by a 5–4 vote. Laws against sodomy had "ancient roots" according to the majority opinion, and against such a legal backdrop the notion that homosexuals had a right to engage in sodomy was, "at best, facetious" (*Bowers*, 192, 193–94).

Seventeen years later, the Supreme Court reconsidered the constitutionality of sodomy laws. Like *Bowers*, *Lawrence v. Texas* (2003) was a test case designed to build on years of political and legal mobilization. By the time Lambda appealed *Lawrence* to the Supreme Court the number of states with sodomy laws had dropped to thirteen; gay rights activists hoped that the high court would strike the remaining laws down. This time they prevailed. In a 6–3 decision, the Court overruled *Bowers*, finding that its "continuance as precedent demean[ed] the lives of homosexual persons" and stating that the gay male couple in the case were "entitled to respect for their private lives" (*Lawrence*, 2482, 2485).

How are we to make sense of the varying ability of Lambda and other litigators to mobilize the law on behalf of gay rights? Existing scholarship on litigation campaigns and legal change offers useful suggestions.

According to the bulk of studies examining litigation campaigns, the primary factor influencing an interest group's or social movement's success in court is its ability to mobilize organizational resources. My reading of the literature finds eight resources to be the most commonly mentioned. They are sufficient staff, preferably "expert," to handle cases in progress and to respond to new litigation opportunities (Manwaring 1962; Meltsner 1973; Sorauf 1976; Tushnet 1987); an internal organization facilitating coordination of litigation efforts (Cowan 1977; Greenberg

1977; Lawrence 1990; Meltsner 1973; Rubin 1987; Sorauf 1976); skill in forming coalitions with allies (Handler 1978; Kluger 1975; Vose 1959); the generation of extra-legal publicity (Cortner 1968; Vose 1959); adequate funding to support the litigation campaign (Cortner 1968; Handler 1978; Olson 1984; Rubin 1987; Sorauf 1976; Tushnet 1987; Vose 1959); control over the initiation and progress of litigation (Kluger 1975; Sorauf 1976; Wasby 1983); a sufficiently long time line to litigate repeatedly (Galanter 1974; Greenberg 1977; Kluger 1975; Vose 1959); and support from the Department of Justice and/or the solicitor general (Cortner 1968; Krislov 1963; Vose 1959).

It seems abundantly clear at this point that any account of Lambda's varying ability to mobilize the law on behalf of gay rights must carefully consider Lambda's access to organizational resources. But an emerging body of scholarship on the courts and legal change suggests that an account that focused solely on Lambda's ability to marshal resources would miss crucial aspects of the story. In recent years, sociolegal scholars have begun to embrace an approach known as "new institutionalism"[6] to examine the circumstances under which legal change does and does not occur. This approach emphasizes the relationship between actors and the sociopolitical institutions within which they operate. In other words, new institutionalist approaches take as their frame of reference what Theda Skocpol (1984, 1) has called "the interplay of meaningful actions and structural contexts."[7]

Scholars working within the vein of new institutionalism have emphasized a wide variety of structural determinants. Some have concerned themselves primarily with endogenous constraints on the courts, examining such factors as the norm of collegiality on multimember courts, the "rule of 4" for granting certiorari in the U.S. Supreme Court, and the legal requirements for filing lawsuits (Epstein and Knight 1998; Kahn 1999; Maltzman, Spriggs, and Wahlbeck 2000). Others have focused more on the constraints placed on the courts by exogenous institutions such as the legislative and executive branches, organized interests, and the population at large (Epp 1998; Epstein and Kobylka 1992; Eskridge and Frickey 1994). Still others have looked at the relationship between courts and deeply embedded social structures such as race, class, and gender (Kahn 1996; Smith 1995). Most commonly, though, scholars pick and choose several different kinds of constraints from the grab bag of institutional possibilities.

From a new institutionalist perspective, any explanation of why Lambda and other organized litigators have been more successful in some cases than in others must weigh Lambda's actions against the larger legal and political institutions within which gay rights claims are made.[8] It follows that this account must also identify *which* of the myriad possible institutional factors are relevant at any particular point and articulate the ways in which these institutional factors interact both with Lambda and with each other to facilitate or retard legal change.

In this book I develop and deploy a theoretical perspective that does just that. Specifically, my legal opportunity structure (LOS) approach seeks to explain the dynamics of legal change through an examination of the institutional and sociolegal factors that shape the decisions made by legal actors. This theoretical perspective draws heavily on recent social movement scholarship on political opportunity structure (POS) and frame alignment processes. I lay out the central features of these two concepts next.

Structuring Political Opportunity

In recent years, the concept of political opportunity structure has emerged as the most promising method of integrating the emergence, progress, and outcomes of social movements with the social context in which they operate. Political opportunity structure refers broadly to the institutional and sociocultural factors that shape social movement options—by making some strategies more appealing and/or feasible than others.

Peter Eisenger coined the term in his study of protest in forty-three American cities.[9] His argument was that the incidence of protest was related to the ability of potential protestors to "gain access to power and to manipulate the political system [from within]" (Eisenger 1973, 25). Likewise, Doug McAdam (1982) found that the rise of black insurgency in the United States in the period from 1930 to 1954 was due in large part to shifting political conditions resulting from greater black urbanization, education, and income levels. In the twenty-five or so years since its origination, the concept of political opportunity has become a staple in the study of social movements. It has been used to examine causes as diverse as the civil rights movement (Button 1989; McAdam 1982); the women's movement (Banaszak 1996; Costain 1992); the labor movement (Burstein 1991; Ruggie 1987); and the antinuclear movement (Kitschelt 1986; Meyer 1993). One of the great strengths of political opportunity structure as a concept is its balancing of agency between state and social movement (Gamson and Meyer 1996). The political configuration of the state shapes the opportunities afforded to movements; shifts in that configuration can open or close "windows" for action. Conversely, social movements can influence the political configuration of the state; through their actions, they can forge opportunities.

A corresponding weakness of the concept is its definitional plasticity. Sidney Tarrow (1988, 430) has argued that political opportunity "may be discerned along so many directions and in so many ways that it is less a variable than a nest of variables—some more readily observable than others." The precise specification of its dimensions has varied, almost scholar by scholar. However, general agreement exists on three dimensions: *access to the formal institutional structure, availability of allies,* and the *configuration of power with respect to relevant issues/challengers* (see, e.g., Kriesi et al. 1992; McAdam, Tarrow, and Tilly 1996; Tarrow 1994).

A fourth dimension—the *underlying political culture*—is more contested. Some scholars argue that cultural factors play an important role in shaping social movement options, while others ignore this dimension. Still others recognize the importance of cultural factors in shaping opportunities for movement activity but argue that they are not properly elements of *political* opportunity.[10]

William Gamson and David Meyer suggest a simple and elegant way to conceptualize political opportunity, one that encompasses underlying political culture as well as the other three dimensions. The core idea weaving together the various threads of political opportunity structure, they argue, is the *opening and closing of space for action:* "Increased opportunity implies more space and fewer constraints. When we compare opportunities, we do so across political systems or over time. Adverse circumstances exist in one system and more favorable ones in another; or within a single system, circumstances become more or less favorable over time" (Gamson and Meyer 1996, 277).

Frame Alignment Processes

A frame, as Erving Goffman defined the term, is composed of the implicit rules that, by defining the situation, shape the meanings generated by that situation. In other words, a frame is a sort of interpretive schematic that allows us "to locate, perceive, identify and label" aspects of an event in ways that make them meaningful (Goffman 1974, 21).

In recent years, scholars have made use of Goffman's notion of frames to explain the progress and outcomes of social movement claims. Successful framing occurs when a speaker's discussion of a subject leads the receiver of the discussion to alter the criteria on which she judges the subject. To succeed in her task, the speaker must package her discussion in a manner that resonates with the beliefs of the receiver. David Snow and his colleagues (Snow et al. 1986) refer to this packaging of claims as the process of frame alignment.

The process of frame alignment mediates between opportunity and action. The ability of social movements to push the right buttons depends on the availability of cultural frames. Movements "draw on the existing cultural stock for images of what is an injustice" (Zald 1996, 266) and to suggest directions for change. This cultural stock in turn shapes the kinds of claims that can be made. So, for example, Mayer Zald (1996) discusses how the feminist claim of a woman's right to her own body makes sense only in a cultural context that embodies notions of individual autonomy and citizen equality. Shifts in the existing cultural stock may open up—or close down—framing opportunities for movements. For example, the occurrence of a critical event such as September 11, Three-Mile Island, the Hill-Thomas hearings, or the murder of Matthew Shepard can draw attention to issues and influence public attitudes. The gradual revelation of what Zald calls "cultural contradictions" (268) can also shift the cultural stock. Cultural contradictions occur when cultural themes that are potentially in conflict (such as individuality and equality) are brought into active conflict by the force of events or, alternately, when articulated ideologies are not reflected in actual practices.

Structuring Legal Opportunity

A core contention of this book is that the concepts of opportunity structures and frame alignment processes can be utilized to provide a theoretical framework for understanding the conditions under which interactions between or among legal actors and the various institutions in which they are embedded operate to facilitate or retard legal change. This approach is not necessarily incompatible with studies that focus on the mobilization of organizational resources in accounting for litigation strategies and outcomes. Factors such as funding and internal organization continue to matter in my telling of the tale, although they recede into the background. What becomes central in my account are the ways in which sociolegal structures shape movement strategies and are shaped by those strategies in turn. As I will show, several of the most commonly articulated dimensions of *political* opportunity structure—access to the formal institutional structure, the configuration of power with respect to relevant issues, and the availability of allies—are also dimensions of *legal* opportunity structure. In the following pages, I lay out the three dimensions of legal opportunity structure (LOS) that have rough equivalents in political opportunity structure. I then lay out the dimension of LOS that makes it distinct from its political counterpart.

Access

Scholars of political opportunity structure have noted with near unanimity that the extent of access to the formal institutional structure (such as legislatures) significantly shapes the emergence, progress, and outcomes of collective action (see, e.g., Kitschelt 1986; Rucht 1996; Tarrow 1994). Peter Eisenger (1973, 15), for example, argues that collective action is most likely to occur in systems that are open to some kinds of political participation but closed to others.

Much as access to political institutions shapes the emergence, progress, and outcomes of collective action, access to courts shapes the emergence, progress, and outcomes of legal action. Eva Rubin summarizes the situation clearly when she says: "Although courts offer an alternate route to policy change, they have their own institutional peculiarities and idiosyncrasies. The mechanics of the judicial process [are] very different from that of the legislative process, and the approach to judicial institutions must be made in the traditional framework of the lawsuit" (Rubin 1987, 33).

The mechanics of the judicial process shape access in a number of important ways, including what may be litigated, who may litigate, and where such litigation may occur. As noted previously, would-be litigants must show that they have standing to sue. The type of claim they make also affects where they can litigate. By way of illustration, claims arising under the federal Constitution may generally be brought in *either* federal or state court, while claims invoking a state's constitutional provisions but not federal constitutional provisions can only be heard in that state's courts.

Legal access requirements thus shape the options available to activists who hope to mobilize the law on behalf of social movement goals. For example, John McCarthy (1996, 146) notes that many American movements have spawned organizations that specialize in legal strategies and tactics. (He refers to them as movement law firms.) The peace movement, however, is a notable exception. The reason the peace movement has not spawned any movement law firms, he argues, is that peace activists have been unable to get standing in U.S. courts to challenge the U.S. government's use of violence abroad.[11]

It is important to recognize here that access to the legal system is not an unmitigated benefit. When access to the courts has been discussed in the larger literature on groups in court, it has been in the context of gaining entry to the courts to secure legal rights.[12] Yet access to the courts is not a one-way street, not simply a matter of the legal system being open or closed to a set of potential litigants. It is also a matter of whether the courts are open to those who would act in opposition.

Configuration of Power

In addition to access to the institutionalized political system, scholars of political opportunity structure have paid much attention to what Hanspeter Kriesi and his colleagues (1992, 220) call "the configuration of elites with respect to a given challenger" and what Doug McAdam (1996, 27) calls "the stability or instability of that broad set of elite alignments that typically undergird a polity." Sidney Tarrow (1994, 88) argues, for example, that conflicts within and among political elites serve as an incentive to resource-poor groups to risk collective action.

The configuration of power similarly serves to influence the emergence, progress, and outcomes of legal action. The elites in LOS are generally judges.[13] Imagine, for example, a universe of judges presented with a particular legal claim. The judges may align themselves in one of three ways: they may uniformly reject the claim, they may uniformly accept the claim, or they may be divided among themselves with respect to the claim's legal implications. Legal claims that are uniformly rejected exit the litigation process. Claims that are uniformly accepted also exit the litigation process, because they get settled out of court. Where judges are divided, however, further litigation of the claim is stimulated and legal ammunition is provided for both sides to the dispute. H. W. Perry illustrates the implications of judicial conflict in his study of the Supreme Court certiorari process. The single most important factor in determining a case's "certworthiness," he argues, is the existence of a conflict among the circuit courts (Perry 1991).

The perspectives of individual judges thus affect the progress and outcomes of social movement litigation. Anyone familiar with appellate litigation knows that judges hearing the same case often come to diametrically opposing conclusions. Whether these disagreements are a product of legal or political differences is unimportant for the moment. What is important is that claims that more directly touch on legal and/or political fissures are more likely to spark significant disagreement among judges. Moreover, turnovers in the population of judges may open (or close) windows of opportunity for legal action.

Alliance and Conflict Systems

The presence or absence of allies is a third aspect of the structure of political opportunities. Craig Jenkins and Charles Perrow (1977), for example, found that the farm worker movement in the 1960s was more successful than its 1940s counterpart largely because of the existence of urban liberal allies in the latter period. Similarly, William Gamson (1975) found that differential success rates on the part of fifty-three challenging groups were closely related to the availability of allies willing and able to support their claims. By creating political openness on their issues of concern, social movements almost always generate their own opposition (Meyer and Staggenborg 1996). "Consensus movements"—those that enjoy widespread support and little opposition—are uncommon, and when they arise they tend to be local and short-lived (McCarthy and Wolfson 1992). Opposition to social movement concerns, when it occurs, may coalesce into one or more countermovements—such as the pro-choice and pro-life movements—or may remain fragmented and sporadic. Regardless of the form that opposition takes, the relationship between movement and state is rarely dyadic but instead is mediated by the movement's opposition.

The presence of allies and/or opponents is also an aspect of legal opportunity structure. Allies can defray the substantial costs of bringing a case. They can offer assistance with devising legal strategies. They can also file amicus curiae (friend of the court) briefs. These briefs can signal the importance of the case under consideration, provide supplemental legal arguments, and add credibility to claims made by challengers.[14] This is precisely the reason why amicus briefs from the solicitor general are widely sought.

Given the adversarial form of the American legal system, articulated opposition to a legal claim is generally a given. Opponents (and their allies) work to undermine legal claims in just the same way that allies work to support them. Claims making is, at heart, a strategic activity. Movement litigators seek to redefine an existing legal condition as unjust and to identify a strategy for redressing the problem. Opposing litigators in turn seek to prevent them from successfully engaging in such redefinition. Opponents can also do something allies cannot, namely, appeal adverse decisions. Ironically, once a challenger wins a case, she loses control of it. Unless the case is decided by a court of last resort, such as the U.S. Supreme Court (and sometimes state supreme courts), her opponent controls what happens next. He may choose to abide by the adverse decision, or he may choose to appeal it to a higher court.

Cultural and Legal Frames

Were the dimensions of LOS limited to those listed previously, it would simply be political opportunity structure by another name. What makes *legal* opportunity different from *political* opportunity are the underlying frames that ground them. As we have seen, movements seeking to effect change within the political system must draw on the existing cultural stock to frame their claims. Movements seeking to effect change within the legal system are likewise constrained by availability of cultural stock. However, they are also constrained by the availability of *legal* stock. That is, they must articulate their claims so that they fall within the categories previously established by an amalgam of constitutional, statutory, administrative, common, and case law. These laws shape the progress and outcome of movement claims in important ways.

First, laws shape the *kinds* of legal claims that can be made as well as the *persuasiveness* of those claims. For example, under Alaska case law, a parent's sexual orientation is considered to be irrelevant in determining custody (*S.N.E. v. R.L.B.*, 1985). In Missouri, however, courts generally have treated homosexuality as prima facie evidence of parental unfitness (*DeLong v. DeLong*, 1998). A (hypothetical) lesbian woman who would have maintained custody of her children were she living in Alaska would likely have lost custody of her children were she living in Missouri.

Second, the laws also structure the *facts that are considered to be relevant*, just as the facts of the case determine the legal categories that will be invoked. For example, hemophiliacs attempting to sue blood banks for transfusion-related AIDS have consistently had to contend with the question of whether blood products are properly categorized as a product or a service. The distinction is crucial because it determines the kinds of things for which blood banks can be held accountable. If the provision of blood products to hemophiliacs (via doctors) by blood banks is a sale, then the provider of the blood product can be held responsible for any damage the product causes when used properly, whether or not negligence is involved.[15] If the provision of blood products is a service, however, then the provider of the service cannot be held liable for damages without a showing of negligence. In other words, if the provision of blood products is a sale, then the fact that hemophiliacs received AIDS from a blood-related transfusion matters. If it is a service, then that fact does not matter, unless negligence on the part of the blood banks is also established.

A major difference between legal and cultural frames is the *relationship of the past to the present*. One of the rules of the game in judicial decision making is that new decisions are constrained by previous ones.[16] To return to the example of hemophiliacs, the ability of courts to make decisions about AIDS was constrained by existing statutes and precedents. Many states have blood shield laws that protect hospitals, doctors, blood banks, and pharmaceutical companies from certain kinds of damage-related claims for the provision of contaminated blood. These laws were originally enacted to protect hospitals and others from liability for hepatitis contamination, which prior to 1985 was endemic in the blood supply. Their existence, however, unavoidably structured later claims about transfusion-related AIDS.

With respect to the law, it is generally *not* the specific factual outcome of a case that structures future litigation in the area but rather the manner in which the outcome is framed. In *Roe v. Wade* (1973), for instance, the U.S. Supreme Court accepted the privacy framing advanced by Roe in her attempt to void Texas's abortion statute. Since that decision, the lion's share of litigation around abortion has concerned the extent to which the state can permissibly limit that right to privacy.[17] Had the Court's decision been framed differently, the path of subsequent litigation would have been significantly altered.[18]

Shifts in legal stock can create (or foreclose) opportunities for movements to frame their claims successfully, independently of shifts in the social stock. However, it is important to understand that the legal and cultural frames do not exist in isolation from each other, nor is there a clear hierarchy among them. Just as judges do not divest themselves of their political sensibilities when they don their robes, the existence of those political sensibilities does not make the doctrinal framework in which they operate irrelevant. Legal and cultural frames are mutually constitutive: cultural symbols and discourses shape legal understandings just as legal discourses and symbols shape cultural understandings. This is precisely why movements throughout American history have invoked *legal* norms and practices in their efforts to promote *social* change and conversely why shifting social norms have often been followed by shifting interpretations of what the law requires.

Litigation Success and Social Reform

This book takes the concept of legal opportunity structure and uses it to explore the varying ability of Lambda and other gay rights litigators to mobilize the law successfully on behalf of gay rights. Much of it focuses on the factors that facilitate or retard success in the courtroom. That is only half the story, however. The other half concerns the impact of litigation on lived experiences. Litigation outcomes are not self-implementing. They must be interpreted and actualized by actors beyond the courtroom. To what extent are legal victories translated into real-world gains for lgb people?

Great disagreement exists about the empirical power of litigation to effect social reform. Gerald Rosenberg is widely considered to be the standard bearer of the proposition that the judiciary's ability to advance progressive social reform is, at best, limited, subject largely to the reactions of the legislative and executive branches (Rosenberg 1991; see also Horowitz 1977). In his book *The Hollow Hope*, Rosenberg sought to assess the conditions under which judicial processes could be utilized to secure significant social change through an examination of several major decisions, including *Brown v. Board of Education* (1954) and *Roe v. Wade* (1973). He concluded that courts are not only poorly designed to advance social change, by acting as "fly-paper," but they may actually impede social change efforts. He writes:

> Turning to courts to produce significant social reform substitutes the myth of America for its reality. It credits courts and judicial decisions with a power they do not have. (Rosenberg 1991, 338)

And also,

> Yet if groups advocating such reform continue to look to the courts for aid, and spend precious resources in litigation, then the courts also limit legal change by deflecting claims from substantive

political battles, where success is possible, to harmless legal ones where it is not. Even when major cases are won, the achievement is often more symbolic than real. Thus, courts may serve an ideological function of luring movements for social reform to an institution that is structurally constrained from serving their needs, providing only an illusion of change. (341)

Even worse, he continues, progressive court decisions are actually more likely to serve as a rallying cry for opponents of social reform than for its proponents. Reformers, he concludes, should largely abandon the courts and instead focus their efforts on the political arena.

A number of scholars have taken issue with Rosenberg's conclusions, arguing, among other things, that legal decisions have been important factors in the generation of sociopolitical reform. A few have directly contradicted his analysis, concluding that legal decisions are responsible for producing major social changes (see especially Schultz 1998). Others have offered more elliptical critiques. In a study commonly treated as a reply to Rosenberg, Michael McCann (1994) examined pay equity reform battles and concluded that litigation and other legal mobilization tactics have the capacity to generate *indirect* effects—such as constituent mobilization and increased leverage in workplace negotiations—even when court rulings themselves fail to directly produce significant social reform.

If Rosenberg's argument is correct, then Lambda and its litigation have played a negligible—perhaps even negative—role in the struggle for gay rights. If his critics have the better argument, then we should expect to see positive real-world impact from Lambda's litigation, whether directly or indirectly. My study of Lambda and its litigation mediates between the positions taken by Rosenberg and his critics. From an LOS perspective, litigation and legal decisions are best treated as creating moments of opportunity bounded by the specific legal and political contexts in which they occur. Activists may or may not be successful in exploiting these opportunities, both because of their own strategic choices and because of the bounded nature of the opportunities presented. As we shall see in subsequent chapters, litigation can thus have consequences both intended and unintended. Most notably, courtroom victories can result in political losses rather than gains, just as courtroom losses can actually help to produce political gains. An LOS perspective, then, can help to illuminate both the promise and the limits of legal mobilization as a tactic for securing social reform.

I begin this study by exploring the question of why litigation emerged as a tactic in the gay rights movement when it did (chapter 2) and by presenting a general overview of Lambda and its litigation from its emergence in 1973 through June of 2003 (chapter 3). These two chapters show that the emergence and progress of gay rights litigation were products of both shifts in the LOS and the increasing capacity of gay rights litigators to respond to those opportunities.

I then turn to an examination of the efforts of Lambda and other gay rights litigators to mobilize the law in three different issue areas: sodomy reform, antigay initiatives, and same-sex marriage. Chapters 4 and 5 focus on the stop-and-start progress of sodomy reform efforts. They show that shifts in the structure of legal opportunities over time have variously opened up and closed down spaces for successful legal and political challenges to sodomy laws. The disjoint between the political and legal outcomes of antigay initiatives is the subject of chapter 6. This chapter illustrates the very real differences between the structure of legal opportunities and the structure of political opportunities. Chapter 7 explores the ongoing controversy over the question of same-sex marriage, paying particular attention to the ways in which LOS can vary from state to state and the ways in which changes in the structure of legal opportunities are mediated by the existing structure of political opportunities. Chapter 8 draws the three case studies together, illuminating the complex relationship between the structure of legal opportunities and the varied legal fortune of gay rights claims and asking critical questions about the value of legal rights. A short afterword updates this study to include a discussion of the recent Massachusetts marriage case, *Goodrich v. Dept. of Public Health* (2003).

TWO

LOS and the Emergence of Gay Rights Litigation

A cursory glance at the legal treatment of (suspected) homosexuals before the formation of Lambda indicates that Bill Thom was right: gay men and lesbians needed legal representation, and they needed it badly. Prior to the 1970s, every state in the nation except Illinois criminalized sodomy, and although almost all laws prohibited *both* opposite-sex and same-sex sodomy, enforcement activities were directed primarily at gay men. Police surveillance of locations where "known homosexuals" congregated was not uncommon. Bars were especially susceptible; patrons were regularly arrested and liquor licenses often revoked. John D'Emilio has estimated that tens of thousands of lgb people were arrested each year during the 1950s (D'Emilio 1986, 919).[1]

Of course, the legal problems of lgb people went far beyond bar raids. Under the Immigration and Nationality Act of 1952,[2] for example, homosexuality was considered to reflect a "psychopathic personality" and constituted a ground for deportation—a policy upheld by the Supreme Court in 1967 in *Boutellier v. Immigration and Naturalization Service* (1967). Lesbians and gay men were also barred from many jobs in government. Governmental documents show that nearly five thousand people were discharged from military or other governmental employment because of their homosexuality in the years between 1947 and 1950, while an additional seventeen hundred applicants for governmental positions were refused employment because of their homosexuality (Adam 1995). In the early 1950s, the military discharged some two thousand lgb people a year; by the early 1960s, the figure rose to an average of three thousand a year (D'Emilio 1983). The military policy was particularly problematic, because those suspected of homosexuality were subject to court-martial and discharge under "other than honorable" conditions.

The McCarthy hearings in the 1950s made the reasons for this policy explicit: homosexuals were unsuitable for government service because the criminality of sodomy both revealed their "low morality" and made them susceptible to blackmail. In the words of then–senator Kenneth Wherry: "You can't hardly separate homosexuals from subversives. . . . Mind you, I don't say every homosexual is a subversive, and I don't say every subversive is a homosexual. But [people] of low morality are a menace in the government, whatever [they are], and they are all tied up together" (quoted in Faderman 1991, 143).

Despite—and perhaps because of—the pervasive climate of hostility, lgb people rarely challenged the treatment they received at the hands of police, employers, and government in general. Those swept up in police raids, for example, rarely contested their arrests.[3] As one defense lawyer practicing during the 1950s and 1960s noted, "Most of the gay men who were arrested were so ridden with guilt and so afraid of exposure that they couldn't imagine facing a jury trial" (quoted in Marcus 1992, 148). And even when lesbians and gay men fought for their rights in court, they tended to raise procedural rather than substantive challenges to the legality of governmental actions. For instance, when Frannie Clackum was dishonorably discharged from the Air Force in 1952 on the basis of her alleged lesbianism, the Air Force refused to inform her of the specific charges against her and refused to allow her a trial by court-martial so she could defend herself.[4] Clackum subsequently challenged the *way* she was discharged rather than the *right* of the military to discharge her. (In fact, she consistently denied allegations of lesbianism.)[5]

To make matters even more difficult, those lgb people willing to fight for their rights often had a difficult time finding lawyers willing to take on cases involving homosexuality. Whether this was because of personal distaste, legal analysis, or the fear of being thought gay themselves is unknown. Even the ACLU regularly refused to take on gay rights cases, arguing that there was no constitutional right to "practice homosexual acts." A policy statement the group issued in 1957 supported the constitutionality of sodomy statutes as well as federal security regulations excluding homosexuals from employment.[6]

As this overview shows, lesbians and gay men faced myriad legal consequences because of their sexual orientation. By emphasizing the kinds of concerns that appeared in court, however, I do not mean to imply that these were the only issues of legal consequence. Like gender and race, sexual orientation deeply affects individual living experiences in a wide variety of contexts. Prior to the 1970s, many of the core sociolegal concerns of lesbians and gay men had never been addressed by the courts. The range of issues *not* litigated included discrimination in private employment, housing, and public accommodations. With the notable exception of divorce, family law matters were virtually absent as well.[7] In her comprehensive survey of the civil cases dealing with homosexuality, Rhonda Rivera (1979) uncovered only three custody cases involving parental homosexuality.[8] Questions of marriage or other mechanisms for protecting same-sex partnerships were certainly never raised, nor were adoption, foster care, or guardianship.

It was not until the late 1960s and early 1970s that litigation began to assume any sort of prominent role as a tactic to advance the interests of lgb people. The ACLU was the first organized entity to enter the fray, when in 1967 it reversed its policy stance and started challenging governmental regulation of homosexuality across a number of fronts, including police harassment, employment, and immigration. Lambda filed its incorporation papers in 1972. By the end of the decade, the New York–based Lambda was joined by several other groups dedicated to litigating on behalf of lgb people, including the Gay Rights Advocates (GRA) and the Lesbian Rights Project—both based in San Francisco— the Boston-based Gay and Lesbian Advocates and Defenders (GLAD), and the Texas Human Rights Foundation.

Why did organized litigation on behalf of gay rights appear when it did? In the following pages, I show that the emergence of this litigation was precipitated by several changes in the LOS, including shifts in both the legal and the cultural stock and the increased visibility of elite divisions over the criminalization of consensual sexual behavior.

Conflicts among Legal Elites: The Model Penal Code

The American Law Institute (ALI) is an organization of some fifteen hundred legal scholars and practitioners whose work in drafting model laws has influenced the development of many different legal areas. In the 1950s, it began drafting a Model Penal Code, designed to standardize and simplify the myriad laws of the fifty states. A draft was published in 1955 and the code was completed in 1962. Part of the document made what its drafters called a "fundamental departure from prior law" in decriminalizing all "deviate sexual intercourse" performed in private by consenting adults as well as adultery and fornication (ALI 1962). By *deviate intercourse* the ALI meant all forms of anal and oral sex, as well as mutual masturbation and penetration by inanimate objects.

The organization's primary reason for departing from prior law concerned the distinction between civil and religious responsibilities. As the

ALI saw it, adultery, fornication, and "atypical" sexual practices performed in private by consenting adults fell under the provenance of spiritual rather than civil authorities because they did not harm the secular interests of the community. Moreover, the ALI argued, individuals were fundamentally entitled to protection against state interference in their personal affairs so long as they were not hurting others.[9]

The proposal to decriminalize deviate sexual intercourse sparked controversy within the ALI's own ranks. Its Advisory Committee was the first to consider the recommendations made by the committee in charge of drafting the Model Penal Code; after consideration, it endorsed the code and sent it on to the Governing Council. The council, however, endorsed continued criminalization in a sharply divided vote that pitted two influential federal judges against each other. Judge Learned Hand of the U.S. Court of Appeals (Second Circuit) led the push for decriminalization. Judge John H. Parker of the U.S. Court of Appeals (Fourth Circuit) pushed for the continued criminalization of such conduct, seeing it as either the symptom or cause of moral decay. Parker's position prevailed, garnering support both from members of the council who agreed with his reasoning and from members who feared that the decriminalization provision might engender enough opposition in state legislatures to endanger acceptance of the Model Penal Code as a whole. The council's vote to uphold sodomy laws was in turn overruled by the membership as a whole at the ALI's 1955 meeting.

The ALI's adoption of the Model Penal Code revealed the existence of significant conflict among legal elites with respect to sodomy statutes and the numerical dominance of the decriminalization camp. That a number of lawyers and jurists supported the reform of laws pertaining to sodomy was further indicated by the endorsement of the ALI's stance by the International Congress on Penal Law and by the steady flow of supportive articles in legal journals.[10]

Shifts in the Legal Stock: *Griswold* and the Right to Privacy

The Model Penal Code was not the only indication that judicial elites were grappling with matters of sexual privacy. In 1965, the Supreme Court handed down a landmark decision articulating the notion of a fundamental right to privacy. *Griswold v. Connecticut* concerned a Connecticut statute prohibiting the use of contraceptives by married couples. Justice Douglas, writing for the Court, found that the statute operated "directly on an intimate relationship of husband and wife" (*Griswold*, 482), thereby violating a fundamental right of privacy that existed in the penumbras of various guarantees of the Bill of Rights. "Would we allow the police to search the sacred precincts of marital bedrooms for telltale signs of the use of contraceptives?" he queried. "The very idea is repulsive to the notions of privacy surrounding the marriage relationship."[11]

Over the next several years, the Supreme Court extended the parameters of the right to privacy significantly. In *Stanley v. Georgia* (1969) the Court ruled that the possession of obscene materials in the home was constitutionally protected, even though it could be criminalized outside the home.[12] In *Eisenstadt v. Baird* (1972) the Court expanded *Griswold*'s ruling to protect the rights of single people to use contraceptives.[13] The next year, the Court developed the contours of the right to privacy in sexual matters even more in the controversial *Roe v. Wade* (1973), which held that the right to privacy encompassed a woman's decision whether or not to terminate her pregnancy.

Griswold and its progeny opened the door to some potentially useful legal arguments for lgb people. The cases made it clear that at least some aspects of sexuality were protected by the right of privacy. But just how far did the right to sexual privacy extend? If the right of privacy included the *outcomes* of sexual activity, might it not also include the activity itself?

Unfortunately for gay rights advocates, some of the language of *Griswold* seemed to specifically exclude homosexuality from the right to privacy. As Justice Goldberg wrote in his concurrence:

> Finally, it should be said of the Court's holding today that it no way interferes with a State's regulation of sexual promiscuity or misconduct. As my Brother Harlan so well stated in his dissenting opinion in *Poe v. Ullman:*

> Adultery, homosexuality and the like are sexual intimacies which the State forbids. . . . but the intimacy of husband and wife is necessarily an essential and accepted feature of the institution of marriage, an institution which the State must not only allow, but which always and in every age it has fostered and protected. It is one thing when the State exerts its power either to forbid extramarital sexuality . . . or to say who may marry, but it is quite another when, having acknowledged a marriage and the intimacies inherent in it, it undertakes to regulate by means of the criminal law the details of that intimacy.[14]

Although this language pointedly excluded lgb relationships from the zone of sexual privacy protected by the Constitution, its potential damage to gay rights claims was tempered by the fact that it was a concurring rather than a majority opinion and therefore had no force of law. It was further tempered by *Eisenstadt,* which specifically expanded *Griswold* to cover the use of contraceptives outside marriage, thereby chipping away at the distinction between marital and nonmarital sexuality.

Despite its shortcomings, the right to privacy articulated in *Griswold* and expanded in subsequent cases sparked interest in using the courts to advance gay rights claims. Nowhere is this more evident than with the ACLU. The organization's 1957 policy supporting the constitutionality of sodomy statutes and employment restrictions had provoked some dissent among ACLU affiliates, more notably the Washington, D.C., New York, and southern California branches, all of which supported and occasionally litigated gay issues.[15] They lobbied the national organization to change its policy position vis-à-vis homosexuality, and by the early 1960s the national ACLU began to signal a reconsideration of its earlier position.[16] *Griswold* was influential in this regard. The national ACLU was involved in the case and recognized its potential significance with respect to the wider sphere of sexual behavior. As then–ACLU associate director Alan Reitman wrote during the course of the litigation, "Once we have the high court's opinion in [*Griswold*], we will be in a position to determine our policy on the civil liberties aspect of a variety of sexual practices, including homosexuality."[17]

Organizational deliberation within the national ACLU began in earnest after the 1965 victory in *Griswold.* Two years later, in 1967, the ACLU formally reversed its stand on homosexuality. The criminalization of private, consensual sexual activities between adults, it said, constituted an impermissible infringement on the fundamental right to privacy. It added sexual privacy cases to its pantheon of interests.

Griswold and its progeny altered the LOS surrounding gay rights in two important ways. The articulation of a right to sexual privacy offered a new legal ground upon which to base rights claims, especially in the context of sodomy. As we shall see in later chapters, privacy-based arguments would become a staple in what might be called the repertoire of litigation around gay rights.[18] In addition, it garnered the first powerful ally for lgb people. For years to come—until it was surpassed by Lambda itself—the ACLU would be the most important litigator of gay rights concerns.

Shifts in the Cultural Stock: Stonewall as a Critical Event

So I was drinking at the [Stonewall Inn], and the police came in to get their payoff as usual. . . . I don't know if it was the customers or if it was the police, but that night everything just clicked. Everybody was like, "Why the fuck are we doing all this for? Why should we be chastised? Why do we have to pay the Mafia all this kind of money to drink in a lousy fuckin' bar? And still be harassed by the police?" It didn't make any sense. The people at them bars, especially at the Stonewall, were involved in other movements. And everybody was like, "We got to do our thing. We're gonna go for it!" When they ushered us out, they very nicely put us out the door. Then we were standing across the street in Sheridan Square Park. But why? Everybody's looking at each other. "Why do we have to keep putting up with this?" Suddenly, the nickels, dimes, pennies, and quarters started flying. . . .

To be there was so beautiful. It was so exciting. I said, "Well, great, now it's my time. I'm out there being a revolutionary for everybody else, and now it's time to do my own thing for my own people." I was like, "Wow, we're doing it! We're doing it! We're fucking their nerves!" The police thought that they could come in and say, "Get out," and nothing was going to happen. . . . So we're throwing the pennies, and everything is going off really fab. The cops locked themselves in the bar. It was getting vicious. Then someone set fire to the Stonewall. The cops, they just panicked. They had no backup. They didn't expect any of this retaliation. But they should have. People were very angry for so long. How long can you live in the closet like that? (Rey Rivera, quoted in Marcus 1992, 191–92)

Changes in the structure of legal opportunities can open (or close) space for legal claims making by social movements. Such opportunities will go unrealized, however, without internal movement frames and organizational forms that allow them to be perceived and acted upon (see Snow et al. 1986). The Stonewall Riot facilitated the generation of new movement frames and forms that allowed lgb people to recognize and respond to the opportunities around them.

In the early morning hours of June 28, 1969, the police raided the Stonewall Inn, a gay bar in New York City's Greenwich Village. As I noted earlier, raids of this sort were not uncommon at the time. What *was* uncommon was that the patrons fought back, sparking three nights of rioting. That a new and distinctively gay militancy was in the offing quickly became apparent. On the second night of the riot, over two thousand people converged on Greenwich Village, clashing violently with the police and shouting slogans ranging from the overtly political ("Gay Power Now") to the quintessentially campy ("We are the Stonewall girls / We wear our hair in curls / We wear our dungarees / Above our nelly knees").[19] In one memorable incident, police were confronted with an impromptu chorus line—and promptly wielded their nightsticks to disperse it. By the third day, "gay power" graffiti was scrawled all over Christopher Street, where the Stonewall Inn was located, and gay liberation "manifestos" were appearing around Greenwich Village.

Why Stonewall occurred when it did and why it had the effect that it had are questions that have received considered attention by many other scholars (see especially Altman 1971; Duberman 1993; Teal 1971). Whatever the reasons, Stonewall's impact on the politics of homosexuality was extraordinary. Within weeks of the riot several "gay liberation" groups formed, an organizational mobilization that continued for the next several years. While this mobilization was centered in New York City, it extended across the nation. By way of comparison, approximately fifty gay-related organizations existed nationwide at the time of Stonewall; four years later such organizations numbered in excess of eight hundred (D'Emilio 1983).

It is important to recognize here that Stonewall did not occur in a vacuum. It came on the heels of a cycle of protest that swept through the United States and the other industrialized democracies in the 1960s, a cycle that encompassed activism around civil rights, the Vietnam War, and women's liberation. Many of the people mobilized in Stonewall's aftermath had initially cut their activist teeth in one or more of these other movements. When they turned their attention to the societal treatment of lgb people, they brought the organizational templates and collective action frames they had acquired from those other movements with them.

Of these, the most significant was the invocation of legal conventions and discourses. Social movements throughout American history have drawn on the concept of legal rights to reframe existing social conditions as unjust. As Stuart Scheingold noted in his seminal book *The Politics of Rights* (1974), movements that can cast their social goals in terms of legal rights lend legitimacy to those goals, because rights connote entitlement.

The invocation of rights can thus initiate and sustain mobilization around particular social movement concerns. Not surprisingly, movements framing their claims in terms of rights commonly turn to the courts to advance their goals, whether directly—by winning cases and developing precedents—or indirectly—by mobilizing potential adherents, generating public support, and/or countering antagonists.[20]

The NAACP and its Legal Defense and Educational Fund are the prototypic example of litigation as a social movement tactic. Formed in 1909 in response to the rising tide of white violence against blacks, the NAACP turned to litigation early on, generally in defense of black men accused of attacking whites. In the late 1920s, however, the NAACP began to use the courts proactively to attack discriminatory social practices. Although it continued to respond to white violence as necessary, it initiated legal challenges to restrictive housing covenants, exclusionary voting practices, and segregated schooling.[21] Its evident successes in these areas—most notably *Brown v. Board of Education* (1954)—in turn caught the attention of myriad other social change movements, resulting in a proliferation of "legal defense funds" and other public interest litigation.[22]

Because of their involvement with civil rights and other movements, many of the activists newly mobilized around gay-related issues were acutely aware that rights talk and the litigation it implied could be used to ameliorate the social conditions faced by lgb people. The courts quickly became a locus of activism. Willingness to challenge sodomy-related arrests increased, as did willingness to contest the legality of gay-related firings and military discharges.[23] Activists likewise began filing suits to force the recognition of lgb organizations, most notably in the university context.[24] The cases that most symbolized Stonewall's impact on lgb consciousness, however, concerned same-sex marriage. Within five years of the riot, litigants in three different cases raised a previously unheard of claim: the right to marry their same-sex partners.[25]

Conclusion

Organized litigation on behalf of gay rights emerged when it did for several reasons. Changing legal frames opened an opportunity for litigation on behalf of gay rights, as did the existence of conflicts among legal elites vis-à-vis criminal regulation of consensual same-sex intimacy. Stonewall, finally, lit a match to the kindling of legal opportunity, facilitating the development of movement frames and forms that allowed lgb people to recognize and respond to the opportunities surrounding them. Given the myriad legal consequences of homosexuality, the burst of organizational mobilization in the aftermath of Stonewall, and the rights-based framing utilized successfully by earlier social movements, it was only a matter of time before the formation of an organization dedicated specifically to litigating on behalf of gay rights. According to Bill Thom, the idea was "in the air . . . even overdue" in 1972, when he made the decision to form Lambda in order to work "through the legal process, to insure equal protection of the laws and the protection of civil rights of homosexuals" (LLDEF 1998, 4). In the next chapter, we turn to an examination of Lambda and its litigation.

THREE

An Overview of Lambda and Its Litigation

L ambda opened its doors for business on October 18, 1973. In its first year of business it handled only three cases and raised about four thousand dollars. Its "office" was Bill Thom's apartment, and its staff consisted of a few attorneys willing to volunteer their time to handle calls for assistance and to consider whether potential cases could and should be pursued. Much changed during the next thirty years. By the end of 2002, Lambda had handled over five hundred cases and boasted an annual budget of nearly eight million dollars. It had seventy-three people on staff and offices in New York, Los Angeles, Chicago, Atlanta, and Dallas.

Because it is both the oldest and the largest organization dedicated to litigating gay rights claims, the history of the Lambda Legal Defense and Education Fund is in no short measure the history of gay rights litigation in the United States. Lambda has involved itself in every major area of legal concern to lesbian, gay, and bisexual people. Its litigation has reflected the ever-widening spectrum of gay rights claims. Its actions have also had a major hand in shaping those claims.

In this chapter, I provide a general overview of Lambda and its litigation from its emergence in 1973 through the middle of 2003, when the U.S. Supreme Court handed down *Lawrence v. Texas*. My aim is twofold. The first is to lay the groundwork for the case studies that follow. The second is to tease out the sometimes subtle relationships between Lambda's actions and the underlying structure of legal opportunities. I argue that Lambda's growth over time is a product of both shifts in the LOS and the increasing capacity of Lambda and other organized litigators to recognize and respond to the opportunities created by those shifts. I also show that Lambda's actions helped to shape the LOS. For ease of presentation, I break the material down by decade, first describing Lambda's organizational resources and its litigation and then examining the underlying LOS.

Lambda's First Decade: 1973–82

The early years of Lambda's existence were inauspicious. The newly minted organization operated under several debilitating handicaps. One major problem was that Lambda had virtually no money. It did not even have an office until 1979, when it moved into space in the New York Civil Liberties Union. According to Thom, he "had an unrealistic notion that we'd apply to liberal foundations and partake of the same largess as other legal defense funds. That proved to be false" (LLDEF 1998, 5). Only a few foundations gave money, usually in small amounts. Lambda's money came almost entirely from individual contributions and occasional fund-raising events. A comment in Lambda's very first newsletter, published in 1976, illustrates the extremity of its financial problems. Noting that it operated "more or less on the edge of insolvency," Lambda claimed that it had "enough in the bank, barring unforeseen circumstances, for about the next 60 days" (LLDEF 1976, 2).

The organization was often forced to turn away cases for lack of money. For example, in its second newsletter, under the title "Money," Lambda noted two cases it turned down for financial reasons (1977). The first of these was *Matlovich v. Secretary of the Air Force* (1974), a military expulsion case that the ACLU had declined to pursue further after a loss in federal district court. Carrington Boggan, Lambda's chief legal counsel (and Bill Thom's law partner), chose to litigate the case privately, after Matlovich agreed to shoulder much of the out-of-pocket costs himself. The second was *Honeycutt v. Malcolm* (1977), a case involving gay prisoners. Although invited by a U.S. District Court in New York to represent the prisoners, Lambda was forced to decline when it could not find a funding source.

Lambda's financial constraints were reflected in its staffing. The organization operated entirely on a volunteer basis until 1978, when Barbara Levy was given a nominal salary as Lambda's first executive director. (Levy was the lone paid staff member until 1980, when a full-time secretary was hired.) Lambda's litigation priorities were set by a volunteer board of directors in its early years. The role of the board was to decide which cases to pursue and to locate attorneys to litigate them pro bono. Finding lawyers, however, was problematic. Few attorneys—even gay ones—were willing to litigate gay rights cases, largely because they were unwilling to risk being perceived as homosexual. As Bill Thom put it, "If you were outed at work you were out of work" (LLDEF 1998, 5). Moreover, attorneys at that time could be disbarred if their homosexuality became known. Lambda's small board of directors comprised a large percentage of the universe of New York lawyers willing to handle gay rights cases. Founding board member Shepherd Raimi recalled that the early board was composed of "every gay lawyer or law student willing to go on the letterhead" (LLDEF 1998, 15). In practice, those board members ended up litigating most of Lambda's early cases.

Lambda was further hobbled by its limited ability to identify and track potential test cases outside the New York metropolitan area. When Lambda first opened its doors for business, the universe of gay rights litigation was ad hoc and atomistic. Litigators bringing gay rights cases worked in virtual isolation from each other, because mechanisms for communication and coordination were largely absent. Friendship networks between gay rights litigators were in their infancy. The media rarely covered gay rights issues, probably because very few reached the higher courts. And although the ACLU was taking on occasional gay rights cases, it did not have any staff members dedicated solely to the subject. As a result, Lambda was often unaware of cases in progress outside of New York City, where its small pool of volunteer attorneys was centered. In fact, in the 1970s, learning about *decided* cases was often difficult.[1] Only when cases outside the New York metropolitan area became highly visible—by appearing before a federal appeals court (*Gay Students Organization of the University of New Hampshire v. Bonner,* 1974) or through the filing of a writ of certiorari (*Enslin v. North Carolina,* 1976) or a petition for rehearing (*Doe v. Commonwealth's Attorney,* 1976) before the U.S. Supreme Court—did Lambda become aware of and involved in them. In such cases, Lambda's involvement was limited to filing amicus curiae briefs. As the foregoing might suggest, Lambda did not originate gay "rights" litigation, although it was the first organization dedicated to the task. It jumped into a parade already in progress. The mobilization of lesbians and gay men sparked by Stonewall spread rapidly throughout the nation, and much early litigation was initiated by individual gay rights activists in an ad hoc fashion.

The one resource Lambda had during its first period was potential clients. Lambda's board of directors spent much of its time winnowing down the myriad calls for legal assistance to the ones that would make the strongest test cases. Its legal criteria were straightforward. In order to be taken on, potential clients needed to show that they were being discriminated against by a governmental entity[2] because of their homosexuality and *only* because of their homosexuality. Most of the calls for assistance failed this test. Some were calls from people whose problems did not have a "legal" resolution, such as teenagers kicked out of the house when their homosexuality was discovered by their parents. Others were calls from people with legal problems but whose claim was marred by bad facts.

The notion of good and bad facts can be a bit difficult to define, but perhaps the simplest way to conceptualize it is to say that good facts make the harm suffered by a potential client seem more obvious or more egregious while bad facts make the harm seem less obvious or egregious. For example, Lambda was very interested in attacking the constitutionality of sodomy laws, believing that they violated the fundamental right to privacy established by *Griswold* and its progeny. A good factual case for a sodomy challenge might involve someone arrested for engaging in consensual same-sex sex in the privacy of his own home (a place where privacy is constitutionally protected). A bad factual case, on the other hand, might involve someone arrested for sodomy whose sexual activity had occurred in a public location such as a park (where privacy is not constitutionally protected). Many of Lambda's earliest requests for assistance fell into this latter category and so were rejected as potential test cases.

Given all the constraints it faced, it is not surprising that Lambda's early involvement in gay rights litigation was quite limited. The organization took on only forty-two cases during its first decade, and sixteen of those originated in 1981 or 1982.[3] As table 1 shows, Lambda's early impact litigation efforts were centered in four principal areas: sodomy, family law (primarily custody but also the legal status of same-sex relationships), immigration, and first amendment litigation (primarily concerning the regulation of gay-related organizations). Lambda also fought discrimination in employment on five occasions and the military's policy

TABLE 1.   Size and Scope of Lambda's Docket, 1973–82

Type of Case	Docket (%)	Number of Cases
Sodomy	19	8
Family	19	8
Immigration	17	7
Speech/association	14	6
Employment	12	5
Military	5	2
Youth	2	1
Miscellaneous gay	10	4
Non-gay	2	1
Total	100	42

of discharging lgb service members on two occasions. The majority of these cases occurred in and around New York City.

Behind the Litigation: LOS in Lambda's First Decade

Legal Frames, Cultural Frames, and Judicial Perspectives

A closer examination of Lambda's docket during its first decade of existence illustrates several features of the legal and cultural frames operating at that time. For example, thirty-one of its forty-two cases involved the public sphere rather than the private sphere. Custody cases were the principal exception to this rule. Lambda's focus on governmental regulations and actions rather than the actions of private individuals was based on the legal principle of "rationality." Stated briefly, private actors may do anything that is not explicitly illegal. Private employers may, for example, fire employees for being gay unless there is a law expressly prohibiting it. Governmental regulations and the actions of public officials, on the other hand, must have, at a minimum, a rational basis. Unlike private employers, public employers may not discharge employees without a reasonable cause. In circumstances where fundamental rights—such as the right to freedom of speech—are concerned, the government must have a compelling reason for restricting the exercise of those rights.

A core reason for Lambda's focus on the public sphere in the 1970s was that laws forbidding discrimination on the basis of sexual orientation were extremely rare. Without specific laws to hang an argument on, Lambda simply had no legal recourse to offer people who had suffered harm at the hands of private individuals because of their sexual orientation. However, to the extent it could convince courts that a particular public policy—such as barring homosexuals from immigrating, excluding them from military service, or preventing them from teaching children—was *irrational*, Lambda did have legal recourse. As increasing numbers of gay rights ordinances were passed in the 1980s and 1990s, Lambda's ability to bring suit on behalf of lgb people likewise increased.

Another feature of the legal and cultural frames in operation during Lambda's first decade can be seen through an examination of the claims made by Lambda's opponents in its cases. In virtually every case Lambda involved itself in, the criminalization of same-sex sexual conduct was invoked by opposing counsel to justify the disparate treatment of the lgb litigant.[4] In *Gay Students Organization v. Bonner* (1974), for example, the University of New Hampshire sought to justify its denial of recognition of a newly formed gay and lesbian student group on campus in part by arguing that students attending the group's functions would be likely to engage in sodomy as a consequence.

Given the invocation of sodomy laws to justify discrimination against lgb people in myriad legal contexts, it should come as no surprise that Lambda's board of directors considered the overturning of sodomy laws to be Lambda's most important priority. During its first decade of existence the organization confronted the constitutionality of sodomy statutes head-on in seven cases, while an eighth challenged a New York statute criminalizing "loitering for the purpose of engaging in deviant sex."[5] It had some measure of success. In 1980, Lambda won a landmark victory when New York's Court of Appeals struck down the state's sodomy law. *People v. Onofre* (1980) marked the first time a state high court had found a sodomy statute unconstitutional in the context of same-sex sexual activity.

Although Lambda chose to focus on sodomy cases, custody cases were actually the most commonly litigated gay rights concern in the 1970s (Rivera 1979). The great majority of this litigation took the form of custody disputes between ex-spouses, where one (usually the father) sued for custody based on the homosexuality of the other (usually the mother). In a variation on the standard custody proceeding, lesbian and gay parents sometimes found themselves in the position of fighting their own parents or even grandparents over the custody of children. Lambda involved itself in three custody disputes during its first decade of operation, two involving disputes between ex-spouses and one involving a lesbian mother and her mother.[6]

Given that custody disputes were a more common problem for lesbians and gay men than were sodomy arrests, why did Lambda emphasize the latter over the former? The answer partly has to do with the personal preferences of Lambda's board of directors, which determined the cases Lambda would take on. But it also had to do with the existing cultural and legal frames.

Put simply, sodomy cases seemed more winnable than custody cases to Lambda's board of directors. Many judges, they knew, thought that consensual sodomy should be decriminalized. And the constitutional right to privacy articulated in *Griswold v. Connecticut* and its progeny, they reasoned, presented a legal hook on which to hang their contention that sodomy statutes should be abolished. As we shall see in chapter 4, privacy-based arguments about the constitutionality of sodomy statutes proved more problematic to the courts than gay rights litigators had hoped they would be. However, in Lambda's early years, such arguments seemed particularly potent.

The legal and cultural frames surrounding parents and children in the 1970s made custody cases seem much less winnable to Lambda. A legal emphasis on furthering the "best interests of the child" lies at the heart of all custody cases. The idea here is that judges are supposed to take into consideration all the "relevant circumstances"[7] of the particular case at hand and decide that case in the manner best calculated to secure the proper care, attention, and education for the children involved.

Because the determination of a child's "best interests" is so subjective, the outcomes of these cases are necessarily more a product of a judge's sociopolitical beliefs than an objective application of legal principles. What are the qualities of a good mother or father? What does a healthy, adjusted child look like? Which influences on a child's life are proper and which are not? The answers to these questions are derived more from cultural frames than from legal ones.

While many judges believed that consensual sodomy should be decriminalized, it did not necessarily follow that they thought lesbians and gay men were proper influences on children. Hitchens and Price published a survey of lesbian custody cases in 1978 in which they identified a number of commonly held judicial beliefs about the implications of lesbian parenting. Many judges, they found, viewed lesbians as mentally ill, unpredictable, and irresponsible people who took on either "male" or "female" roles in relationships and had a propensity to molest children or at least to engage in sexual activity in front of them. Accordingly, lesbian parenting was seen as endangering children in a number of different ways. The children were perceived to be at higher risk for sexual abuse, either by their mothers, their mothers' partners, or their mothers' lesbian friends. They were also thought to be at higher risk of becoming homosexual themselves and/or becoming confused in their gender identity. Furthermore, judges were concerned about the implications of lesbian parenting on children because they believed children would grow up believing in the social acceptability of same-sex relationships. Finally, Hitchens and Price found that judges commonly believed that children would be socially stigmatized as a result of living in a lesbian household.

In short, the prevailing judicial conception about lesbian parents in the 1970s was hostile. It's not surprising that under the circumstances lesbians and gay men rarely initiated custody cases. Rather they were forced into court when ex-spouses or other parties initiated legal action seeking to remove custody and/or restrict them from being able to see their children. Lambda was hesitant to step into cases that seemed likely to lose, especially since their fact specificity made them more expensive than many other kinds of cases to prepare.

In sum, legal frames, cultural frames, and judicial beliefs about the nature of homosexuality all affected the kinds of cases Lambda chose to litigate in the 1970s. The lack of specific statutes forbidding discrimination on the basis of sexual orientation meant that Lambda was unable to address a wide array of discriminatory actions. The ever-widening scope of the right to privacy (first encompassing contraceptive use within marriage, then contraceptive use outside of marriage, then abortion) offered a potentially potent ground to challenge sodomy statutes, one that Lambda had some success in exploiting. The "best interests of the child" standard in custody cases, by contrast, made success difficult, largely because of the cultural frames about homosexuality invoked by presiding judges. In Lambda's second decade of operation, the legal and cultural frames surrounding homosexuality would change enormously, opening up many avenues of litigation and shutting down others.

Alliance Systems, Conflict Systems, and the Configuration of Power

When Lambda first opened its doors for business, it was the only organization in existence dedicated to litigating on behalf of gay rights. By the close of its first decade, the alliance structure surrounding gay rights litigation had changed. Lambda was joined by several other gay rights law firms, most notably the Gay Rights Advocates and the Lesbian Rights Project (both formed in 1977),[8] GLAD (formed in 1978), and the Texas Human Rights Foundation (formed in 1979).[9]

From Lambda's perspective, the ACLU was by far its most important ally. When Lambda moved out of Bill Thom's apartment in 1979, it moved into the New York offices of the ACLU. Although the two organizations retained separate identities, sharing office space encouraged the formation of close working relationships between the then-tiny Lambda and the comparatively enormous ACLU. This relationship benefited Lambda in several respects as the 1970s turned into the 1980s. It gave Lambda access to the ACLU's resources, including its litigation expertise and organizational networks.[10] But the benefits of the relationship were not entirely one-sided. The ACLU also tapped into the litigation expertise of Lambda's staff and, based in part on Lambda's urging, launched its own gay rights project in 1985.[11]

Just as the alliance system surrounding litigation was beginning to coalesce by the close of the 1970s, so was the conflict system. The visible successes of gay rights activists in the 1970s sparked vocal opposition among those opposed to gay rights, most notably so in the context of newly enacted gay rights laws.

Laws forbidding discrimination on the basis of sexual orientation were unheard of at the time of the Stonewall Riot in 1969. Ten years later, forty-four different communities—mostly large cities or college towns—had instituted laws prohibiting some forms of sexual orientation–based discrimination.[12] The passage of these ordinances sometimes sparked enormous controversy. For example, in Boulder, Colorado, the 1974 passage of a citywide gay rights law sparked such a debate between supporters and opponents of the measure that the city council finally put the ordinance on the ballot for consideration by the entire electorate. It was repealed by a nearly 2–1 margin (Button, Rienzo, and Wald 1997, 86; Keen and Goldberg 1998, 6).

When in 1977 Dade County, Florida, became the first southern city to ban discrimination on the basis of sexual orientation in employment, housing, and accommodations, a similar backlash occurred. Conservative Christian singer Anita Bryant quickly announced that she would mount a campaign to repeal the ordinance through a ballot referendum. She formed a group, "Save Our Children (From Homosexuality) Inc.," which depicted homosexuals (especially gay men) as immoral, predatory, and especially dangerous to the physical and moral welfare of children. Bryant summed up her message in a phrase that was quoted repeatedly by her supporters: "Homosexuals cannot reproduce so they must recruit" (Shilts 1982, 156).

Bryant's repeal effort tapped into a wellspring of public opposition to the notion of gay rights: within five weeks of the ordinance's passage, the proposed repeal measure had garnered more than six times the number of votes needed to qualify it for the ballot. Less than six months after the gay rights law passed, Dade County voters repealed it by a margin of 78 percent to 22 percent. Buoyed by the victory, Bryant embarked on a national tour to promote the repeal of similar laws in other localities. By the end of 1978, Bryant and her supporters had utilized citizen lawmaking to repeal gay rights provisions in three additional cities—Wichita, Kansas, where the repeal referendum garnered an 83 percent majority; St. Paul, Minnesota, 63 percent; and Eugene, Oregon, also 63 percent.[13]

Attempts to repeal gay rights ordinances were part of a larger mobilization of "New Right" activists in the late 1970s and early 1980s. The New Right coalesced around what they saw as the spiritual and moral weakening of America, as exemplified by legalized abortion, the rising divorce rate, the proposed Equal Rights Amendment, the absence of prayer in public schools, and the very notion of "gay" rights.[14] The Republican party was particularly solicitous of the concerns of these activists, including for the first time a plank in its 1980 platform specifically opposing any form of governmental endorsement for gay rights.[15]

The election of the New Right's favored presidential candidate, Ronald Reagan, combined with the Republican capture of the Senate, signaled that, at least in the near future, the national political system would be far more open to New Right activists than to gay rights activists. The passage of antigay legislation in Congress further emphasized the power disparity between gay rights advocates and their opponents. In 1980, for example, Congress approved the McDonald Amendment, which prevented the Legal Services Corporation from providing "legal assistance for any litigation which seeks to adjudicate the legalization of homosexuality." Then in 1981, it voted overwhelmingly to require the District of Columbia to retain its sodomy law.

In sum, Lambda witnessed the shaping up of both the alliance and the conflict systems surrounding gay rights during its first decade. These systems would become significantly stronger in the 1980s and 1990s. Allies would begin to work in concert, increasing Lambda's ability to mobilize resources on behalf of gay rights litigation. New Right activists would find yet another symbol of moral decay around which to mobilize: AIDS. Events in the early 1980s also highlighted the lack of opportunity for advancing gay rights in the national political realm. This inhospitality would last throughout Lambda's second decade as well.

Lambda's Second Decade: 1983–92

Lambda's capacity to mobilize resources in support of its gay rights litigation grew dramatically during its second decade. In 1983 it was housed in the offices of the New York Civil Liberties Union and had an annual income of about $133,000. By the close of 1992, Lambda's annual income totaled over $1.6 million, and it had its own suite of offices in New York City, as well as two regional offices: one in Los Angeles and one in Chicago. Its paid staff grew from three to twenty-two during that time period and from one full-time litigator to five.

A major engine of Lambda's growth was the organizational and fund-raising abilities of its staff, particularly its executive directors. For example, Tim Sweeney became Lambda's executive director at the start of 1982, a position he held through the end of 1985. A non-lawyer, he dedicated his time to building Lambda's extralegal infrastructure, engaging in continual fund-raising, and using that money to hire a public information director, organize seminars, disseminate informational materials, and increase Lambda's visibility and membership base. A year after Sweeney's arrival, the organization was finally able to hire an attorney to coordinate the development and implementation of litigation.

Abby Rubenfeld became Lambda's first managing attorney in 1983, bringing with her a voiced commitment to developing a coherent set of litigation strategies and to improving communication and coordination among the growing community of gay rights litigators. As we shall see later in this chapter, Rubenfeld was instrumental in establishing the first mechanism for bringing together the growing community of gay rights litigators and in expanding the scope of Lambda's docket. The combined efforts of Sweeney and Rubenfeld shored up Lambda's financial base, expanded its outreach to the larger lesbian and gay community, and increased the communication and coordination network among litigators. By the end of 1985, when Sweeney stepped down as executive director, Lambda's budget had increased from $80,000 to $300,000.

That said, Lambda's visibility in the gay rights movement was still fairly low in 1985. Hiring Tom Stoddard as executive director was a coup: telegenic and personable, Stoddard was well known in New York's gay activist circles and widely respected for his work as the legislative director of the New York Civil Liberties Union and for his coauthorship of New York City's lesbian and gay rights ordinance. Under Stoddard's leadership, Lambda's visibility rose enormously. He pushed the organization into mainstream media outlets, writing editorials and appearing on television programs. This increased visibility "legitimated Lambda in the eyes of . . . a lot of donors, including big donors" (Robert Murphy, quoted in Freiberg 1997). As a result, Lambda's organizational capacities grew immensely. During Stoddard's tenure, Lambda not only moved into its own offices for the first time (in 1987) but opened a second office in Los Angeles (in 1990). When he stepped down at the end of 1991, the organization's budget topped $1.6 million, and there were four full-time litigators in a staff of twenty-two.

Lambda's docket likewise grew. It took on 191 new cases between 1983 and 1992. As table 2 shows, the scope and emphasis of Lambda's litigation shifted considerably in its second decade. Emphasis on AIDS is

the most striking change. About 30 percent of Lambda's new cases grap-
pled with sociolegal repercussions of the epidemic (about which more
presently). At its peak in 1989, AIDS litigation swallowed up close to 40
percent of Lambda's docket. The percentage of Lambda's docket allotted
to sodomy and immigration challenges, in contrast, fell off sharply.

That the proportion of docket space allotted to these issues dropped
should not be taken to mean that they were no longer priorities for
Lambda. The number of cases litigated in a given area is an imperfect
marker of the importance of that area. Indeed, the number of AIDS cases
on Lambda's docket surpassed sodomy cases in the midst of *Bowers v.
Hardwick,* one of the most important gay rights cases ever litigated.
Sodomy reform simply moved from being the major concern of gay rights
litigators to being one of several major concerns.

One of these new priorities was family law. Rhetoric about the "gay
agenda" aside, it is more accurate to speak of multiple gay communities
than of a singular entity. Gender is one obvious marker of community
boundaries, and gender-based conflicts have pervaded the movement for
gay rights. For example, men greatly outnumbered women in early liberation groups and tended to focus on gay male concerns such as sodomy
law reform, bar raids, and police entrapment to the virtual exclusion of
custody, child care, wage discrimination, and other core lesbian-feminist
concerns. Lesbians were far less likely to be entrapped and/or arrested
than were gay men because as a rule they were less likely to solicit virtual

TABLE 2.   Comparison of Lambda's Docket in Its First and Second Decades

Type of Case	Decade 1 Docket (%)	Decade 1 Number of Cases	Decade 2 Docket (%)	Decade 2 Number of Cases
Sodomy	19	8	5	9
Family	19	8	20	38
Speech/association	14	6	14	27
Employment	12	5	11	21
Immigration	17	7	2	3
Military	5	2	6	12
AIDS	0	0	30	58
Legislation	0	0	2	4
Youth	2	1	<1	1
Miscellaneous gay	10	4	4	7
Non-gay	2	1	6	11
Total	100	42	101[a]	191

[a]Percentage does not equal 100 due to rounding.

strangers for sex or to engage in semipublic sexual activity; they were angry that those concerns were viewed as more central to "gay" liberation than were the issues that more directly affected their lives.[16]

Lambda was not immune to these tensions. Its early emphasis on sodomy-related litigation made it vulnerable to the charge of being male centered—all the more so because the group's intake records in the early 1980s showed that requests for assistance from lesbian mothers in custody battles outnumbered any other kind of request. The group's efforts to reach out to the lesbian community underscored the existence of gender-related tensions. Lambda formally added family issues and relationships to its list of litigation priorities in 1983. Shortly thereafter, it pointed to two new "lesbian teacher" cases as evidence of its "commitment to working more extensively on lesbian issues" (*Lambda Update* 1984, 2).

Lambda was aided in its decision to diversity its docket by the arrival of Abby Rubenfeld as Lambda's first managing attorney. Rubenfeld came to the position with a background in family law and pushed Lambda to take on more family law cases. She did not see this interest as taking away from the importance of sodomy law reform. In fact, she saw sodomy law reform as essential to advancing gay rights claims in the context of family law. Rubenfeld illustrated this linkage in her recounting of her first solo trial as an attorney, representing a lesbian mother in a child custody case.

I was a young lawyer, well prepared, and had a great case. There was a five year old child with cerebral palsy who could get all the services and physical therapy he needed in the public school system in Nashville, where his mother lived. The father and the grandparents wanted to bring the child back to Cleveland, Tennessee, and put him in a private school that could not offer the child any of the therapy that he needed. The school was not accessible to the handicapped, so the child could not even get into the school. To me it looked like an easy case. It turned out to be anything but easy.

I put on my case, and the other lawyer stood up and said, "But your honor, this woman is a criminal." This was basically true. She was a violator of the state's sodomy law. While status is not a crime, the fact is that gay men and lesbians violate the law by their sexual activity, and they are engaging in criminal acts. We are criminals in the eyes of the law and that is used against us. That is why these sodomy laws have to go; they are the nails in the closet doors. (Rubenfeld 1986, 61)

Lambda also began litigating a "new" kind of case in the 1980s, namely, ones based on the passage of laws forbidding discrimination on the basis of sexual orientation. These laws opened up additional avenues for gay rights litigation. In one case, Lambda initiated an enforcement action to try to give Wisconsin's new gay rights law teeth, calling it "an opportunity to make precedent under the only state-wide gay rights law in the country" (*Lambda Update*, summer 1988, 10).[17] In another instance, Lambda attempted to defend a new gay rights measure against backlash. In 1984 the Salvation Army, the Roman Catholic Archdiocese of New York, and Agudath Israel challenged then–New York City mayor Ed Koch's authority to issue an executive order requiring contractors with the city to certify that they did not discriminate on the basis of various categories, including sexual orientation (*Salvation Army v. Koch*, 1985). Lambda filed an amicus brief defending the order and also coordinated the submission of a brief from a coalition of civil rights groups.

Although litigation remained at the core of Lambda's activities during its second decade, its work was not limited to the courtroom. Tim Sweeney and Tom Stoddard both placed a lot of emphasis on public education. Lambda began engaging in myriad extrajudicial activities under their leadership. In 1983, for example, Lambda testified before a subcommittee of the House Committee on Government Operations concerning issues of confidentiality in AIDS surveillance and research. Similarly, Lambda cosponsored a day-long conference called "Lesbians Choosing Motherhood" in the fall of 1984.[18] Perhaps the single most important extrajudicial project Lambda involved itself in was the creation of the Ad-Hoc Task Force to Challenge Sodomy Laws. We turn to a discussion of that group now.

Behind the Litigation: LOS in Lambda's Second Decade

A Developing Alliance System

As noted previously, Lambda's status as the only dedicated gay rights law firm lasted for only a few years. By the close of the 1970s, it was joined by a handful of other groups scattered across the nation. The ACLU also continued to litigate gay rights cases and in 1986 formally created the Lesbian and Gay Rights Project. These groups would form the backbone of the alliance system surrounding gay rights.

Lambda's relationship with the other gay legal organizations was a complicated one. On the one hand, the organizations competed with each other for a limited pool of money, prestige, and public recognition (see Vaid 1995). Lambda and the Boston-based GLAD frequently engaged in "turf" battles in the 1980s as each organization attempted to expand its sphere of influence.[19] On the other hand, the groups quickly became intertwined with one another—trading staff, filing amicus briefs in each other's cases, and coordinating litigation processes.

The web of connections tying the groups together often led through the ACLU. When Lambda moved out of Bill Thom's apartment and into dedicated office space in 1979, it was in the ACLU's New York building. Because the prestige of the ACLU and its affiliates lent credibility to gay rights claims, gay legal groups sought out ACLU involvement or sought to piggyback on ACLU-backed cases. Staff from gay legal groups sometimes sat on the boards of regional civil liberties unions. Kevin Cathcart's recollection of the formation of the ACLU's Lesbian and Gay Rights Project illustrates the web of relationships tying the groups together.

> Years ago, this is in the mid-80s . . . Lambda was in the ACLU building over on 43rd Street in New York. There was no ACLU project. And we lobbied the ACLU very hard about "Why aren't you doing more? Why don't you have a project? Why don't you create a job?" . . . [A]nd I was at that point at GLAD not at Lambda and Lambda was a much bigger player, a much, much bigger player because they were there [in New York]. Tom [Stoddard] was involved and Tom also worked at the New York Civil Liberties Union and Tom was on the ACLU National Board and when I was at GLAD I was on the board of the Civil Liberties Union in Massachusetts, so we all have lots of overlaps with the various civil liberties unions. . . . We pushed them to do this. We wanted them to do this. I don't see it as a bad thing that they do it. I don't see it as competition. I see it as: it would be shocking if the ACLU did not have a project.[20]

The single most important connection in the alliance system surrounding gay rights litigation was forged on November 20, 1983, when, at the urging of then–Lambda legal director Abby Rubenfeld, Lambda and the ACLU hosted a nationwide meeting of gay rights litigators working on sodomy law reform. It was not the first effort to bring together the various groups working on gay rights.[21] It differed from earlier meetings, though, in that it led to the formation of the Ad-Hoc Task Force to Challenge Sodomy Laws, the first ongoing mechanism for communication and coordination between the myriad sodomy reform litigators across the nation. The core purpose of the Ad-Hoc Task Force was to be what one litigator called "a central place to discuss constitutional theory and litigation strategies" (quoted in *Lambda Update* winter 1985, 5). The task force's immediate objectives included targeting a few states for sodomy challenges, creating appropriate litigation strategies, and amassing a central directory of information and resources to use in future challenges to sodomy laws (*Lambda Update*, February 1984).

The Ad-Hoc Task Force became a formal project of Lambda in 1985. In 1986, after the Supreme Court's decision in *Bowers v. Hardwick*, the task force rechristened itself the Litigators' Roundtable and shifted its emphasis from eradicating sodomy laws to containing the damage wrought by the decision and pursuing litigation in other areas. The Litigators' Roundtable is widely credited among gay rights litigators as providing a forum for hashing out legal theories, considering rhetorical approaches, forging agreement between the various groups, and coordinating the process of litigating (see, e.g., Freiberg 1997; Vaid 1995).

I do not want to leave the impression that the existence of the Litigators' Roundtable has erased intracommunity conflict. The gay rights movement has never been homogeneous: the membership of the community, the goals of the movement, and the vehicles for achieving those goals have all been matter of intense debate.[22] These conflicts did not disappear with the formation of the Litigators' Roundtable. As we shall see in subsequent chapters, significant intracommunity conflict existed over how to attack sodomy laws and antigay initiatives as well as whether to pursue the right to marry. However, it seems clear that the Litigators' Roundtable has served as a useful tool for resolving many disagreements and for achieving intergroup consensus about legal strategies vis-à-vis divisive issues; it has also minimized duplication of effort among the various gay rights groups and facilitated the conduct of litigation.

Two Sudden Shifts in Cultural and Legal Frames: AIDS and *Bowers*

Although evidence of the existence of AIDS in the United States can be traced back to the early 1970s, it escaped medical attention until the early 1980s.[23] The general public paid it little attention until June 24, 1985—the day actor Rock Hudson announced he had AIDS. Hudson's illness ignited a panic about AIDS among heterosexuals. New York City's AIDS hotline, for instance, reported a fivefold jump in daily calls after Hudson's announcement, largely from anxious heterosexuals (Rimer 1985).[24] "Contagion-fear" among heterosexuals mounted through 1988. Much of the media coverage during this time was alarmist, emphasizing the crossover of AIDS from the gay male population to the heterosexual population.[25]

The emergence of the AIDS epidemic had myriad effects on the course of the gay rights movement. One of them was to increase the prominence of litigation. In fact, by 1990, AIDS had stimulated more litigation than any other disease in the United States, in absolute numbers and across all time (Gostin 1990, 1961). Much of this litigation related only indirectly to gay rights per se, involving instead questions of blood banks' liability for transfusion-related AIDS, the legality of insurance caps on AIDS-related medical payments, and the rights and responsibilities of health-care workers vis-à-vis AIDS. But because of the association of AIDS with male homosexuality in the United States, litigation around AIDS and gay rights was inevitably intertwined. As Nan Hunter (1993, 1706) noted, "Although legal and social reaction ostensibly focused on the disease, the disease itself was so closely associated with gay men in the first years of the epidemic that much of the reaction seemed a euphemism for opinions of male homosexuality."

Opponents of gay rights forwarded the theoretical possibility of HIV transmission as a reason to deny a variety of gay rights claims. As we shall see in chapter 4, opponents of sodomy reform used AIDS to argue that homosexuality posed a public health threat, arguing that sodomy laws were necessary to stem the spread of the epidemic. But gay rights opponents also raised the specter of AIDS—often successfully—in cases not directly involving sexual activity. Among other things, they pointed to the syndrome as a reason to prevent gay men and lesbians from forming gay rights groups, working with the public (especially in the food and health-care industries), and securing custody and visitation rights to their children.[26] In 1985, Lambda's then–executive director Tim Sweeney phrased the impact of AIDS on gay rights this way: "There is no question that AIDS now puts a veneer over the top of every civil rights issue I see. Last month a Vermont legislator tried to make it a felony for a gay man to give blood" (Specter 1985, 4).

AIDS clearly acted as a critical event in refocusing Lambda's litigation priorities. Lambda became actively involved in the area at its outset: in

1983 it litigated the first AIDS-related discrimination lawsuit in the country.[27] By the mid-1980s Lambda was confronting an avalanche of requests for help from gay men encountering AIDS-related discrimination in housing, employment, insurance, and a host of other areas. According to the group's intake records, for example, requests for AIDS-related assistance increased 300 percent between 1984 and 1985. Lambda responded to this outpouring of need by incorporating AIDS-related litigation into its mission, a route that its sister organizations by and large did not take.

One of the most important effects of this decision was that it dramatically improved Lambda's ability to raise money. Mainstream foundations that had previously shied away from underwriting gay rights efforts donated money for Lambda's AIDS-related work.[28] The impact these grants had on Lambda's bottom line can be seen in table 3, which itemizes Lambda's annual income from 1980 through 2002. Table 3 also shows what is perhaps the most symbolically resonant impact of AIDS on Lambda's organizational growth: the addition of bequests as a revenue source in the late 1980s.

Of course, AIDS was not the only generator of income for Lambda. If AIDS was a long-term critical event stimulating lesbian and gay mobilization, the 1986 Supreme Court decision in *Bowers v. Hardwick* was a suddenly imposed grievance.[29] In a scathingly worded opinion written by Justice Byron White, the Supreme Court found the claim of a "fundamental right to engage in sodomy" to be "at best, facetious." Chief Justice Warren Burger took the additional step of writing a concurrence to emphasize his abhorrence of homosexuality, based on what he described as "millenia of moral teaching."

Lambda attorney Evan Wolfson, who drafted Lambda's amicus brief in *Bowers,* referred to *Bowers* and AIDS as "the two towering paradigm shifters of the '80s."[30] Wolfson described *Bowers*'s impact thus: "It energized a grass-roots movement and tapped into a deeper anger and politicized people. Lambda mushroomed after [*Bowers*], as did a number of other groups. [*Bowers*] had a whole galvanizing effect [in addition to its legal effects]."[31]

Lesbians and gay men were clearly angered by the Court's ruling. Within hours of its announcement, small protests erupted in several cities across the nation. The largest of these occurred in New York City, where more than one thousand protestors marched on a federal court house, clashing with police during the process. The case was also a major impetus for the 1987 March on Washington for Lesbian and Gay Rights, which drew over half a million participants. A prominent feature of the march was a mass protest on the steps of the Supreme Court building in which some 600 people were arrested, making it the largest single act of civil disobedience in the United States since the anti-Vietnam War demonstrations.[32]

Lambda moved quickly to capitalize on the anger *Bowers* provoked within the lgb community. Solicitation letters were mailed out within a week of the decision and *Bowers* became the cornerstone of Lambda's fundraising appeals for the next year.[33] Using favorable and unfavorable court decisions is a tried-and-true method for raising funds. Although there is no way to know for certain how much additional funding Lambda was able to leverage out of *Hardwick,* the threefold increase in

TABLE 3.   Breakdown of Lambda's Income by Source, 1980–2002[a]

	Individual Contributions	Bequests	Grants	Special[b] Events	Other[c]	Total[d]
1980	18,625	—	6,000	8,519	522	33,666
1981	46,981	—	—	5,716	326	53,023
1982	38,518	—	23,500	13,994	3,515	79,527
1983	64,308	—	41,500	24,458	3,207	133,473
1984	116,893	—	60,000	13,452	5,323	195,668
1985	181,239	—	52,800	39,705	26,110	299,854
1986	553,402	—	—	49,933	16,379	897,814
1987						1,019,642
1988	475,343	49,102	187,107	135,615	50,647	897,814
1989	688,525	87,740	276,181	193,217	77,704	1,323,367
1990[e]	630,966	145,670	177,050	162,862	46,940	1,163,488
1991	943,565	124,890	277,580	263,053	69,744	1,678,832
1992	907,951	223,514	278,399	162,473	46,957	1,619,294
1993	968,542	387,611	197,955	211,460	52,019	1,817,587
1994	1,102,422	194,354	280,406	398,073	191,395	2,166,650
1995	1,303,486	864,170	322,941	477,680	124,738	3,093,015
1996	1,393,475	2,196,843	217,612	486,415	141,471	4,435,816
1997[f]	1,500,000	1,500,000	348,000	512,000	388,000	4,300,000
1998	1,940,477	783,705	397,348	722,026	168,522	4,062,078
1999	2,266,070	934,162	623,919	832,768	291,569	4,948,488
2000	2,205,828	1,193,486	890,102	980,181	187,479	5,457,076
2001	2,682,167	924,792	949,618	1,063,173	(271,317)	5,348,433
2002	2,797,824	2,326,910	1,448,372	1,139,023	119,636	7,831,765

[a]Data collected by author from Lambda's audited financial reports. Categorical data for 1987 unavailable.

[b]Fund-raisers of various types.

[c]Attorney fees, speaking engagements, publications, interest, and other miscellany.

[d]Excluding the value of donated services. In 2002, donated services were valued at over $1.5 million.

[e]1990 figures are for nine months only, because Lambda switched from calendar to fiscal year accounting.

[f]1997 figures are rounded.

individual contributions in 1986 compared to 1985 suggests that Lambda was reasonably successful in using a litigation defeat to mobilize support. A comparison of the organization's budgeted and actual income in 1987 is also suggestive. Lambda projected an income of $500,000; its actual income was twice that. The increased visibility that both AIDS and *Bowers* gave the gay rights movement likewise resulted in increased giving from corporations and other organized entities. For instance, in 1987, three prominent law firms held a then-unprecedented fundraiser for Lambda, raising more in one evening (about $50,000) than Lambda had raised in the first four years of its existence.[34]

Lambda was able to take the money it raised in the aftermath of AIDS and *Bowers* and expand its organizational base. The group opened a western regional office in Los Angeles in 1990, followed by a midwestern regional office in 1992.[35] It was also able to increase its litigation capacity. Much of this increased capacity was dedicated to AIDS-related litigation, of course. But Lambda also expanded its litigation in its more "traditional" areas—including family law, employment law, and military challenges—utilizing the funds generated from *Bowers* and AIDS. Ironically, AIDS and *Bowers* often made it harder for Lambda to litigate successfully in those areas, a subject explored in more detail in chapter 4.

In the end, the emergence of the AIDS epidemic and the Supreme Court decision in *Bowers v. Hardwick* radically impacted both the legal and the cultural contexts of gay rights. AIDS opened up a vast new sphere of litigation even as *Bowers* brought a decade of litigation efforts to a screeching halt. Both served as rallying points for a massive lesbian and gay mobilization. And both increased the sociopolitical visibility of homosexuality in the United States, garnering new support from heterosexual allies even as they emboldened gay rights' opponents. In Lambda's third decade, the battle over gay rights would only grow larger. And litigation would be at the heart of the fray.

Lambda's Third Decade: 1993–2002

Lambda exploded in size during its third decade. It opened two new regional offices, one in Atlanta, the other in Dallas. Its annual income nearly quadrupled, from $1.6 million in 1992 to $7.8 million in 2002.[36] Its staff grew from twenty-two to seventy-three; the number of litigators from five to fifteen. Lambda was far and away the dominant player in gay rights litigation by this point, in terms of both the size of its litigation staff and its financial wherewithal. Table 4 compares Lambda's budget and staffing figures in 1996 to those of the other organized gay rights litigators. (There is nothing special about the year 1996 for the purposes of this table. It is simply the year for which comparative data were most readily available.) As it shows, the relative positions of Lambda and the ACLU had decisively switched by this point in time; Lambda out-massed the ACLU's Lesbian and Gay Rights Project by a fourfold margin. Lambda retained its size advantage even factoring in spending by the ACLU's state affiliates on gay rights litigation. Matt Coles, the executive director of the ACLU's Lesbian and Gay Rights Project, put affiliate spending on gay rights in the realm of $1.5 million in 1996, bringing the ACLU total up to some $2.2 million—only two-thirds of Lambda's spending (Freiberg 1997).

As in its second decade, a major engine of Lambda's growth in its third decade was the organizational and fund-raising abilities of its staff, particularly Kevin Cathcart, its executive director. Although Tom Stoddard's leadership had helped to propel Lambda into the center of the gay rights movement, day-to-day management of the organization was not his strong suit. When Cathcart took over as executive director in 1992, organizational management was a core priority; Lambda grew exponentially under his leadership.

The size of Lambda's docket grew along with its organizational resources. During its third decade, Lambda took on 269 cases (table 5). A perusal of these cases reveals that gay rights claims broadened

TABLE 4.　Comparison of Lambda with Other Gay Legal Groups, 1996

Organization	Year Founded	Budget[a]	Legal Staff[a]
Lambda Legal Defense and Education Fund	1973	$3.1 million	12
ACLU National Lesbian and Gay Rights Project	1985	$700,000	3
ACLU state affiliates		$1.5 million	
Gay and Lesbian Advocates and Defenders (GLAD)	1978	$650,000	3
National Center for Lesbian Rights (NCLR)[b]	1977	$500,000	2
Servicemembers Legal Defense Network (SLDN)	1993	$448,000	3

[a]Budget and staffing data come from Freiberg 1997 (21).
[b]Formerly the Lesbian Rights Project, a project of the Equal Rights Advocates.

significantly in the 1990s. Lambda's "family" litigation is illustrative of this trend.

While litigation arising from the AIDS epidemic continued to occupy a prominent place on Lambda's docket during the years between 1993 and 2002, it was superseded in numerical prominence by litigation centered on the familial relationships of lgb people. About a quarter of Lambda's family docket involved custody disputes between formerly married parents, a kind of case Lambda had been litigating since its inception. A handful of cases concerned openly lgb people attempting to adopt or foster children as single parents, another issue that Lambda had been litigating for some time. But much of Lambda's family docket involved "new" legal claims.

For example, Lambda's docket included a dozen second-parent adoption cases, where the same-sex partner of a biological or adoptive parent was attempting to establish formal legal ties with the children of the relationship. It also included about a dozen same-sex coparent custody disputes, where people in a dissolved same-sex relationship battled over custodial and visitation rights to the children of that relationship.[37]

The "new" cases on Lambda's family docket that garnered the most public attention, though, concerned marriage. In its third decade, Lambda became a major proponent of the legal theory that same-sex couples had a constitutional right to marry. It advanced this position in a

TABLE 5. Comparison of Lambda's Docket in Its Second and Third Decades

Type of Case	Decade 2		Decade 3	
	Docket (%)	Number of Cases	Docket (%)	Number of Cases
Sodomy	5	9	6	17
Family	20	38	30	82
Speech/association	14	27	5	13
Employment	11	21	11	29
Immigration	2	3	3	7
Military	6	12	2	6
AIDS	30	58	22	58
Legislation	2	4	9	23
Youth	<1	1	5	12
Miscellaenous gay	4	7	5	13
Non-gay	6	11	3	9
Total	101[a]	191	101[a]	269

[a]Percentages do not equal 100 due to rounding.

number of high-profile cases, including Hawaii's *Baehr v. Lewin,* Vermont's *Baker v. Vermont,* and New Jersey's *Lewis v. Harris.*[38]

Increased diversity of gay rights claims can also be seen in other areas of Lambda's litigation. In the 1980s, for instance, Lambda took cases to enforce recently enacted gay rights measures. It also confronted a new variation on lawmaking targeted at lgb people, namely, measures designed to "fence gay people out"[39] of the political process by prohibiting the future enactment of gay rights laws. It initiated a handful of suits designed to derail these measures, most famously *Romer v. Evans.*[40]

By the mid-1990s, Lambda also began to take cases that gay rights groups had tended to avoid in prior years: cases involving lgb children. Some of its cases were designed to force schools to protect lgb students from antigay violence. For example, one of Lambda's first cases in this area involved the refusal of school officials to intervene to protect an openly gay boy from constant harassment and beatings by his fellow students, despite the boy's repeated requests for help (*Nabozny v. Podlesny,* 1996).[41] Lambda also began to bring cases to force schools to allow lgb student groups to meet.[42] In a related vein, Lambda also filed suit to force the Boy Scouts to accept openly gay scout leaders. In the most well-known of these cases, *Boy Scouts of America v. Dale* (2000), Lambda convinced the New Jersey Supreme Court that the Boy Scouts should be viewed as a public accommodation and hence subject to New Jersey's law prohibiting antigay discrimination in public accommodations. On appeal to the U.S. Supreme Court, however, this ruling was overturned on the basis of the Boy Scouts' First Amendment right to freedom of association.

Lambda also involved itself in a handful of cases dealing with the rights of transgendered people during its third decade. For example, it represented the mother of Brandon Teena in a case arising from his brutal rape and murder when Teena's status as a biological female had been discovered.[43] It also filed an amicus brief in a case dealing with the validity of a marriage between a man and a postoperative transsexual woman.[44]

The contours of Lambda's litigation broadened in yet another way in the 1990s. It began to immerse itself more heavily in the earlier stages of litigation rather than entering cases in the appeals stage or filing an amicus curiae brief. All things being equal, organized litigators generally prefer to be a part of cases from their inception rather than joining them at a later stage or acting as amicus curiae. By acting as counsel from the inception of a case, litigators can shape the factual issues and legal theories that are presented to the court. The drawback to this approach is its burden on a group's financial and staff resources.

Participation as an amicus curiae enables a group to advance its concerns and forward legal theories in a less expensive fashion. Limiting involvement to amicus status allows a group to spread limited resources across more issue areas, while still allowing it to leverage the case at hand to mobilize adherents and educate the public. Its major drawback as a strategy concerns the control, or lack thereof, of a case's progress. An amicus can offer additional sociolegal arguments, but it cannot control the issues, facts, or venue. It is, in Joseph Kobylka's words, "fixing its argument to a wagon of someone else's design" (1987, 14).

Lambda has always pursued a blend of direct involvement and amicus participation. Even in the cases in which it has directly involved itself, however, the group has traditionally waited until after the trial stage, entering only on appeal. This approach reflects the tension between depth and breadth. The trial stage is generally the most expensive and labor-intensive part of litigation. By waiting to join promising cases that have already made it past the trial stage, Lambda has sought to conserve its limited resources. In the 1990s, Lambda altered the relative allocation of its resources somewhat, developing an increasing number of legal challenges from scratch. This shift in litigation strategy largely reflected Lambda's increasing ability to absorb the costs involved.

Lambda's increasing organizational capacity also allowed it to alter the parameters of its mission. One key change instituted during Lambda's third decade was the expansion of its extrajudicial activities. Lambda created several programs—including the Marriage Project, the Foster Care Initiative Project, the Youth and Schools Project, and the Education and Public Awareness Department—whose emphasis was more on fostering sociopolitical change and public education than on litigation per se.

The Foster Care Initiative Project is illustrative of Lambda's expanded focus. Supported by a Ford Foundation grant, Lambda examined the foster care policies and services of fourteen states as they pertained to the needs of lesbian, gay, bisexual, and transgendered (lgbt) youth.[45] Based on its findings, Lambda developed several proposals for reform and then shopped them around to relevant state agencies and institutional actors. It also created a toll-free number for lgbt youth in foster care to report discrimination and distributed posters containing this number to foster care agencies across the nation.

The scope and direction of Lambda's actions during its third decade both reflected and shaped the structure of legal opportunities surrounding gay rights. Since chapters 5 though 7 explore the interaction of LOS and gay rights litigation in the specific contexts of sodomy, antigay initiatives, and marriage, I limit my discussion here to a few brief highlights.

Behind the Litigation: LOS in Lambda's Third Decade

The 1992 Elections

If the 1980 elections signaled the increasing prominence of the New Right in American politics, the 1992 elections announced the arrival of gay rights at the center of political discourse. Every Democratic presidential candidate actively courted the gay vote. Opposition to gay rights was a key feature of the Republican national convention.[46] An article published in the *New York Times Magazine* at the height of the presidential election campaign, titled "Gay Politics Goes Mainstream," explored the context of the political debate over gay rights.

> For some political strategists, especially those in the Presidential race, this is a game, with the gay issue to be manipulated from state to state for maximum electoral advantage. But for many on both sides of the sexual-orientation divide, it is a holy war—an inevitable confrontation of two forces that have been building strength for a decade. And it is ugly. The religious right and some other conservatives push the fear button, linking homosexuality to child molesting, while homosexuals tug at compassion one minute, invoking AIDS, then spew venom the next, outing conservative gay Congressmen and the gay and lesbian children of Government officials and right-wingers.
>
> Strictly speaking, this is a battle about specific issues, like whether homosexuals have a right to equal job opportunities or to serve in the military. (Clinton stresses that his commitment to gay rights ends there.) But it is really a bigger and more complex fight over whether America can accept homosexuality, over whether it is O.K. to be gay. (Schmalz 1992, 18)

With Clinton's election, lgb people gained their first presidential ally. Lambda sought to benefit from this turn of events. Shortly after Clinton's election, Lambda attorneys met with high-ranking White House officials to discuss matters related to gay rights and AIDS (Cathcart 1993). Such access to administration officials had been unavailable to gay rights advocates under prior administrations. Throughout the Clinton years, Lambda and other gay rights organizations sought to take advantage of the relative openness of the administration to press their claims.[47]

Notwithstanding the importance of Clinton's election in shifting the configuration of power with respect to gay rights, other aspects of the 1992 elections proved equally, if not more, important to Lambda. Measures on the ballots of two states (Oregon and Colorado) and two cities (Portland, Maine, and Tampa, Florida) were designed to tap into the reservoir of public opposition to gay rights. While the measures in Oregon and Portland failed, the measures in Colorado and Tampa passed. Of the latter, Colorado's was the more significant because it amended the state's constitution to invalidate all existing state and local provisions barring discrimination on the basis of sexual orientation and to prohibit the future enactment of any such legislation.

The passage of Colorado's Amendment 2 prompted Lambda to turn its focus to defeating antigay ballot measures. Together with the ACLU and the Colorado Legal Initiatives Project, Lambda filed suit to block the implementation of Colorado's Amendment 2. Lambda also began preparing for the onslaught of copycat measures that antigay activists were attempting to place on ballots across the nation. Over the next few years, Lambda filed myriad preelection challenges designed to disqualify antigay measures from making it onto ballots. It encouraged get-out-the-vote campaigns and other sorts of political activism designed to defeat those measures that made it to the ballot. And it litigated the constitutionality of antigay ballot measures that passed. Lambda's activism in this areas continued unabated through 1996, when the U.S. Supreme Court ruled in *Romer v. Evans* that Colorado's antigay measure was unconstitutional. At that point, attempts to pass antigay measures slowed to a trickle and Lambda was able to focus more heavily on its other gay rights concerns. Among these, the most prominent was clearly same-sex marriage.

A Radical Shift in Legal Frames: Baehr and Its Aftermath

Were one to try to rank the most important shifts in the LOS surrounding gay rights during the 1990s, the 1993 decision by the Hawaii Supreme Court in *Baehr v. Lewin* would have a strong claim to the number one spot. In ruling that Hawaii's ban on same-sex marriage constituted sex discrimination under the state's constitution and remanding the case for a trial to determine whether this discrimination was permissible, the Hawaii Supreme Court fractured a long-standing judicial consensus that marriage was solely the province of opposite-sex couples.

This decision had widespread repercussions both for Lambda and for the larger movement for gay rights. For one thing, it hijacked Lambda's agenda. Prior to the 1993 decision in *Baehr*, Lambda had been struggling internally with the question of whether to pursue equal marriage rights for same-sex couples.[48] The Hawaii Supreme Court effectively silenced this debate, because the stakes had become too high for Lambda to ignore. Lambda added marriage to its formal list of priorities and became cocounsel in *Baehr*.[49] It also developed the Marriage Project, taking the unusual step of dedicating several staff members to work full-time on political organizing around marriage. Lambda's reasons for doing so reflected its recognition that the door opened by *Baehr* could be closed again through the legislative process.

And indeed, realizing that the legal scales had shifted against them, opponents turned to state and federal legislatures. Dozens of bills to deny recognition to same-sex marriages were introduced in states across the nation. Lambda expended much energy mobilizing opposition to those bills when its calculations suggested that they might be defeated. And although many of them were deflected, over thirty states and the federal government had passed laws denying recognition to same-sex marriages by the time the Hawaii Supreme Court issued its final decision in *Baehr* in 1999. Ironically, the court ultimately ruled that there was no right for same-sex couples to marry in Hawaii.[50]

The final ruling in *Baehr* did not end the conflict over same-sex marriage, because by the time it came down copycat suits had been filed in several other states. One of these cases, *Baker v. State of Vermont*, resulted in a decision that came down nine days after the final ruling in *Baehr*. In counterpoint to *Baehr*, *Baker* held that the state of Vermont was required to grant same-sex couples all the rights and benefits it provided to married couples. Although the decision stopped short of saying that same-sex couples had the right to marry it came closer than any other court in the nation had.

As Lambda's third decade drew to a close, a new wave of copycat litigation was under way. GLAD, which was cocounsel in *Baker*, promptly challenged the constitutionality of Massachusetts's ban on same-sex marriage (*Goodridge v. Dept. of Public Health,* 2003). Lambda instituted a parallel challenge to New Jersey's law in 2002 (*Lewis v. Harris,* in progress.) Activists in Indiana and Arizona similarly initiated lawsuits seeking to compel their states to recognize marriages among same-sex couples.[51]

Legal Frames and Judicial Perspectives

Shifts in the legal frames surrounding gay rights extended far beyond *Baehr* and *Baker.* A key reason Lambda was able to broaden the contours of its litigation in the 1990s was the increased availability of helpful legal frames in general. By the close of 2002, thirteen states had passed reasonably comprehensive gay rights laws.[52] Eight additional states had measures prohibiting antigay discrimination in public employment.[53] Hundreds of localities had instituted similar provisions. By one estimate, over one-third of the U.S. population lived in an area that had a state or local gay rights law in 1999 (van der Meide 2000). The existence of these laws increased Lambda's ability to raise several kinds of gay rights claims, mostly involving employment but also including issues such as housing and access to public accommodations.

The increased availability of legal frames was not limited to legislative and executive enactments. Case law also began to become more favorable. Nowhere is this more evident than in Lambda's custody and adoption cases. By the 1990s, judges were increasingly unwilling to say that lgb parents were unfit per se to raise children. An evolving majority rule required a showing of some nexus between parental homosexuality and harm to children. One study indicated that less than one-third of American jurisdictions in the 1990s presumed that parental homosexuality was harmful to children, while more than two-thirds required affirmative proof of any allegations of harm to children based on parental homosexuality (Stein 1996). While courts in some states continued to react with hostility to the concept of lgb parents,[54] other courts were increasingly willing to place a judicial stamp of approval on homes headed by lgb parents. For example, in 1999, the Illinois Court of Appeals had this to say about two pairs of lgb parents seeking second-parent adoptions: "Petitioners in both of these cases came to our state court system in order to be allowed to adopt children, children with whom they had already formed a loving relationship over a period of time. A higher purpose cannot be imagined" (*In Matter of Petition of C.M.A. / In Matter of Petition of M.M. & J.S.,* 1068).

Alliance and Conflict Systems

The alliance and conflict systems surrounding gay rights grew much larger in the 1990s. The breadth of these systems can be seen clearly in the political battles and litigation surrounding antigay initiatives and same-sex marriage. In both instances, one of Lambda's major goals was to build alliances with a wide range of non-gay actors and organizations. Civil rights groups and religious groups were seen as particularly desirable allies.

Lambda's alliance-building efforts in the context of antigay initiatives were largely focused on soliciting amicus briefs in *Romer v. Evans*. By the time *Romer* came before the U.S. Supreme Court, more than three dozen organizations had signed on to amicus briefs supporting Lambda's position. Included among them were several groups representing the interests of other minority groups, such as the NAACP Legal Defense and Educational Fund, the Puerto Rican and Asian American Legal Defense and Education Funds, the National Council of La Raza, and the National Organization for Women. Also represented were a number of religious groups, including the Union of American Hebrew Congregations, the Anti-Defamation League, and the United Church Coalition for Lesbian/Gay Concerns. Other prominent amici included the American Psychiatric and Psychological Associations and the National Association of Social Workers. The crown jewel of Lambda' coalition-building efforts, however, can be seen in two amicus briefs. Seven states and the District of Columbia joined together to submit an amicus brief opposing Amendment 2.[55] Ten cities likewise submitted a joint brief.[56]

Lambda's alliance-building efforts in the context of marriage differed somewhat from its efforts in the context of antigay initiatives. Although it sought amicus support, it placed heavy emphasis on gathering signatories for its "Marriage Resolution," a document setting forth reasons why same-sex couples should be permitted to marry. Lambda used the "Marriage Resolution" for several purposes: stimulating discussion and public education around the issue of same-sex marriage, mobilizing potential adherents, and demonstrating the breadth of support for same-sex marriage. Over the course of several years, Lambda garnered the signatures of a wide range of non-gay actors and organizations, including a number of religious figures and denominations.[57] Three cities signed on, as did the state Democratic parties of California and Washington and several politicians.[58]

Lambda was not alone in forging alliances. The opposition system surrounding gay rights also grew stronger during the 1990s and focused heavily on same-sex marriage. Preventing same-sex marriage became a rallying cry that mobilized conservatives and religious groups to political activism (see especially Goldberg-Hiller 2002; Herman 1997; Patton 1997). Among the most prominent of these groups were the Church of Latter Day Saints (Mormons), the Lutheran Church (Missouri Synod), Agudath Israel of America, the Catholic Church, and Focus on the Family. Seven states joined together to file an amicus brief supporting Colorado's antigay amendment in *Romer*.[59] Eleven states filed an amicus brief opposing same-sex marriage in *Baehr*.[60]

In sum, Lambda's actions during its third decade came about largely in response to consequential events in the public sphere. New laws and policies—and in some cases the *possibility* of new laws and policies—catapulted the subject of gay rights into the center of public discourse. Tensions over homosexuality were played out in the ballot box and in the halls of Congress and dozens of state legislatures, as well as in the Supreme Court and the high courts of many states. The alliance and conflict systems surrounding gay rights broadened. The configuration of power shifted. And once again, changing legal and cultural frames opened up some areas of litigation and shut down others.

Conclusion

Shifts in the structure of legal opportunities may open spaces for legal challenge, but unless movements have the capacity to recognize and respond to such opportunities, they will pass unnoticed (Sawyers and Meyer 1999). In this chapter, I have argued that Lambda's growth is a product of both shifts in the LOS and the increasing capacity of Lambda and other organized litigators to recognize and respond to new opportunities.

I wish to be clear here that shifts in the LOS did not automatically translate into increased resources for Lambda, nor did they account for all of Lambda's growth. Shifts in the legal structure provide *opportunities* for action, not the action itself. That depends on the agency of social movement actors. In the case at hand, Lambda recognized these shifts as opportunities for mobilization and worked to translate the opportunity into the reality. For example, Lambda chose to involve itself in AIDS-related litigation from the outset of the epidemic, unlike some other groups, which drew a sharp division between AIDS and gay rights. Lambda (and the ACLU) also made a conscious decision to bring together the various organizations and individuals involved in sodomy litigation. Similarly, Lambda chose to respond to the decision in *Baehr* by engaging in political as well as legal activism around the right to marry.

I also wish to be clear that Lambda's actions in turn helped shape the structure of legal opportunities in which it operated. The notion of LOS implies a balancing of agency between state and social movement. Social movement organizations like Lambda are not merely passive entities forced to wait for opportunities to arise; they can actively help to produce them. As just one example, Lambda helped engineer the shift in legal opportunities created by *Bowers, Romer,* and *Baehr*. Of course, the fact that actors such as Lambda can produce changes in the LOS does not mean that those changes will always be desirable ones. The very notion of social movement agency necessarily implies that actors may make poor choices as well as smart ones. We shall pursue this theme in greater detail in chapter 4 when we explore the decisions Lambda and other organized litigators made in their efforts to eradicate sodomy laws.

A related feature of LOS is that it is often multidimensional. *Bowers* is a good example of this feature. While the case clearly presaged a closing of *legal* space for action, Lambda was able to take this legal loss and use it as an agent for lgb mobilization. *Romer* also shows the multidimensionality of LOS. The passage of Colorado's Amendment 2 presaged a closing of space for *political* action but opened up space for *legal* action; by turning to the courts Lambda was able to subvert a localized political loss into a nationwide legal gain. *Baehr* too illustrates the multidimensionality of LOS. The 1993 Hawaii Supreme Court ruling initiated a cascade of both legal and political opportunities. It served as an agent for lgb and antigay mobilization. Legal opportunities, in short, may be available to multiple actors operating in multiple domains.

An obvious implication of this is that legal opportunity and legal change do not flow unproblematically from each other. Shifts in the LOS do not necessarily provide clear road maps for action. They are subject to multiple interpretations, and movement actors responding to them may misinterpret them, miss them, or be outmaneuvered by countermovement actors also responding to them. Unfortunately for social movement litigators, the value of any particular shift in legal opportunity, like Schrödinger's cat, exists only as a wave of probabilities until the box is opened, that is, until movement actors attempt to capitalize on it. In the next four chapters, we examine the relationship between legal opportunity structure and litigation success.

FOUR

Sodomy Reform from
Stonewall to *Bowers*

On June 26, 2003, the U.S. Supreme Court handed down a decision that Lambda's executive director, Kevin Cathcart (2003), described as "the most significant ruling ever for our civil rights." *Lawrence v. Texas* struck down Texas's "Homosexual Conduct" law, which criminalized oral and anal sex when performed by same-sex couples. The government, according to the Court, had no business policing the intimate personal relationships of consenting adults.

> Adults may choose to enter upon this relationship in the confines of their homes and their own private lives and still retain their dignity as free persons. When sexuality finds overt expression in intimate conduct with another person, the conduct can be but one element in a personal bond that is more enduring. The liberty protected by the Constitution allows homosexual persons the right to make this choice. (2478)

Lawrence was an unqualified legal victory for Lambda. Prohibitions against sodomy had long been invoked to justify the legality of discrimination against lgb people in multiple domains, including employment, military service, housing, public accommodations, immigration, speech and association, custody, adoption, marriage, and the provision of government benefits (see Achtenberg 1996; Rivera 1979, 1985, 1986).[1] In short, sodomy laws have been "the chief systematic way that society as a whole tells gays they are scum" (Mohr 1986, 53).

Not only did *Lawrence* invalidate Texas's sodomy law and, by extension, all other state sodomy laws, it did so in language that made it clear that lgb people deserved legal respect. As Justice Kennedy's majority opinion put it: "The petitioners are entitled to respect for their private lives. The State cannot demean their existence or control their destiny by making their private sexual conduct a crime" (*Lawrence*, 2485).

This victory, however, took a long time coming. Lambda had viewed the eradication of sodomy laws as a core priority since its creation in 1973. In the thirty years leading up to its final victory in *Lawrence*, Lambda attacked the constitutionality of sodomy laws twenty-four times, acting as counsel in eleven cases and filing amicus briefs in the other thirteen. As we shall see, a number of Lambda's cases were in fact successful, leading several states to judicially void their laws. But until *Lawrence*, Lambda's biggest sodomy case was a paradigmatic example of a test case gone badly awry.

Bowers v. Hardwick came before the U.S. Supreme Court in 1986. Like *Lawrence*, *Bowers* asked the high court to find that a (Georgia) state law criminalizing anal and oral sex violated the right of privacy under the federal Constitution.[2] The *Bowers* Court's reaction to this request was dramatically different from the *Lawrence* Court's. In a scathingly worded decision, the Supreme Court decreed that the notion of a "fundamental right to engage in homosexual sodomy" was, "at best, facetious" (*Bowers*, 193). It upheld Georgia's power to criminalize sodomy and, by extension, the power of all other states to do so as well. Lower courts subsequently relied on *Bowers* to justify discrimination against lgb people in a wide variety of legal contexts.

In this chapter and the next I examine the long campaign by Lambda and other gay rights litigators to eradicate sodomy laws. This chapter traces the progress of sodomy law reform from its beginnings in the early 1970s through the Supreme Court's decision in *Bowers v. Hardwick*. Chapter 5 tells the tale of litigating in *Bowers*'s shadow and continues through to the Supreme Court's decision in *Lawrence v. Texas*. The primary focus of my inquiry is on the shifting ability of Lambda and other gay rights litigators to mobilize the law successfully in the context of sodomy reform. Why did gay rights advocates lose *Bowers* but win *Lawrence*? More broadly, under what circumstances have rights claims about same-sex sexuality been more or less likely to prevail in court?

In the following pages, I show that sodomy reform has been a start-and-stop process proceeding in four distinct stages. I then examine Lambda's actions and the prevailing structure of legal opportuniites in each of those stages. Ultimately, I argue that the progress of Lambda's thirty-year campaign against sodomy laws is best understood as a product of shifts in the LOS and the strategic responses of Lambda and other organized litigators to those shifts.

The Stages of Sodomy Reform

The legal status of sodomy laws has changed enormously in the years since Stonewall. In 1969, every state in the nation except Illinois had a sodomy law on the books.[3] By 2003, when the Supreme Court issued its decision in *Lawrence,* the number of states with sodomy laws had dropped to thirteen.

Figure 1 charts the progress of sodomy reform between 1960 and 2003. (The starting point for the graph is arbitrary. Had it started earlier, nothing would have changed; the graph would show sodomy laws in all fifty states.) It reveals that sodomy reform has proceeded in four relatively distinct stages. Stage 1 can be considered to be the status quo ante. It runs from 1960 to 1970. In 1971, Connecticut became the second state in the nation to erase its sodomy statute, inaugurating a period of reform that lasted for thirteen years, coming to a close in 1983 (stage 2). During stage 2, the number of states with operational sodomy laws dropped from forty-nine to twenty-four (line A). During this same period of time, a number of states embarked on an alternate path, exempting heterosexual sodomy from prosecution but retaining prohibitions on same-sex sodomy (line C).

Stage 3 runs from 1984 through 1991 and marks a period of backsliding with respect to sodomy reform. The trend toward repeal (line A) leveled off while the specification trend (line C) continued to gather momentum, rising to ten states by the close of the period. The *Bowers* decision came down during this stage. Although the 1986 decision in the case is commonly considered to mark a transition from a period of reform to a period of backlash, figure 1 suggests that *Bowers* symbolized the period of backsliding rather than generating it.

Stage 4 marks the final era. It runs from 1992, the year Kentucky became the first post-*Bowers* state to invalidate its sodomy law (*Kentucky v. Wasson*), to June 2003, when the Supreme Court invalidated all remaining state sodomy laws. Much like stage 2, stage 4 represents a period of reform. The number of states with sodomy laws dropped from twenty-four to fourteen in the years between *Bowers* and *Lawrence*—a number that includes one state, Michigan, where the enforceability of the law became questionable.[4] The District of Columbia likewise repealed its sodomy law during stage 4. Most notable among the states invalidating their laws was Georgia, the state whose sodomy law birthed *Bowers v. Hardwick* (*Powell v. State,* 1998).

number of states

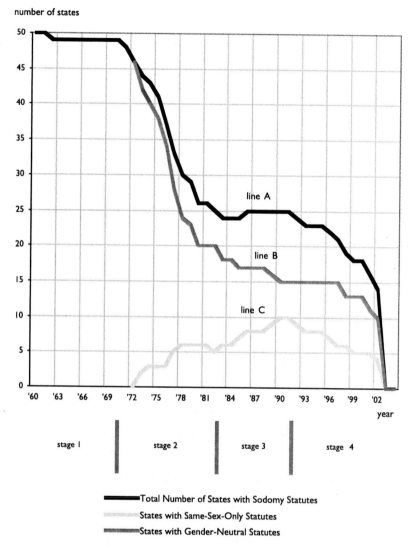

Fig. 1.   The stages of sodomy reform, 1960–2003

Why these sudden shifts in the course of sodomy reform? Why does it begin suddenly in the early 1970s and then ground to a (temporary) halt in the mid-1980s? And what happened to jump-start reform again in the 1990s? In the following pages, I examine the first three phases of sodomy reform in depth. I leave consideration of the fourth phase until chapter 5.

Stage I (1960–70): The Status Quo Ante

Laws regulating sexual activities have been a staple of American jurisprudence since colonial times. For example, when Plymouth became the first settlement to codify a set of laws, four of the eight offenses punishable by death concerned sex: sodomy, buggery, rape, and adultery.[5] The criminalization of sexual acts such as sodomy and buggery was widespread as the nation coalesced; eleven of the thirteen original states had statutory prohibitions against such acts.[6] The penalties for these acts ranged from death to life imprisonment to whipping to public humiliation to disqualification from property ownership (Katz 1983).

In marked contrast to the widespread prohibitions of sodomy and buggery, there was little legal elaboration of what these crimes actually entailed. Anal intercourse seems to have clearly fallen within their purview, but the criminality of other acts was uncertain. For example, courts differed over whether sodomy required penetration, ejaculation, or both; mutual masturbation and tribadism thus fell into murky legal waters. Likewise, courts differed over whether sodomy encompassed oral-genital contact. The first court to answer the question ruled that "however vile and detestable" fellatio was, it did not fall within the crime of sodomy (*Prindle v. State*, 1893). Others disagreed, finding fellatio to be as heinous as—or even more heinous than—anal intercourse.[7]

By 1940, the definition of sodomy had more or less stabilized. Almost all states criminalized oral-genital as well as anal-genital contact, via either statutory language or judicial interpretation. At this point in time, prohibitions against sodomy either made no reference to the gender of the actors or expressly included heterosexual conduct; many statutes even reached nonprocreative sexual activity between married couples. The penalties for engaging in sodomy ranged from three years to life imprisonment. Laws in a number of states permitted sexual "psychopaths" to be held until "cured."

Although stage 1 marks a period of outward calm with respect to sodomy reform, tensions over the criminalization of private, consensual sexual activity were bubbling beneath the surface. As discussed in chapter 3, the LOS altered in several respects in the 1950s and 1960s. *Griswold v. Connecticut* and its progeny suggested the existence of a right to sexual privacy. The ACLU added sexual privacy cases to its pantheon of interests. Perhaps most important is that the ALI's Model Penal Code exempted certain private consensual activities, including sodomy, from prosecution. The impact of the Model Penal Code on sodomy reform first became apparent in Illinois. In 1961, it adopted the massive Model Penal Code in toto and in the process became the first state in the nation to decriminalize sodomy.

Stage 2 (1971–83): Rapid Reform

Illinois remained alone in its stance until 1971, when Connecticut became the second state in the nation to erase sodomy statutes from its books. Within three years, five additional states followed the path of Illinois and Connecticut.[8] By 1979, Stonewall's tenth anniversary, fully twenty-one states had invalidated their sodomy laws. By 1983, the close of stage 2, the number of states with operational sodomy laws had dropped from forty-nine to twenty-four.

Why such a dramatic shift in the 1970s? Because the trend of rapid reform followed so soon on the heels of Stonewall, it is tempting to ascribe it mainly to the influence of the gay rights movement. In fact, although gay rights advocates pushed for sodomy law reform in several states, the major instigator of reform was the Model Penal Code. Of the twenty-five states shedding sodomy statutes in the years between 1971 and 1983, only three resulted from judicial rather than legislative action; in all other states, sodomy reform piggybacked on a larger project of penal reform.

Thirty-four states incorporated some or all of the Model Penal Code between 1971 and 1983. Of these thirty-four states, twenty-two basically adopted the text of the Model Penal Code wholesale (Hunter, Michaelson, and Stoddard 1992, 120). There is doubt as to whether legislators in some states were even aware that adoption of the Model Penal Code would result in the decriminalization of sodomy (Shilts 1993, 170), although legislators in at least one state (California) decriminalized sodomy after considering it separately and specifically.

Of the twelve states that did not adopt the Model Penal Code wholesale, five chose to keep their sodomy provisions untouched. The other seven states rewrote their sodomy statutes to prohibit oral and/or anal sex only between same-sex partners.[9] Missouri's rewritten statute was the most comprehensive, outlawing "any sex act involving the genitals of one person and the mouth, tongue, hand or anus of another person of the same sex." That some states chose not to reform their sodomy statutes or engaged in a process of specification highlights the fact that, in at least some states, sodomy laws were not simply relics from earlier eras but rather active tools of public policy.

Although very little of the sodomy reform occurring in stage 2 can be traced directly to the emergence of the gay rights movement, this does not mean that lgb legal activists did not try to influence the course of sodomy reform. Indeed, stage 2 saw two notable court decisions striking down state sodomy laws: New York's *People v. Onofre* (1980) and Texas's *Baker v. Wade* (1982). These cases significantly affected subsequent sodomy litigation and will be examined in detail later in this chapter. For the moment, though, I wish to emphasize that would-be reformers such as Lambda were hampered in their quest to use the courts by sizeable roadblocks. One roadblock was the general dearth of resources available to gay rights activists in the 1970s. Another, more specific, roadblock emanated from the mechanics of the legal process. Lambda and other gay rights advocates seeking to reform sodomy statutes consistently encountered difficulties in getting access to the courts for a simple but frustrating reason: the indirect nature of the harms caused by sodomy laws.

Sodomy and Standing

Sodomy laws have rarely been enforced in the context of private, consensual conduct.[10] The general nonenforcement of these laws posed an enormous legal hurdle for gay rights activists. As a rule, in order to obtain standing to challenge the legality of a statute, would-be plaintiffs must show that they have suffered actual or threatened injury large enough to give them a real and personal stake in the outcome. People who have not *actually* been injured by a statute and who seek to challenge a statute because of the *threat* it poses to them generally need to satisfy two requirements: they must show that they are likely to engage in the proscribed conduct and that the government is likely to prosecute them for it.[11] Since prosecutions for consensual sodomy were extremely rare, finding plaintiffs who could show actual harm (i.e., arrest and/or conviction) from the statute was correspondingly difficult. This pattern of nonenforcement also made it hard to show a credible threat of future prosecution.

The facts surrounding *Bowers v. Hardwick* provide a striking illustration of just how rarely private, consensual conduct served as the basis for arrest. In 1982, Michael Hardwick was arrested in his own bedroom when a police officer looked through the room's partially open door and saw him engaging in mutual oral sex with another man. The officer was in the house to serve a warrant on Hardwick for failure to appear in court. (Hardwick, in fact, had already resolved the legal matter, which involved a charge of public drinking.) A houseguest had let the officer into the house and gestured in the direction of Hardwick's bedroom. Upon reaching the bedroom and witnessing the sexual activity, the officer arrested the men for violating Georgia's sodomy statute, which proscribed "perform[ing] or submit[ting] to any sexual act involving the sex organs of one person and the mouth or anus of another" under penalty of up to twenty years' imprisonment.[12]

Members of the Georgia affiliate of the ACLU had been searching for a good test case to challenge the state's sodomy statute and approached Hardwick within a week of his arrest. We shall turn to *Bowers*'s litigation presently, but for the moment the important point is that the Georgia litigators had been looking for a good case for five years prior to Hardwick's arrest and during that time were unable to come up with a *single instance* of a conviction for sodomy that was not the result of a plea bargain agreement in which a more serious charge (such as rape) was dismissed in return for a guilty plea on the sodomy charge.[13] As it turns out, Michael Hardwick was the first person to be arrested in the state of Georgia for adult, private, consensual same-sex conduct *in nearly fifty years.*

Lambda's first attempt at using the courts to reform New York's sex laws is likewise illustrative with respect to the problem of standing. In *Dudal v. Codd* (1975), Lambda represented a man who had been charged with "loitering for the purposes of deviant sex" in violation of New York's Penal Code. These kinds of charges were commonly pressed against gay men caught frequenting areas where "known homosexuals" congregated. They rarely went to trial, however. Either the suspect pleaded guilty in return for a fine rather than jail time, or the police dropped the charges after locking the suspect up overnight. When Dudal, represented by Lambda, chose to fight the charge, the district attorney's office declined to prosecute. Lambda then initiated suit, seeking to have the statute declared unconstitutional, but ran into the standing hurdle. Since the charges against Dudal had been dismissed, the court ruled, he no longer had standing to challenge the statute.

Legal Frames and Legal Access: The Problem of Doe v. Commonwealth's Attorney

The problems faced by activists seeking to use the courts to effect sodomy reform in stage 2 were exacerbated by a case called *Doe v. Commonwealth's Attorney*. In 1975, two gay male plaintiffs filed suit in federal court challenging the constitutionality of Virginia's "crime against nature" statute.

The case was filed shortly after several gay activists spoke with Justice William Douglas at an open forum held on Staten Island. Douglas had opined during the forum that a sodomy challenge might succeed if the litigants could show that they were in genuine jeopardy of persecution under the law and that they lived otherwise impeccable lives (Shilts 1993, 283). One of the activists present at the forum subsequently initiated *Doe* to test Douglas's hypothesis. The two plaintiffs in the case asserted that they regularly engaged in private, consensual conduct falling within the provisions of Virginia's statute and feared arrest. (One of the two, in fact, had previously been prosecuted under the statute.) They sought to declare the statute unconstitutional on a host of constitutional grounds, including their rights to privacy and free expression, as well as their right to be free from cruel and unusual punishment.

The three-judge panel of the federal district court assigned to hear the case rejected all of these claims, citing Justice Goldberg's concurrence in *Griswold* distinguishing homosexuality from sexual intimacy within marriage (see chap. 2). Homosexual conduct, said the *Doe* court, was "obviously no portion of marriage, home or family life" and therefore did not fall within the parameters of the right to privacy (*Doe*, 1202).

In a classic example of making a bad decision worse, the gay male plaintiffs chose to take their case to the Supreme Court via a mechanism of appeal that has since been largely discontinued. Requests for Supreme Court review are typically made via a writ of certiorari. The Court may choose whether or not to hear the case; if it chooses not to hear it (which is what happens the great majority of the time), no precedential value is attached to its decision not to decide.[14] The *Doe* case, however, came before the Court via a process whereby federal constitutional challenges to state statutes were heard by a three-judge panel of district judges and then appealed directly to the Supreme Court (bypassing the U.S. Court of Appeals). Under this procedure, the Court had to take the case and summarily affirm it or summarily reverse the decision of the district court. Precedential value was attached to the Court's decision no matter what.

The Supreme Court's response to the *Doe* appeal was to summarily affirm the decision of the federal district court. Although Justices William Brennan, Thurgood Marshall, and John Paul Stevens[15]—the three justices with the most liberal voting records on civil rights issues—voted to hear the case, they were overruled by their more conservative brethren.

With the Supreme Court's summary affirmance in *Doe*, efforts to use the courts to effect sodomy reform took a step backward. The access hurdle became that much higher to jump, because *Doe* shifted the legal frames encompassing sodomy laws. Unsurprising, and without exception, district attorneys and other sodomy law defenders claimed that *Doe* was an authoritative ruling on the constitutionality of sodomy laws.

Despite the arguments made by district attorneys and other sodomy law defenders, the Supreme Court's ruling in *Doe* did not knock all future sodomy reform litigation out of the judicial ballpark. Summary affirmations are, by definition, not accompanied by an explanation of the Court's reasoning in the case. Thus, the nature of the precedent emanating from them is necessarily inchoate.[16] The Supreme Court might agree with both the lower court's disposition of the case and its reasoning. Alternately, it might agree with the disposition but reject the reasoning. Without an opinion, it is impossible to know.

The ambiguity of the ruling in *Doe* thus left some "wiggle room" for later challenges. Lambda's litigation is illustrative here. In every sodomy reform case it litigated post-*Doe* (and pre-*Bowers*), the organization had to contend with the opposing counsel's assertion that *Doe* had already determined the constitutionality of sodomy laws. Lambda took a number of different paths to circumvent *Doe*: it asserted the essential indeterminacy of summary affirmances; it argued that *Doe* was limited to the specific facts of the Virginia challenge (a declaratory action against possible future police enforcement) and that other factual situations (such as an actual arrest) were beyond *Doe*'s reach; and it also forwarded state constitutional arguments to get around the damaging federal precedent.

Fortunately, a Supreme Court case decided one year after *Doe* gave Lambda and other sodomy law reformers a legal wedge with which to prop open the doorway to the courts. In *Carey v. Population Services* (1977), the Court struck down a handful of New York laws regulating the advertisement and distribution of contraceptives. Justice Brennan's opinion for the Court reiterated the privacy interest at the heart of *Roe v. Wade* and also explicitly linked abortion and sodomy jurisprudence. After noting that the outer limits of the right to privacy had not yet been defined, Brennan stated: "[T]he Court has not definitively answered the difficult question whether and to what extent the Constitution prohibits State statutes regulating private consensual sexual behavior among adults . . . and we do not purport to answer that question now" (*Carey*, 688 n. 5).

The value of *Carey* to Lambda and other gay rights advocates was that it indicated that the Court itself did not find *Doe* to be dispositive vis-à-vis sodomy laws and that the issue of their constitutionality was still an open question. Of course, whatever else it was, *Doe* could not be construed as an indictment of sodomy laws. This inconvenient fact continued to cause litigators problems as they sought to convince the courts to invalidate state statutes.

Ultimately, courts hearing sodomy challenges during stage 2 split over *Carey*'s effect on *Doe*. Courts in Michigan and Maryland drew on *Doe* to uphold sodomy statutes facing privacy challenges, notwithstanding *Carey*.[17] Some courts even used *Doe* to deny gay rights claims in contexts not explicitly involving sexual activity.[18] Courts in New York, Pennsylvania, and Texas, however, relied on *Carey* to strike down the sodomy statutes in those states.[19]

The Wisdom of Litigating Bowers

Like Monday morning quarterbacks, many people have questioned the wisdom of litigating *Bowers v. Hardwick,* arguing that gay rights litigators failed to develop a body of precedent over several years before bringing a case to the Supreme Court and that their hasty actions only magnified the impact of *Doe.* But at the time, Lambda and gay rights advocates had real reason to believe that the stage was set for a successful federal challenge to the constitutionality of sodomy laws if a case with the "right" facts could be found. This belief was based largely on the outcomes of two cases: New York's *People v. Onofre* and Texas's *Baker v. Wade.* An examination of these two cases offers insight into why some gay rights litigators believed that a broad attack on the constitutionality of sodomy statutes might be received favorably by the courts.

People v. Onofre

Ronald Onofre was that most unusual of plaintiffs in sodomy challenges: a gay man who had actually been convicted of engaging in consensual sodomy in his own home. He was arrested in 1977, after a seventeen-year-old male accused him of forcible sodomy. During the trial, though, the young man recanted his accusation, admitting that he had lied to the police and that the relationship had been entirely consensual. On this admission, the district attorney's office dismissed all charges related to the use of force but refused to dismiss the sodomy charge (under New York law, consent was not a defense to sodomy). Onofre's private attorney unsuccessfully sought to have that charge dismissed as well, arguing that the statute violated Onofre's right to privacy and denied him the equal protection of the laws. Relying in part on *Doe v. Commonwealth's Attorney*, the trial court upheld the constitutionality of New York's sodomy statutes, convicted Onofre, and sentenced him to a year's probation.[20]

While the fact that Onofre's own partner had initially accused him of forcible sodomy might not have made Onofre the most sympathetic figure, the issue of sexual privacy stood in sharp relief: Onofre had been convicted of engaging in consensual sodomy in his own home. Lambda entered the case as cocounsel on the appeal, which alleged that New York's statute violated Onofre's rights to privacy and equal protection under both the federal Constitution and New York's constitution. His privacy argument drew on *Griswold* and its progeny. His equal protection argument drew on the fact that New York only criminalized sodomy when engaged in by "persons not married to each other."

The state of New York, in response, alleged that the statute advanced three governmental interests: the general promotion of morality, the preservation of marriage and the family, and the prevention of injury. Its brief was extremely graphic in depicting the physical injuries sodomy supposedly caused.

> One of the activities for which the respondent was convicted was his penetration into the anus of the victim with his penis. . . . This deviate sexual practice can result in anal ulcer or fissure as well as "extensive changes in the anus and rectum both by friction and as a result of infection" since the anal canal was not evolved for such activity. Another of the activities committed by the respondent . . . was fellatio (the placing of his penis into the victim's mouth). Injury from this activity has also been reported. (*Onofre*, Appellant's Brief, 10, citations omitted)

Moreover, the state argued, striking down the statute would endanger society by creating a slippery slope that would lead to the legitimization of other immoral but consensual acts, including bigamy, prostitution, self-mutilation, consensual murder, and the distribution of drugs (*Onofre*, Appellant's Brief, 16–17).

The New York Court of Appeals unequivocally rejected each of the state's arguments. It found no evidence for the proposition that private, consensual sodomy was harmful either to the participants or to society in general. It also found no rational reason to distinguish between married and unmarried people. New York's sodomy statute, the court ruled, violated Onofre's right to privacy and equal protection under the federal Constitution.

In its ruling, the Court of Appeals specifically distinguished between public morality, which it saw as the legitimate province of state regulation, and private morality, which was beyond the reach of the state, finding that consensual sodomy statutes reached into the forbidden sphere of private morality without advancing public morality in any way. Personal distaste, it ruled, was not a sufficient rationale for intruding into an area of "important personal decision" (*Onofre,* 942).

The 1980 New York Court of Appeals decision in Onofre was not the first judicial decision to invalidate state prohibitions on private consensual activity.[21] It was, however, the first to do so when same-sex acts were directly at issue. That the court had considered and rejected a wide variety of reasons for upholding consensual sodomy statutes suggested to Lambda (and other gay rights advocates) that, if they could just overcome the standing hurdle, they might be successful in other courts as well.

Lambda's perception was reinforced by the subsequent actions of the U.S. Supreme Court. Unwilling to concede defeat, the district attorney prosecuting *Onofre* petitioned the Supreme Court for a writ of certiorari. The Court turned down the opportunity to clarify its decision in *Doe v. Commonwealth's Attorney.* Although denials of certiorari have no precedential value, Lambda interpreted the Court's decision as further support that Doe should not be read to preclude privacy-based sodomy challenges (*Lambda Update* 1981, 1). At least one federal court interpreted the Court's actions similarly (*Rich v. Secretary of the Army,* 1984).

Baker v. Wade

In 1982, two years after *Onofre,* gay rights activists succeeded in overturning Texas's sodomy statute. The case, *Baker v. Wade,* was in many ways the antithesis of *Onofre. Onofre* was brought in state court; *Baker* was a federal suit. *Onofre* involved a man actually convicted for consensual sodomy; *Baker* involved a man who had never been arrested for violating Texas's sodomy statute but argued that the law's existence posed a real and immediate threat to him. Ronald Onofre may have been less than sympathetic as a plaintiff; Don Baker had clearly lived the kind of "impeccable" life that Justice Douglas had suggested would be a vital component in a successful challenge. He had served in the Navy for four years during the Vietnam War and had an excellent service record. He was a former Dallas schoolteacher with a master's degree in education;

his school district regarded him as an "excellent teacher." He had not been open about his sexuality while teaching, nor did he "advocate homosexuality to the students." He was an "active and devout Christian." In addition, he was a "good citizen, having served as precinct chairman and as a delegate to two state Democratic Party conventions." But for his sexual orientation, he was a model citizen.[22]

As did Onofre, Baker argued that the sodomy statute at issue violated his right to privacy and equal protection under the federal Constitution. The legal basis for Baker's equal protection claim differed somewhat from Onofre's: New York's law distinguished between married and unmarried partners while Texas's statute distinguished between same-sex and opposite-sex partners, forbidding sodomy in the first instance but permitting it in the second.

Over the course of the twenty-two-day trial in the case, both sides presented reams of testimony about the nature of homosexuality, the sexual practices of gay men, and the impact of consensual sodomy on the participants and public at large.[23] The *Baker* litigation marked the entrance of dueling experts into sodomy law litigation. Several expert witnesses testified on behalf of Baker, including a psychiatrist, a sociologist, and a theologian. These experts presented "social facts" about homosexuality, including the number of lesbians and gay men in Texas, the intractable nature of sexual orientation, the American Psychiatric Association's removal of homosexuality from its list of mental disorders, and the lack of any evidence that homosexuals had any greater criminal propensity than heterosexuals (other than through violation of the sodomy law under dispute).

The state of Texas responded to these experts by presenting one of its own: a legal psychiatrist. He claimed that sodomy laws benefited both children and homosexuals, the former by reinforcing the "culture of society's norm pattern or expected pattern of behavior" and the latter by encouraging homosexuals to seek help to resolve "their problems."[24] Homosexuals were less stable than heterosexuals, he said, and had more pathological illnesses. The state also introduced explicit depictions of what it termed "common homosexual practices," including anal sex, fisting, and "golden showers" (urination). Relying heavily on its expert, the state advanced four interests justifying the sodomy law: morality and decency, public health, welfare and safety, and procreation.

In August 1982, the U.S. District Court ruled that Texas's sodomy law unconstitutionally denied Baker his rights to privacy and equal protection. Said the court: "The right of two individuals to choose what type of sexual conduct they will enjoy in private is just as personal, just as important, just as sensitive—*indeed, even more so*—than the decision by the same couple to engage in sex using a contraceptive to prevent unwanted pregnancy" (*Baker*, 1140; emphasis added). Moreover, the district court concluded, the state of Texas had failed to show that its law met the minimal requirement of being rationally related to a legitimate state purpose, much less show that the statute advanced a compelling governmental interest (which was the legal standard in the case).

The *Baker* court was the first federal court to consider a sodomy challenge since the Supreme Court's ambiguous affirmation in *Doe*. That it found the statute to be unconstitutional was a clear gay rights victory, especially because it had come down after an extended trial. That the federal district court had heard reams of testimony about the meaning of sex, sexuality, and privacy and *then* decided in favor of Baker seemed to signal a new judicial openness to gay rights claims. The decision by the Texas attorney general not to appeal *Baker* to the Fifth Circuit lent further support to this perception, suggesting that the state's antigay stance was shallow.

Baker and *Onofre*, then, gave Lambda and other gay rights advocates real reason to believe that a carefully crafted attack on the constitutionality of sodomy laws might succeed. The courts in both cases had considered and rejected a wide variety of rationales for maintaining such laws, even after being presented by opposing counsel with graphic depictions of some of the conduct that would be protected if the laws were struck down. Both courts in turn issued broadly worded opinions striking down sodomy statutes as impermissibly infringing on the rights of privacy and equal protection guaranteed by the U.S. Constitution.

Stage 3 (1984–91): Backsliding

In 1982, when Michael Hardwick filed a challenge to Georgia's sodomy statute in federal district court, the timing seemed ripe. With the benefit of hindsight, we can see that the first period of rapid sodomy reform was drawing to a close even as *Bowers* was starting its litigation journey. Figure 2 compares the legislative response to the Model Penal Code's recommendation regarding sodomy statutes in stages 2 and 3. It shows that, of the twelve states considering the Model Penal Code in the years from 1984 through 1991, not a single one repealed its sodomy statute. This stands in stark contrast to the trend in stage 2, when nearly two-thirds of the states considering the Model Penal Code repealed their sodomy

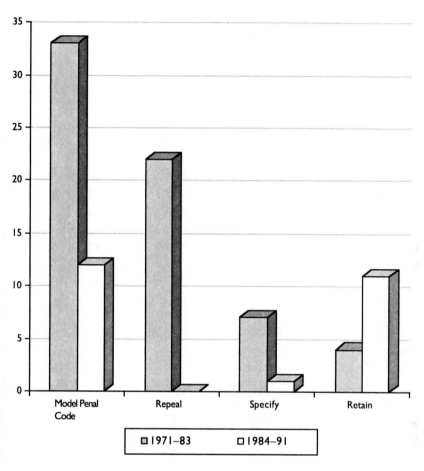

Fig. 2. Comparison of states considering Model Penal Code in stages 2 and 3

statutes. Legislative repeal, in fact, tapered off after 1980. The only state to repeal its sodomy statute in the 1980s was Wisconsin, which did so in 1983.

The course of sodomy reform in the courts likewise stalled in the period between 1984 and 1991. Challenges to sodomy laws were heard by several state trial courts, two state supreme courts, one federal district court, two federal courts of appeal, and the U.S. Supreme Court in stage 3. In the end, not a single state's sodomy law was overturned insofar as it applied to same-sex acts.

Bowers v. Hardwick is, of course, the most obvious example of the judiciary's unwillingness to strike down sodomy laws in stage 3. In a bitterly contested 5–4 vote, the Supreme Court upheld the constitutionality of Georgia's statute. Writing for the Court, Justice Byron White distinguished *Bowers* from the line of privacy cases preceding it. Earlier cases, he said, concerned issues related to procreation, child rearing, marriage, and family relationships: "[W]e think it evident that none of the rights announced in these cases bears any resemblance to the claimed constitutional right of homosexuals to engage in acts of sodomy that is asserted in this case. No connection between family, marriage, or procreation on the one hand and homosexual activity on the other has been demonstrated, either by the Court of Appeals or by [Hardwick]" (*Bowers*, 190–91). "Proscriptions against that conduct have ancient roots," he continued (192). Against such a backdrop, the notion that Hardwick possessed a fundamental right to have same-sex sex was, "at best, facetious" (*Bowers*, 193–94).

Given the Supreme Court's role as the authoritative interpreter of the U.S. Constitution and its unambiguous ruling in *Bowers*, it should come as no surprise that federal challenges to laws prohibiting same-sex sodomy either failed or were withdrawn in the immediate aftermath of the decision.[25] I argue, however, that stage 3 began in 1984, some two years *before* the decision in *Bowers*, while the case was still working its way up through the federal courts and while litigators still had real reason to believe that a carefully crafted federal challenge to state sodomy laws would be successful. My reason for placing the start of stage 3 in 1984 reflects the fact that at this point in time the trend toward legislative sodomy reform ceased, supplanted by a spate of bills seeking to recriminalize same-sex sodomy. It also reflects the fact that *Baker v. Wade* unraveled in 1985, when the Fifth Circuit reinstated Texas's sodomy law.

It may be that others will disagree with this decision and will place the line of demarcation between stages 2 and 3 closer to 1986. The ambiguity of this temporal boundary highlights the fact that shifts in the structure of legal opportuniites do not always occur at discrete points in time. Some changes, such at *Bowers*'s alteration of the legal frames available to sodomy reformers, are immediately apparent. On June 29, 1986, the federal constitutional right to privacy arguably encompassed consensual intimacy between partners of the same sex. On July 1, 1986, the federal constitutional right to privacy definitely did not encompass consensual intimacy between partners of the same sex. Other events, such as the emergence of the AIDS epidemic, clearly altered the LOS but took place over longer periods of time and cannot be pinned down to a single moment.

In any event, during stage 3 sodomy reform stagnated and even reversed course. Why? I argue in the following pages that this backsliding was powered by several conceptually distinct but analytically intertwined factors, including fallout from the 1980 elections, shifts in the membership of the federal courts, the mounting backlash against abortion and the notion of a right to sexual privacy, the emergence of the AIDS epidemic, and doctrinal and access-related constraints. These factors combined variously to staunch the reform of sodomy laws in both the legislative and judicial branches, despite (and occasionally because of) the best efforts of Lambda and other gay rights advocates to eradicate them.

The 1980 Election and Judicial Turnover

The 1980 presidential election was a critical event for gay rights advocates, albeit one whose direct effects on gay rights litigation took a few years to manifest themselves. Ronald Reagan was an ardent pro-lifer who disagreed strongly with the notion of a right to privacy that encompassed abortion. His platform included a promise to rein in what he saw as an "activist" judiciary, that is, a judiciary whose rulings emerged from the political values (read: liberal beliefs) of judges rather than from the dictates of law per se. He vowed, if elected president, to nominate jurists to the federal bench who shared his ideological values on a range of issues, most notably abortion (Schwartz 1988). While he never explicitly discussed sodomy, the common doctrinal grounding of abortion and sodomy jurisprudence meant that, to the extent that Reagan's antipathy to the notion of a constitutional right to abortion was reflected in his appointments to the bench, a major doctrinal argument for voiding sodomy laws would be undermined.[26]

In the end, the "promise" of Reagan's election was fulfilled. Reagan's appointees were far more likely to rule in favor of pro-life claims than were Carter's appointees (Alumbaugh and Rowland 1990). The impact of Reagan's ideological litmus test was augmented by the sheer number of lower court judges he appointed. During the course of his presidency, he successfully brokered the nominations of 378 judges to the federal bench. The most significant of these were his Supreme Court appointments. Over the course of his two-term presidency, Reagan placed three new justices on the Court: Sandra Day O'Connor, Antonin Scalia, and Anthony Kennedy. In addition, he selected sitting justice William Rehnquist to serve as Chief Justice of the Supreme Court.

In all but one instance, Reagan's Supreme Court nominees were as or more conservative than their predecessors (table 6).[27] Rehnquist's elevation to Chief Justice is emblematic of Reagan's ideological designs. Of the justices then sitting on the Supreme Court, Rehnquist's voting record with respect to civil liberties cases was by far the most conservative. By one measure, Rehnquist supported the liberal position in civil liberties cases only 19 percent of the time. As such, he stood in sharp contrast to justices such as Brennan and Marshall, who consistently supported the liberal position in such cases.

It should be noted here that most of Reagan's opportunities to shape the contours of the Supreme Court occurred in the last few years of his presidency. Reagan appointed only one justice in the years before *Bowers*: Sandra Day O'Connor.[28] As table 6 shows, O'Connor's position on civil liberties issues fell considerably to the right of Potter Stewart's, the justice whose seat she filled. While Stewart had supported the liberal position in civil liberties cases some 44 percent of the time in the years from 1958 (when he arrived on the Court) to 1981, O'Connor supported such positions only 28 percent of the time in the years between 1981 and 1985. The ideological difference between the two justices was exemplified by their positions on abortion-related cases. Stewart had been a member of the majority in *Roe v. Wade* and had voted pro-choice in a number of subsequent cases. Although O'Connor would vote to "save" *Roe* in *Planned Parenthood v. Casey* (1992), in the 1980s she consistently argued for rolling back the right to abortion.[29]

In 1986, O'Connor provided one of the five votes to uphold Georgia's sodomy law in *Bowers*. Ultimately, there is no way to ascertain the direct effect of judicial turnover in the case; there is no way to know whether Stewart would have taken a different position in *Bowers*, providing the

TABLE 6. Comparison of Outgoing and Incoming Justices during Reagan's Presidency

Departing Justices	Civil Liberties (%)[a]	Replacement Justices	Civil Liberties (%)[b]
Burger, Chief Justice		Rehnquist,	
(1969–86)	28	Chief Justice (1986–)	19
Stewart (1958–81)	44	O'Connor (1981–)	28
Rehnquist (1972–86)	19	Scalia (1986–)	30
Powell (1971–87)	35	Kennedy (1988–)	35

[a]Percentages represent justices' support for the liberal position in civil liberties cases from arrival on the Supreme Court through 1985. Source for data is Segal and Spaeth 1989.

[b]Percentages represent justices' support for the liberal position in civil liberties cases from their arrival on the Supreme Court through 1995. Source for data is Epstein and Knight 1998.

fifth vote to strike down Georgia's sodomy law rather than the fifth vote to uphold it. However, comparing the justices' votes in *Bowers* with their voting record on civil liberties cases more generally is suggestive.

Table 7 lays out the justices on the *Bowers* Court according to their Baum scores. Baum scores rank the relative ideological stances of the twenty-six justices who sat on the Supreme Court in the years between 1946 and 1985. The lower the Baum score, the more liberal the voting record in cases that split along a left-right schema. As table 7 shows, the four most liberal members of the *Bowers* Court all believed that Georgia's sodomy law violated Michael Hardwick's right to privacy, while the five most conservative members all voted to sustain the law. O'Connor's Baum score was twenty out of twenty-six, making her the third most conservative member of the *Bowers* Court, ranking just beneath Rehnquist and Burger. Stewart's Baum score, on the other hand, was eleven out of twenty-six. Had he remained on the Court for *Bowers,* he would have been the fourth most liberal justice hearing the case. To the extent that Stewart's Baum score can be used as a predictor of his vote in *Bowers* (and this is a big caveat), Georgia's sodomy statute would have fallen had he, not O'Connor, heard the case.

In sum, the 1980 elections shifted the structure of legal opportunities

TABLE 7. Supreme Court Votes in *Bowers*

Justice	Vote in Bowers	Baum Score[a]	Court Ranking[b]
Rehnquist	Uphold law	25/26	9
Burger	Uphold law	21/26	8
O'Connor	Uphold law	20/26	7
Powell	Uphold law	16/26	6
White	Uphold law	14/26	5
Blackmun	Strike law	13/26	4
[Stewart][c]	—	11/26	
Stevens	Strike law	10/26	3
Brennan	Strike law	5/26	2
Marshall	Strike law	3/26	1

[a]Baum scores rank the relative ideological stance of the twenty-six justices who have sat on the Supreme Court in the years between 1946 and 1985. Marshall's score of 3 indicates that he has the third most liberal voting record with respect to civil liberties issues, while Rehnquist's score of 25 indicates that he has the second most conservative voting record on the Court during the period studied. Source for data is Baum 1989.

[b]Court ranking adjusts the Baum scores to reflect the relative ideological stances of the nine justices sitting on the Supreme Court in 1986, when *Bowers* was decided.

[c]Justice Stewart's name is in brackets because he was not actually on the Supreme Court in 1986, when *Bowers* was decided.

with respect to sodomy reform, because they put into office a president whose judicial philosophy was antithetical to the privacy doctrine that grounded most sodomy challenges. This president in turn used the power of his office to nominate jurists who shared his philosophy, resulting in a federal bench that grew increasing hostile to the notion of sexual privacy rights. One of these jurists, Justice Sandra Day O'Connor, replaced a member of the pro-choice majority on the Supreme Court and subsequently voted to limit the right to abortion in a number of cases. In 1986, she provided the fifth vote to deny Michael Hardwick's challenge to the constitutionality of Georgia's sodomy statute.

The Emergence of AIDS

Like the 1980 elections, the AIDS epidemic began several years before stage 3 began. Again like the 1980 elections, it was a critical event whose direct effects on the course of gay rights and sodomy reform took a few years to manifest themselves. Ultimately, however, the emergence of the AIDS epidemic shifted the LOS surrounding sodomy reform by sparking a backlash against homosexuality more generally and gay male sexuality more specifically.

Events in Texas during 1983 illustrate the impact of AIDS on sodomy reform. Remember that in *Baker v. Wade* (1982) a U.S. District Court ruled that Texas's sodomy law violated Don Baker's constitutional rights to privacy and equal protection. Although Texas's attorney general decided not to appeal the decision in *Baker* to the Fifth Circuit, a district attorney from Amarillo by the name of Danny Hill appealed the case (and the attorney general's choice not to pursue *Baker*) in a variety of judicial fora, including the U.S. District Court, the Fifth Circuit, and the Texas Supreme Court.[30]

Under the legal rules governing Hill's federal appeals, he had to show either the existence of newly discovered evidence or some other reason (such as fraud) important enough to require a different result in the case in order to get the original decision set aside. The thrust of his "newly discovered evidence" argument was the public threat posed by homosexuality. His proof: AIDS.

The incidence of AIDS in persons who engage in homosexual conduct and its deathly public health threat are newly discovered evidence. Although AIDS had been discovered at the time of trial, its direct relationship to homosexual conduct was not fully established. AIDS is recognized by the medical community as one of the most deadly and proliferic [*sic*] diseases in recent memory and is directly related to homosexual conduct. The court should consider the public health dangers which AIDS poses and its relationship to the type of conduct which is before the Court in this action. (*Baker*, Brief in Support of Motion to Set Aside Final Judgment and Reopen the Evidence, 4)

Shortly after Hill filed his appeal in *Baker*, Bill Ceverha, a Texas state legislator, approached the subject of sodomy laws from a different direction. He introduced a bill, HB 2138, that was designed to broaden Texas's sodomy statute (depending on the outcome of the court appeal) to prohibit all "homosexual conduct" and to dramatically increase the penalties involved.[31] The stated purpose of the bill was to prevent homosexuals from destroying the nation's health.

Hill and Ceverha were connected by a newly formed group called Dallas Doctors Against AIDS (DDAA).[32] One of the group's founding members served as Danny Hill's lawyer and also helped draft HB 2138. Although DDAA presented itself as an objective research-oriented group, its efforts were clearly directed toward restricting the civil liberties of lgb people in a wide variety of contexts. The amicus brief it filed in the *Baker* appeal detailed the "AIDS-threat" posed by homosexual (by which it meant gay male) activities. DDAA also solicited Dr. Paul Cameron to testify on behalf of HB 2138 and to serve as an expert witness in the *Baker* appeal. Cameron was—and is—a notorious opponent of gay rights.[33] Most telling is the fact that DDAA also involved itself in a concurrent lawsuit over the formation of an lgb student group at Texas A&M University (*Gay Student Services v. Texas A&M University*, 1984). The student group should be prevented from forming, they argued, because it would encourage the commission of sodomy and thereby further the transmission of AIDS.[34]

Ultimately, both the legislative and judicial attempts to use AIDS in order to derail sodomy reform failed. HB 2138 died in committee when the legislative session ended. The U.S. District Court rejected Hill's (and DDAA's) arguments that sodomy laws were needed to combat AIDS. Although the Fifth Circuit reversed the U.S. District Court's decision in *Baker* and reinstated Texas's sodomy law, it did not base its decision on the perceived threat to public health.

Nevertheless, HB 2138 and Hill's appeal both signaled the potential power of AIDS to reframe sodomy from an issue of privacy to a matter of public health. AIDS put sodomy law reformers into a difficult position. On the one hand, they needed to respond to the public health arguments raised by their opponents. On the other hand, they wanted to avoid graphic discussions of the mechanics of the sexual activities at issue, concentrating instead on the liberty interests infringed on by state intrusion into one of the "fundamental experiences" through which "people define the meaning of their lives."[35] Opponents of sodomy law reform, conversely, usually embraced explicit discussions of sex acts, as Danny Hill's appeal illustrates.

> The [U.S. District] Court was offered very little evidence concerning what homosexuals do and why homosexual conduct poses such a severe public health threat to the citizens of the State of Texas. *The case was tried on the basis of homosexuality as a state of being or lifestyle rather than on the specific acts of "homosexual conduct."* Common homosexual practices such as "rimming," "scat," "handballing," "golden showers," the insertion of various objects into the anus of individuals and oral/anal, oral/penal and penal/anal conduct were not referred to or discussed in depth. The variety of sexual conduct, in conjunction with the frequency of anonymous sexual partners, poses substantial considerations which were not presented to the Court in the trial of this matter. (*Baker*, Brief in Support of Motion to Set Aside Final Judgment and Reopen the Evidence, 4; emphasis added)

By explicitly treating homosexuality as a set of sexual practices, Hill sought simultaneously to inspire revulsion by the reader, to situate gay men (lesbians being virtually absent) as different from "normal" people, and to exclude the conclusion that homosexuality was a fundamental component of identity. AIDS played into this strategy neatly, because it forced consideration of gay male sexual practices and their potential threat to public health. Literally thousands of pages of medical articles about AIDS were introduced into the *Baker* appeal, an occurrence that was repeated in several other sodomy challenges, including *Bowers*.

That legislative repeal of sodomy statutes ceased just as the AIDS epidemic became visible may be coincidental, although the simultaneous appearance of bills designed to recriminalize and/or increase the criminal penalties associated with same-sex sodomy suggests otherwise. The evidence that judicial openness to repealing sodomy statutes was affected by the emergence of AIDS is more direct; some decisions explicitly invoked the epidemic. The most notable example of this is the Missouri Supreme Court, which in 1986 upheld the constitutionality of the state's sodomy statute, holding in part that the statute was

> rationally related to the State's concededly legitimate interest in protecting the public health. The State has argued that forbidding homosexual activity will inhibit the spread of sexually communicable disease like [AIDS]. . . . [T]he General Assembly could have reasonably concluded that the general promiscuity characteristic of the homosexual lifestyle made such acts among homosexuals particularly deserving of regulation. (*State v. Walsh*, 1986)

In sum, the emergence of the AIDS epidemic shifted the structure of legal opportunities surrounding sodomy reform in several ways. It served as a catalyst for mobilization on the part of those who opposed gay rights in general. It altered the persuasiveness of the sociolegal arguments about the (de)merits of sodomy laws by giving those opponents of sodomy reform a documented public health issue to support their long-standing "homosexual danger" claims. It sparked the introduction of legislative bills designed to heighten the criminal penalties associated with same-sex sodomy. It probably contributed to the abrupt end of legislative repeal. It certainly undercut the efforts of gay rights litigators to frame homosexuality as a core aspect of identity rather than as a taste for certain sexual activities, in the process weakening the privacy argument at the heart of most sodomy challenges. And it was invoked as a basis for upholding sodomy laws in a number of legal challenges.

The Wisdom of Litigating Bowers, *Revisited*

The foregoing discussion of the impact of the 1980 elections and the AIDS epidemic on the course of sodomy reform inevitably calls into question the wisdom of litigating *Bowers* in the first place. By their actions, Lambda, the ACLU, and the other litigators involved in the case worsened the legal position of lgb people—at least temporarily—rather than improving it. Why did they not read the shifting political winds correctly? The answer to this is multifaceted, but a large part of it is that what seems clear in retrospect can be fuzzy while it is ongoing. When *Bowers* was initiated in 1982, the scope of sodomy reform seemed to be expanding, not contracting. Broadly worded decisions in *Onofre* and *Baker* seemed to indicate that a carefully crafted attack on the constitutionality of sodomy laws might well be successful. AIDS was not yet a potent political threat to gay rights.

Moreover, the 1980 elections, while clearly auguring that the federal bench would grow more conservative, did not suggest an obvious course of action to gay rights litigators. On the one hand, the fact that the space available for legal activism around sodomy reform would likely decrease in the future indicated that sodomy reformers should seek alternate routes for achieving their sociopolitical goals. On the other hand, the fact that the courts would likely grow less friendly to sodomy reform suggested that gay rights activists should press cases quickly, before Reagan had the opportunity to appoint new judges to the bench. The appropriate litigation response to the 1980 elections was in fact a source of tension among gay rights groups.

This intergroup tension over tactics can be seen clearly in *National Gay Task Force (NGTF) v. Board of Education of Oklahoma*. The case was brought by the GRA and the Oklahoma affiliate of the ACLU. It involved a challenge to the constitutionality of a law making "public homosexual conduct or activity" grounds for firing (or refusing to hire) schoolteachers. *Conduct* was defined as "advocating, soliciting, imposing, encouraging or promoting public or private homosexual activity in a manner that creates a substantial risk that the conduct will come to the attention of school children or school employees."[36] The constitutionality of sodomy laws themselves was not directly at issue, although "homosexual sodomy" was clearly at the heart of the dispute.

The U.S. District Court upheld the statute's constitutionality when the matter came before it in 1982, but in dicta[37] accompanying the decision the court construed the reach of the provision narrowly. The court said that the Oklahoma law did not permit the school board to dismiss or otherwise discipline a teacher "who merely advocates equality or tolerance of homosexuality, . . . who openly discusses homosexuality, . . . who assigns for class study articles and books written by advocates of gay rights, . . . who expresses an opinion, publicly or privately on the subject of homosexuality; or . . . who advocates the enactment of laws establishing civil rights for homosexuals" (*NGTF*, 32–33). The court continued, "If, under the Act, a school board could declare a teacher unfit for doing any of the foregoing or refuse to hire one for similar reasons, it would likely not meet constitutional muster" (33).

At the time, the GRA was pursuing a policy of seeking high court review of all its cases, hoping to have them decided before Reagan could appoint more conservative judges to the bench. It immediately filed an appeal of the district court ruling to the Tenth Circuit. Lambda, however, fearing the growing conservatism of the federal bench, believed that the GRA should cut its losses. In a letter dated August 3, 1982, Lambda wrote:

> We realize that the notice of appeal has been filed and that substantial publicity about the appeal has been sent out. We believe, however, that the risk of a negative decision from the 10th Circuit is significant enough to warrant reconsideration of your decision. We also believe that a decision not to proceed with the appeal, if based on a thorough review of the legal precedent and an analysis of the risks involved, could be effectively communicated to the gay community. . . .
>
> The question of what we have to lose by proceeding with this appeal has been raised. There is some positive dicta in the court's opinion [referring to the district court's narrow reading mentioned previously] which leaves the door open for a possible challenge at a later date if the statute is applied to a teacher solely on the basis of his or her speech or for a possible challenge if we can clearly demonstrate that teachers are restricting their discussion of gay issues because of this legislation. A negative decision from the 10th Circuit might preclude such a challenge, eliminating even the positive dicta in the decision. A negative decision might also affect future cases in other Circuits.[38]

Lambda was not alone in its concerns. The national ACLU also opposed the appeal. The day after Lambda sent its missive, the national ACLU sent a virtually identical letter to its Oklahoma affiliate, urging it to reverse course. The recipients of these letters were not persuaded and continued their litigation.[39]

Hindsight reveals that Lambda and the national ACLU need not have worried about *NGTF*. In 1984, the Tenth Circuit came down with a mixed but reasonably favorable ruling holding that the Oklahoma law violated the First Amendment speech rights of schoolteachers. In 1985, the Supreme Court summarily affirmed the Tenth Circuit's decision, albeit by the narrowest of margins: a 4–4 tie.[40]

Ironically, given the ultimate outcome in *Bowers,* the Tenth Circuit and Supreme Court decisions in *NGTF* soothed Lambda's concerns about the tactical wisdom of seeking high court review of gay rights cases. And *Bowers* seemed to offer an unparalleled opportunity to attack state sodomy statutes.

Hardwick's arrest clearly gave him standing to challenge Georgia's sodomy law. The location of the arrest (Hardwick's own bedroom) made the privacy interest at stake very clear, with respect to both its decisional and its spatial aspects. Hardwick's willingness to expose himself to the potential trauma of extended litigation about his private sexual activities constituted yet a third reason for bringing the case.[41] As Goldstein (1993, 1792) phrased it, "Hardwick seemed to be the perfect plaintiff to challenge the law—he was arrested in the bedroom of his own home with another consenting adult; he worked in a gay bar, so his job would not be endangered by a public fight and he was already out to his mother." Given the infrequency of the law's enforcement in the context of private, consensual sexual activity, the likelihood of finding another case with as good a fact pattern was remote. In short, even though Lambda recognized that Reagan's election augured a change in judicial winds, *Bowers* seemed to be as good a means to challenge sodomy laws as gay rights advocates were likely to find.

That said, the decision to press *Bowers* was quite controversial within the universe of sodomy-reform litigators. Discord surfaced immediately. Kathy Wilde, an Atlanta attorney in private practice, had agreed to serve as Hardwick's counsel on behalf of the Georgia ACLU, which had initiated the case.[42] As she told me in a telephone interview, she began to receive calls from gay rights activists around the country within days of filing the case.[43] Many were upset with her for initiating *Bowers*, arguing that Georgia was a "bad" state in which to pursue sodomy reform through the courts. Unlike the sodomy statutes of New York and Texas, Georgia's statute did not offer a clear equal protection claim. Although Wilde suspected that Georgia's sodomy statute was being disproportionately enforced against gay men, no hard evidence was at hand. Many of Wilde's callers believed that a combined equal protection/privacy challenge was more likely to succeed and that sodomy reformers should bring cases only in those states whose statutes offered that option.

Intracommunity tensions over *Bowers*'s viability heightened early in 1983, when the U.S. District Court dismissed the case, ruling that Hardwick's privacy claim had been foreclosed by the Supreme Court's summary affirmance in *Doe v. Commonwealth's Attorney*. Wilde immediately appealed the ruling to the Eleventh Circuit. The Georgia ACLU, however, declined to sponsor the appeal. As Wilde recalled it, the affiliate was more divided over the politics of having a heterosexual woman press the case than the lack of an equal protection argument. (Much as the NAACP felt it was important for black lawyers to press major civil rights cases, some members of the affiliate apparently felt that a lesbian or gay lawyer should litigate *Bowers*.)

No matter what the reason for the affiliate's withdrawal from the case, Wilde needed to find another group to underwrite the costs of the appeal. She approached the national ACLU, but it declined the case based on its affiliate's decision. Lambda then offered to fund the appeal (although a review of its financial status in 1983 indicates that the organization would have been hard-pressed to cover the not inconsiderable costs of continuing the litigation).

Ultimately, Lambda did not need to find the money to finance the case. Lambda was physically located at the ACLU's New York offices in 1983, and Lambda's managing attorney, Abby Rubenfeld, had been using her geographical proximity to ACLU decision makers to pressure the organization to lend its stature to gay rights litigation by creating its own project rather than continue to take cases on an ad hoc basis. She was joined in her informal campaign by several of the ACLU's own litigators. Based in part on pressure from Lambda and its own litigators, the national ACLU ultimately reversed its decision and agreed to underwrite *Bowers* (although it would not establish the Lesbian and Gay Rights Project until 1986).

Although Lambda had lobbied for the ACLU to lend its institutional credibility to the case, the then-small organization was eager to establish its own importance as a gay rights litigator and did not want its role in *Bowers* to be entirely usurped by the larger, more established litigator. Lambda thus took on the task of defusing tensions and increasing communication among the fragmented network of gay rights litigators.

Late in 1983, Rubenfeld brought key sodomy reform advocates together for an unprecedented meeting, hosted jointly by Lambda and the ACLU. Representatives from the five other gay legal groups then in existence attended the meeting,[44] as did key private litigators such as Wilde and Jim Kellogg, the attorney in *Baker*. From this meeting emerged a coalition—infelicitously named the Ad-Hoc Task Force to Challenge Sodomy Laws—that would serve as a crucial mechanism for communication and coordination among gay legal activists.

The task force met periodically to hash out legal theories, consider rhetorical approaches, and forge agreements among the various litigators. One of the major subjects of discussion was, obviously, *Bowers*. The other was the increasingly complicated litigation in *Baker v. Wade*. There was ongoing debate among task force members over how best to handle the two cases. Some argued that *Bowers* should be dropped in favor of *Baker,* despite the latter case's procedural complications, because its combined equal protection/privacy challenge offered more bases under which the sodomy law could be struck down. Some task force members also felt that Don Baker would be a more sympathetic figure to the justices on the Supreme Court than would Michael Hardwick. Baker, after all, had lived an "impeccable life" and was a "model citizen" but for his sexual orientation. Hardwick worked in a gay bar, had been cited for public drinking, and had been arrested for engaging in mutual oral sex with a one-night stand. Since both cases were federal challenges, they reasoned, a negative decision in *Bowers* might damage *Baker*'s chances.

Other members of the task force felt that the facts in *Bowers* made such a compelling privacy case that the lack of an equal protection argument would not matter. In addition, they argued, bifurcating privacy arguments from equal protection arguments would lessen the negative impact of *Bowers* in the event the case ended badly. While privacy arguments based on the federal Constitution would be foreclosed, equal protection arguments would remain available to gay rights litigators. Still other members of the task force hoped to consolidate the two cases at the Supreme Court level, if both made it that far. Consolidating the cases, they felt, would present the Supreme Court with the most compelling illustration of the harms engendered by sodomy statutes.

The task force members ultimately chose not to sacrifice one case for the other, opting instead to devote their energies to developing the two parallel challenges.[45] They also decided not to seek consolidation of the two cases at the Supreme Court level, opting instead to keep the cases separate. In retrospect, these were bad decisions. *Bowers* made it to the Supreme Court first. *Baker* was still awaiting word on certiorari when the decision in *Bowers* came down; the Supreme Court subsequently declined to hear the case.

It is impossible to know, though, whether the Supreme Court would have ruled differently had it been faced with the issues in *Baker* rather than—or together with—those in *Bowers.* It is possible that the only "good" legal decision would have been the decision not to litigate either case. It is also possible that the *Baker* adherents were correct and that *Bowers* was simply the weaker case. The important point for the purpose at hand is that the members of the task force diligently attempted to read the courts and made reasonable decisions given the limited information before them.

Losing Bowers

Despite the considered efforts of Wilde, the ACLU, Lambda, and the other litigators involved in the Ad-Hoc Task Force, *Bowers* failed. The impact of the 1980 elections and the AIDS epidemic on the course of sodomy reform more generally has already been noted. In this section, I argue that the mechanics of the legal process also played an important role in *Bowers*'s failure. Despite Michael Hardwick's arrest, the general nonenforcement of sodomy laws bedeviled the litigation in the case.

The Georgia ACLU's original plan was to secure Michael Hardwick's criminal conviction for violating Georgia's sodomy law and then to use that conviction as the basis for a legal challenge to the law as applied. These plans were scratched, however, when the district attorney declined to prosecute the case, despite the eyewitness account of a police officer and despite Hardwick's own statements that he had broken the law and intended to do so again in the future. Instead, Hardwick filed a civil challenge in federal district court, alleging that the statute violated his constitutional right to privacy and bore no rational relationship to any legitimate state interest. Hardwick's lack of a criminal conviction would come back to haunt him in the Supreme Court, because it served as the basis for Justice Lewis Powell's vote.

Powell, Sodomy, and Standing

As table 7 shows, Powell was one of the five-justice majority in *Bowers.* The task force had identified him early on as possessing the crucial swing vote in the case, based on his general ideological leanings and his voting record in other sexual privacy and gay rights cases. While the Supreme Court had provided no authoritative guidance on the constitutionality of sodomy laws in the years between *Doe* and *Bowers,* the reaction of the justices in other cases suggested to the task force that *Bowers* would be close and would probably be decided by a 5–4 margin, win or lose (table 8).

As the task force saw it, Rehnquist, Burger, and White would almost certainly vote to sustain Georgia's sodomy statute, while Marshall, Brennan, Stevens, and Blackmun would almost certainly vote to strike it down. Although some members of the task force felt that O'Connor might be persuaded to strike down Georgia's law, most felt that her vote would go against Hardwick. Powell was the puzzle. His voting record offered scant information on his beliefs about the constitutionality of sodomy laws. On the one hand, he favored the notion of a right of sexual privacy, at least insofar as it applied to abortion. On the other hand, he was concerned about how far that right extended.

The case of *Carey v. Population Services* illustrates the ambiguity of Powell's position. The case involved a New York statute prohibiting the distribution of contraceptives by anyone other than a licensed pharmacist. The Court struck down the statute by a vote of 7–2, which Powell

TABLE 8.   Ad-Hoc Task Force's Predictions in *Bowers*

Predicted Vote	Justice	Prior Decisions[a]	Ranking[b]
Pro-Hardwick	Marshall	Roe, Carey, Akron, *Uplinger*,[c] NGTF[d]	1
	Brennan	Roe, Carey, Akron, *Uplinger*, NGTF	2
	Stevens	*Carey*, Akron, *Uplinger*, NGTF	3
	Blackmun	Roe, Carey, Akron, *Uplinger*, NGTF	4
Uncertain	Powell	Roe, *Carey*, Akron, *Uplinger*	6
Pro-Bowers	O'Connor	Akron, Uplinger, NGTF	7
	White	Roe, Carey, Akron, Uplinger, NGTF	5
	Burger	Roe, Carey, Akron, Uplinger, NGTF	8
	Rehnquist	Roe, Carey, Akron, Uplinger, NGTF	9

[a]Case names without underlining are votes that are considered pro-gay. Case names with underlining are votes that are considered to be antigay. Case names in italics are votes that are ambiguous.

[b]Rankings reflect the relative ideological stances of the nine justices sitting on the Supreme Court in 1985, when certiorari was granted in *Bowers*.

[c]*New York v. Uplinger* (1984) concerned the constitutionality of a New York statute prohibiting solicitation for "deviate sexual intercourse." The case was important vis-à-vis sodomy reform because it presented an opportunity for the high court to rule on the constitutionality of sodomy laws. In an extremely unusual turn of events, the Court granted certiorari, heard oral arguments in the case, and then dismissed certiorari as improvidently granted rather than deciding the case on its merits. Justices Burger, Rehnquist, White, and O'Connor issued a two-sentence dissent from the dismissal of certiorari, arguing that since New York's sodomy statute was invalidated on federal constitutional grounds (in *Onofre*), "the merits of that decision are properly before us and should be addressed" (*Uplinger*, 252). Powell joined the four more liberal members of the Court in voting to dismiss the case. Votes on petitions for certiorari are very imperfect measures of votes on the merits; justices may vote to deny certiorari for reasons having little to do with their beliefs about the merits of the issue raised by the case (see Perry 1991). Thus, Powell's vote gave no real indication of his position on the constitutionality of sodomy statutes.

[d]*National Gay Task Force v. Board of Education of Oklahoma* (1985) was the second gay-related case handled by the Supreme Court in the years between *Doe* and *Bowers*. It involved the constitutionality of an Oklahoma law making "public homosexual conduct or activity" grounds to fire (or refuse to hire) schoolteachers. *Conduct* was defined as "advocating, soliciting, imposing, encouraging or promoting public or private homosexual activity in a manner that creates a substantial risk that the conduct will come to the attention of school children or school employees" (Okla. Stat. Tit. 70, § 6-103.15 (A) (2)). By the time *NGTF* made it to the Supreme Court, the only live issue was whether the statute impermissibly restricted constitutionally protected speech on the part of the school teacher. The constitutionality of sodomy laws themselves was not directly at issue, although "homosexual sodomy" was clearly at the heart of the dispute. The Court summarily affirmed the lower court's holding that Oklahoma's statute violated the First Amendment rights of schoolteachers. It is intriguing that the affirmance was the product of a 4-4 tie. Justice Powell did not participate in *NGTF* because he was recovering from surgery.

joined (Rehnquist and Burger dissented). In articulating the reasons for their decision, Blackmun, Brennan, and Marshall specifically argued that the outer limits of the right to sexual privacy had not yet been marked. Rehnquist's dissenting opinion instead argued that sodomy laws were constitutional. Powell took a middle road, arguing that Blackmun, Brennan, and Marshall had gone too far in protecting sexual privacy rights but giving little indication of where the constitutional lines should be drawn.

Hardwick's legal team[46] thus tailored their arguments to appeal to Powell. Since his jurisprudence had consistently emphasized the constitutional significance accorded to the home, they played up the spatial aspects of the case.

> All that Respondent [Hardwick] argues is that a Georgia citizen is entitled by the Constitution to demand not only a warrant of the Georgia police officer who would enter his bedroom, but also a substantial justification of the Georgia legislature when it declares criminal the consensual intimacies he chooses to engage in there. No less justification is acceptable in a society whose constitutional values have always placed the highest value upon the sanctity of the home against governmental intrusion or control. (*Bowers*, Respondent's Brief, 4)

Despite their attempt to "capture" Powell, he ultimately sided with the conservative wing of the Court. His concurrence laid out his reasoning, which centered on the *lack of injury* incurred by Hardwick: although arrested, Hardwick had not been prosecuted, much less convicted and sentenced. Had he been, wrote Powell, it "would create a serious Eighth Amendment issue. Under the Georgia statute a single act of sodomy, even in the private setting of a home, is a felony comparable in terms of the possible sentence imposed to serious felonies such as aggravated battery, first degree arson, and robbery" (*Bowers*, 197–98, citations omitted).

Powell's reasoning here bears further perusal, both because he provided the crucial fifth vote to uphold Georgia's sodomy statute and because he had originally voted to strike the law down. The papers of Justice Marshall contain a memo written by Powell and circulated to all eight of his colleagues in which he explained his shift.

> At Conference last week, I expressed the view that in some cases it would violate the Eighth Amendment to imprison a person for a private act of homosexual sodomy. I continue to think that in such

cases imprisonment would constitute cruel and unusual punishment. I relied primarily on *Robinson v. California.*

At Conference, given my views as to the Eighth Amendment, my vote was to affirm but on this ground rather than the view of four other Justices that there was a violation of a fundamental substantive constitutional rights—as [the Eleventh Circuit] held. I did not agree that there is a substantive due process right to engage in conduct that for centuries has been recognized as deviant, and not in the best interest of preserving humanity. I may say generally, that I also hesitate to create another substantive due process right.

I write this memorandum today because upon further study as to what is before us, I conclude that my "bottom line" should be to reverse rather than affirm. The only question presented by the parties is the substantive due process issues, and—as several of you noted at Conference—my Eighth Amendment view was not addressed by the court below or by the parties.

In sum, my more carefully considered view is that I will vote to reverse but will write separately to explain my views of this case generally. I will not know, until I see the writing, whether I can join an opinion finding no substantive due process right or simply join the judgment.[47]

Three years after *Bowers,* Powell (who had since retired from the Court) expanded on his reasoning in the case. In an address to a group of law students, he said that he "probably made a mistake in [*Bowers*]." The case, he opined, was a "close call." But, he maintained, "[t]hat case was not a major case, and one of the reasons I voted the way I did was the case was a frivolous case" brought "just to see what the Court would do" (Marcus 1990, A3).

Powell's use of the word *frivolous* to describe *Bowers* drives home the core problem of gay rights litigators seeking to use the courts to effect sodomy reform: the general nonenforcement of sodomy laws made it easy for jurists to conclude that those laws did not harm people. Ironically, by not enforcing their sodomy provisions, states could successfully insulate them from constitutional challenge.

Sodomy and Standing, Revisited

The general nonenforcement of sodomy laws bedeviled *Bowers* in more ways than one. Virtually all commentary on *Bowers* has noted what Halley (1993, 1742) calls the "transparent fictionality" of the Supreme Court's framing of the case. Georgia's sodomy statute made no distinction based on gender, proscribing instead "any sexual act involving the sex organs of one person and the mouth or anus of another" under penalty of up to twenty years' imprisonment. Michael Hardwick challenged this statute on its face, yet the Supreme Court construed the question in the case to be "whether the Federal Constitution confers a fundamental right upon homosexuals to engage in sodomy" (*Bowers*, 190). The Court was able to frame the question in this fashion largely because of the inability of gay rights litigators to completely jump the standing hurdle in the case.

Kathy Wilde, Hardwick's lead counsel in the lower court phases of the case, was well aware of the doctrinal constraints imposed by Georgia's statute. She sought to turn the disadvantage caused by her inability to raise an equal protection claim into an advantage by soliciting a married couple to join the case. John and Mary Doe (pseudonyms) were acquaintances of Hardwick. They claimed that Hardwick's arrest had "chilled and deterred" their sexual intimacy and interfered with their marital relationship. By bringing in the Does, Wilde sought to foreclose the interpretation that *Bowers* was just about homosexual sodomy. The plain language of Georgia's statute applied to all people, heterosexual or homosexual, married or single. The presence of the Does pointed to the fact that the activity for which Michael Hardwick was arrested (oral sex) was an activity engaged in by married heterosexual couples as well and dramatized the scope of the sexual privacy issues at stake: the language of Georgia's statute reached into the privacy of the marital bedroom.

Michael Bowers, Georgia's attorney general, argued in response that the Does did not have standing to challenge Georgia's statute, because they had not been arrested and were unlikely to face arrest in the foreseeable future. Their lack of immediate danger from the statute, he argued, meant that they did not meet the legal requirements to challenge it. The U.S. District Court agreed. The Does, it ruled, lacked standing to challenge the law. Wilde appealed the district court's ruling to the Eleventh Circuit. She argued that the danger was real, even if the Does had never been arrested; were she allowed to proceed with the discovery process, she said, she would present evidence of a number of prosecutions of married couples under Georgia's statute.[48] In response, the state of Georgia reiterated its position that the Does lacked standing, *conceding that their sexual activities were encompassed by the right of privacy.*

The decision handed down by the Eleventh Circuit in May 1985 was in many ways a major victory for gay rights. Analogizing Hardwick's activity to the intimate association of marriage and noting its location (Hardwick's own bed), the court ruled that "[t]he activity he hopes to engage in is quintessentially private and lies at the heart of an intimate association beyond the proper reach of state regulation" (*Bowers* 1985, 1212). This decision marked the first time a federal appellate court had found sodomy laws to violate a fundamental right.

The victory had a major drawback, however. The court ruled that the Does lacked standing. Explained the court:

> Each of them [Hardwick and the Does] claims that their normal course of activity will lead them to violate the statute, completely apart from their desire to have it invalidated. *Hardwick's status as a homosexual adds special credence to his claim.* While a plaintiff hoping only to challenge a statute might overestimate his or her willingness to risk actual prosecution, a plaintiff who genuinely desires to engage in conduct regardless of its legal status presents a court with a more plausible threat of future prosecution. (*Bowers* 1985, 1205; emphasis added)

The court concluded that "the authenticity of Hardwick's desire to engage in the proscribed activity" (1206) together with his actual arrest gave him—but not the Does—standing.

By removing the plaintiffs who linked the case most closely to the right of privacy articulated in *Griswold v. Connecticut* and its progeny, the court of appeals weakened the explicit connection to the larger theory of sexual privacy advanced in the case, even as it issued a ruling in Hardwick's favor. Moreover, it set up a factual context that allowed the Supreme Court to limit its review to "homosexual sodomy" despite the facially neutral language of the statute itself. Had the Does been accorded standing by the Eleventh Circuit, it would have been well-nigh impossible for the Supreme Court to morph the question at issue to exclude the consideration of "heterosexual sodomy."

The Impact of Bowers

Had Hardwick won his case, the sodomy laws of twenty-six states would have fallen. His loss, conversely, gave additional ammunition to opponents of sodomy reform. *Bowers*'s legal impact was immediate. One week after the Court handed down its decision in *Bowers,* it denied certiorari in *Baker v. Wade,* leaving standing the Fifth Circuit ruling upholding the constitutionality of the Texas sodomy law. One week after that, the Missouri Supreme Court upheld the constitutionality of its state's sodomy law, relying primarily on *Bowers (State v. Walsh).* Lambda and its fellow gay rights litigators quickly withdrew all the other sodomy challenges in progress.

Bowers's impact was not limited to sodomy challenges or privacy-based claims. *Padula v. Webster* (1987) was the first gay rights case to reach a federal court of appeals after *Bowers* came down. *Padula* concerned the FBI's refusal to hire an otherwise qualified lesbian applicant. She sued, arguing that the FBI's actions violated her right to equal protection of the laws. In 1987, the case reached the D.C. Court of Appeals, which dismissed the case, ruling that *Bowers* constituted an insurmountable barrier to her claim. Said the court: "If the [Supreme] Court was unwilling to object to laws that criminalize the behavior that defines the class, it is hardly open to a lower court to conclude that state sponsored discrimination against the class is invidious. After all, there can hardly be more palpable discrimination against a class than making the conduct that defines the class criminal" (*Padula,* 103).

Shortly thereafter, a different circuit relied on *Bowers* and *Padula* to rule against a man discharged by the Navy because of his homosexuality (*Woodward v. United States,* 1989). Woodward alleged that the Navy's policy violated the due process clause as well as his right to freedom of association. The federal circuit's response was this: "After [*Bowers v.*] *Hardwick* it cannot logically be asserted that discrimination against homosexuals is constitutionally infirm" (*Woodward,* 1076).

One year later, yet another circuit court relied on *Bowers* to uphold a federal agency's blanket policy of denying security clearances to lgb people (*High Tech Gays v. Defense Industry Security Clearance Office,* 1990). Reasoning that under *Bowers* "there is no fundamental right to engage in homosexual sodomy" the Ninth Circuit found it "incongruous" to claim a right of equal protection based on "homosexual conduct" (571).

Bowers's impact also reverberated in cases much closer to home for most lgb people. Shortly after *Bowers* was announced, the Arizona Court of Appeals relied on it as evidence that a bisexual man was presumptively unacceptable to adopt children (*Appeal in Pima County Juvenile Action B-10489,* 1986). One year later, the New Hampshire Supreme Court similarly relied on *Bowers* in opining that a state statute prohibiting lgb people from fostering or adopting children would pass constitutional muster (*Opinion of the Justices,* 1987).

Reliance on *Bowers* to justify legal discrimination against lgb people in a wide range of contexts would continue until the case was overruled by *Lawrence v. Texas* in 2003. It is important to recognize, though, that the aftermath of *Bowers* was not entirely disheartening for gay rights advocates. There were a few bright spots. One was that newspaper editorials and cartoons across the nation criticized the Court's ruling, often in scathing terms, as grossly undermining the basic privacy rights due all Americans. The *New York Times* (1986), for instance, called *Bowers* a "gratuitous and petty ruling, and an offense to American society's maturing standards of individual dignity." The *Los Angeles Times* (1986) likewise took the Court to task for the "rigid and hostile attitude woven through White's opinion." In addition, a *Newsweek* poll conducted by Gallup the week after *Bowers* was announced found that more people disapproved of the ruling than approved.[49] Of those surveyed, 57 percent also believed that states should not have the power to regulate private consensual sexual practices between homosexuals. While these poll results were not tremendously favorable, they did indicate a reservoir of political tolerance toward lgb people.

By far the most positive result of *Bowers* was that it had what Lambda attorney Evan Wolfson referred to as a "galvanizing effect" on lgb people, spurring them to newfound activism in the gay rights movement.[50] As noted in chapter 3, the decision inspired a number of protests by lgb people, most notably the 1987 March on Washington for Lesbian and Gay Rights. Lambda moved quickly to capitalize on the anger *Bowers* provoked, even as it was halting all its ongoing sodomy challenges. An excerpt from a solicitation letter dated one week after the decision illustrates this effort:

What does the Supreme Court decision mean in terms of your rights?
     For those of who live in states that still have sodomy laws on the books, indeed for all of us, the decision amounts to a reaffirmation of centuries of prejudice. Sodomy laws are often used to legitimate discrimination or harassment against us. For example, in a custody case, the fact that the mother is a lesbian, coupled with a presumption that she therefore is in violation of a state's sodomy law, may be used to deny her parental rights. Or in a debate in a state legislature, sodomy

laws may be used to justify a vote against a bill to ban sexual orientation discrimination.

There is no doubt that the Supreme Court's decision last week will add new vigor to hate campaigns against us, including calls to enforce energetically the sodomy laws already on the books and efforts to reintroduce sodomy laws in the 25 states that are free from them at present.

The letter then went on to analogize the Court's opinion to *Plessy v. Ferguson,* the infamous 1896 case in which the Supreme Court refused to find the practice of racial segregation unconstitutional. The black community mobilized in *Plessy*'s aftermath, then-executive director Tom Stoddard wrote, and the decision was ultimately overturned; gay men and lesbians should do the same.[51]

Table 3 (chap. 3) charts Lambda's income over the years. It shows that individual contributions more than tripled between 1985 and 1986, jumping from $181,239 to $553,402. This dramatic increase suggests that Lambda was reasonably successful in using a litigation defeat to mobilize support for its work. Ironically then, *Bowers* helped to increase mobilization on behalf of gay rights claims, even as it directly harmed the legal interests of lgb people.

Conclusion

Shifts in the structure of legal opportunity can variously open up and close down spaces within which social movements can act to effect their sociolegal goals. In this chapter, I have argued that the pace of sodomy reform in the years between Stonewall and *Bowers* varied quite significantly in response to shifts in the structure of legal opportunities as well as to the decisions made by Lambda and other social movement litigators.

I want to emphasize here that the stop-and-start course of sodomy reform cannot be explained by reference to a single agent. Myriad factors interacted to drive (or stall) the pace of sodomy reform. For example, the period of stagnation and backsliding vis-à-vis sodomy reform that marked stage 3 appears to be a product of the emergence of AIDS, tensions over the right to abortion and the right to privacy, and the growing conservatism of the federal bench, not to mention the Supreme Court's decision in *Bowers*. These factors can be discussed separately, but they operated interactively. Moreover, the composition of the factors driving the pace of sodomy reform altered over time. For example, the Model Penal Code was a major instigator of sodomy repeal during stage 2. Likewise the emergence of AIDS helped to power the period of stagnation and backsliding that characterized stage 3.

While some of the factors driving sodomy reform were unrelated to the actions of gay rights advocates (e.g., the passage of the Model Penal Code or the emergence of the AIDS epidemic), others were a product of decisions made by movement actors (e.g., the pursuit of *Doe v. Commonwealth's Attorney, Onofre, Baker,* and *Bowers*). Studying legal change from a legal opportunity perspective means more than examining the external environment confronting social movement actors. It also means relating a movement's litigation strategies and outcomes to that external environment. Just as shifts in the structure of legal opportunities can open or close space for legal action, that action can shape the structure of legal opportunities.

This is clearly evidenced in *Bowers*. Virtually every aspect of the case was a product of considered choice. The Georgia affiliate of the ACLU had been actively searching for a test case and approached Michael Hardwick with an offer to represent him. When the Georgia affiliate chose to withdraw its sponsorship of *Bowers* after the initial loss in district court, Kathy Wilde actively sought a new funding source. Lambda and the ACLU chose to become involved in the case, chose to create the Ad-Hoc Task Force to Challenge Sodomy Laws, and chose to continue with *Bowers* despite concerns raised by several of the task force members that *Baker v. Wade* was the better legal vehicle with which to challenge the constitutionality of sodomy laws. Their actions directly facilitated the Supreme Court's ruling in the case and the major shift in LOS that occurred as a result of the decision.

With the virtue of 20/20 hindsight, it is clear that Lambda, the ACLU, Kathy Wilde, and the other litigators who pushed the *Bowers* case miscalculated. At the same time, it is unclear whether *Baker v. Wade* would have been a better case to bring before the Supreme Court. Decoding the structure of legal opportunities is not a simple task; there is no Rosetta stone. Actors can do no more than make educated guesses based on the available information. In a world of imperfect information, it should come as no surprise that actors sometimes guess poorly.

The task of decoding the LOS is complicated further by the length of time most cases take to work their way through the courts. For example, the LOS surrounding sodomy reform seemed reasonably advantageous when *Bowers* began. But by the time the case made it to the Supreme Court, the LOS had become less favorable, in part due to the emergence of the AIDS epidemic. Moreover, the "heterosexual panic" that erupted at the revelation that Rock Hudson had AIDS occurred at the worst possible time for the *Bowers* team—just after the Eleventh Circuit struck down Georgia's sodomy law and before the Supreme Court considered whether to accept certiorari in the case.[52] At that point in time, gay rights litigators had no control over the case. The decision to appeal to the U.S. Supreme Court was entirely up to Georgia, and while Hardwick's legal team urged the Supreme Court to turn down the case, it had no power to prevent the Supreme Court from choosing to hear it. While there is no direct evidence that post–Rock Hudson AIDS phobia was a major factor in the Supreme Court's decision to hear the case, it seems plausible to suggest that the social panic about homosexuality and AIDS heightened the salience of Georgia's AIDS-fear arguments.

One of the most interesting things about *Bowers* is that Lambda succeeded in overturning it seventeen years later, despite the Supreme Court's great reluctance to disturb recent precedents. Chapter 5 seeks to understand how and why this occurred.

FIVE

Sodomy Reform from *Bowers* to *Lawrence*

owers v. Hardwick constituted an enormous legal defeat for advocates of sodomy reform in particular and gay rights more generally. By a 5–4 margin, the Supreme Court rejected the claim that the federal constitutional right of privacy encompassed same-sex sexual relationships. In so doing the Court torpedoed a previously potent legal argument in the arsenal of gay rights litigators, forcing Lambda and its allies to develop new rationales for a host of gay rights claims. Moreover, the tone of Justice White's majority opinion was contemptuous, while Justice Burger's concurrence crossed over into downright hostility toward lgb people: condemnation of sodomy, he wrote, was based on "millennia of moral teaching." Lambda's executive director, Tom Stoddard, believed that the tone of the decision was actually more damaging to lgb people than the content. "The most important judicial body in the United States has expressed a certain distaste for gay men and women and suggested they may be treated differently from other Americans" (quoted in Clendenin and Nagourney 1999, 537).

But while *Bowers* did indeed have a measurably negative impact on the rights of lgb people, one early fear never came to pass. Not a single state recriminalized sodomy in response to *Bowers*. In fact, efforts to eradicate sodomy laws began gaining traction within a few years of the Supreme Court's decision. In 1992, Kentucky became the first post-*Bowers* state to invalidate its sodomy law, inaugurating a new period of sodomy law reform (stage 4). Kentucky's repeal was followed in short order by Nevada, the District of Columbia, Tennessee, Montana, Georgia (ironically), Rhode Island, Maryland, Arizona, Minnesota, Massachusetts, and Arkansas. The repeal was accomplished legislatively in four instances (the District of Columbia, Nevada, Rhode Island, and Arizona). In the other eight, repeal was accomplished via legal challenge.

This renaissance of sodomy reform culminated in 2003, when the U.S. Supreme Court invalidated all remaining state sodomy laws as impermissibly infringing on the right of privacy (*Lawrence v. Texas*). *Lawrence* was a landmark decision in several respects. For Lambda and other gay rights advocates, it marked the final victory in a decades-long battle to decriminalize consensual same-sex relations. *Lawrence* also signified the potential revitalization of privacy as a fundamental right, a doctrine much weakened by the Court in the 1980s and 1990s. Finally, in *Lawrence* the Supreme Court did something truly exceptional: it explicitly repudiated a decision less than twenty years old. Said the Court: "*Bowers* was not correct when it was decided and it is not correct today. It ought not to remain binding precedent. *Bowers v. Hardwick* should be and now is overruled" (*Lawrence*, 2484). What explains this reversal of fortune for sodomy law reformers in the years after *Bowers?* Why did states begin again to decriminalize sodomy (stage 4) after a period of retrenchment in the 1980s (stage 3)? And ultimately, why were Lambda and other gay rights advocates able to mobilize the law successfully in *Lawrence* when they had failed so spectacularly in *Bowers?* In this chapter I continue my examination of the long campaign to eradicate sodomy laws waged by Lambda and other gay rights litigators. I begin by describing the emergence, progress, and outcomes of new litigation strategies designed to get around the damaging precedent established by *Bowers.* I then turn my attention to *Lawrence,* seeking to understand why it succeeded when *Bowers* failed. As in chapter 4, my primary aim is to understand the circumstances in which rights claims about same-sex sexuality have been more or less likely to prevail in court. Ultimately, I argue, the reinvigoration of sodomy reform in stage 4 was stimulated by shifts in the structure of legal opportunities and the strategic responses of Lambda and other organized litigators to those shifts.

Litigating in the Shadows of *Bowers*

Bowers's outcome disheartened Lambda and the other members of the Ad-Hoc Task Force. Shortly after the decision was announced, the task force met to consider *Bowers*'s implications for the future of sodomy reform and of gay rights litigation more generally. Some members felt that the shift in climate presaged by *Bowers* would make any further legal challenges to the constitutionality of sodomy laws counterproductive.

> [C]ourt challenges of sodomy laws in state courts will simply consume our collective skills, time, and creative energy. We believe that our time would be much better spent organizing and/or working with local political coalitions to get gay rights and privacy

rights on the political agenda. Not only do we believe that courts will be most reluctant to throw out sodomy laws at this time, but by continuing to focus on the courts, we would perpetuate the myth (which is believed by many people in the gay community) that the court system is the place to vindicate our rights. It is important that we educate our own community that the courts are part of the problem, not part of the solution.[1]

Despite these concerns, exiting the litigation process with respect to sodomy law reform was not seriously contemplated by Lambda or most other task force participants. The reason for this seems to have been at least partly occupational. Lawyers are, after all, trained to think of problems in terms of legal solutions. But the decision was also influenced by the structure of the American legal system. There are multiple constitutions in effect in the United States of America: in addition to the federal Constitution, each state has one (as does the Commonwealth of Puerto Rico). All things being equal, social reform litigators generally prefer to bring cases in federal rather than state court. This preference is largely based on cost-benefit calculations. It consumes fewer resources for groups such as Lambda to become experts on federal law than it does to become experts on fifty different bodies of state law. Moreover, a win in the U.S. Supreme Court encompasses the entire country, while a win in a state's supreme court extends only to that state's borders. State-by-state litigation, in short, is a longer and more cumbersome tactic.

But when constitutional litigation in the federal courts seems unwise or is inapposite, state-based litigation often remains a viable option. This is because the federal Constitution functions as a floor rather than a ceiling. State courts and constitutions may not deprive their citizens of federal constitutional rights. They may, however, afford additional rights to their citizenry. Consequently, while the *Bowers* court found that sodomy laws did not run afoul of the federal constitutional right of privacy, state courts were still free to void sodomy laws based on state constitutional provisions. A second benefit of cases based on state constitutional claims is that they are generally insulated from Supreme Court review. In order for the U.S. Supreme Court to hear a case, that case must present a claim based on federal law. Cases raising claims strictly limited to a state's own laws end at that state's high court. A decision striking down a sodomy law based on a state's constitution, then, would not be subject to review from a hostile U.S. Supreme Court.

The potential utility of a state-by-state approach to eradicating sodomy laws was highlighted for the task force by the early success of *Kentucky v. Wasson. Wasson* involved the 1985 arrest and prosecution of a gay man for solicitation, in violation of a Kentucky law that prohibited "deviate sexual intercourse with another person of the same sex."[2] The case began while *Bowers* was still pending before the Supreme Court. It was not brought under the auspices of the task force (it was litigated by attorneys in private practice), although the task force was well aware of its inception and progress.

Wasson's attorneys initially argued that Kentucky's law violated his federal constitutional rights to privacy and equal protection (the law criminalized only same-sex sodomy). When the Supreme Court's subsequent ruling in *Bowers* foreclosed this legal argument, at least insofar as privacy was concerned, Wasson's attorneys reformulated his defense strategy to argue that the law violated Wasson's rights under Kentucky's constitution. Cluing into Justice Powell's concurrence in *Bowers,* they also argued that Kentucky's sodomy law violated federal and state protections against cruel and unusual punishment. On October 3, 1986, a mere three months after *Bowers,* the trial court in *Wasson* stuck down the state's sodomy law, finding that the Kentucky Constitution afforded Wasson a greater right to privacy than did the U.S. Constitution, though it rejected Wasson's equal protection and cruel and unusual punishment claims. Although the state of Kentucky immediately appealed, the trial court ruling in *Wasson* made it clear that *Bowers* had not entirely foreclosed the possibility of achieving sodomy reform through litigation. Members of the task force turned their attention to litigation based on state constitutional claims, compiling a database of constitutional provisions and pertinent case law for each of the twenty-four states with sodomy laws still on the books.

Despite the hope dangled by *Wasson*'s early success, the initial round of state constitutional challenges to sodomy laws faltered. In 1987, for example, a state challenge to Georgia's sodomy law based on equal protection grounds failed (*Gordon v. State*). That same year, two courts in Louisiana upheld the constitutionality of that state's sodomy law (*State of Louisiana v. Mills* and *State of Louisiana v. Neal*). All three cases were brought by private litigators operating independently of the task force.

Lambda's first post-*Bowers* foray into sodomy reform litigation was somewhat more successful. In 1988 it filed suit in conjunction with the Michigan Organization for Human Rights (MOHR), a local gay rights group, and the Michigan affiliate of the ACLU, alleging that a handful of statutes criminalizing sodomy violated the right to privacy under Michigan's constitution (*MOHR v. Kelly*). The trial court agreed and in 1990 found those laws unconstitutional insofar as they applied to consensual sexual conduct in the home. This auspicious start was stymied, however, by an unorthodox move on the part of the state's attorney general, the named defendant in the case. He refused to appeal the adverse ruling of the trial court, without indicating agreement with the decision. His (in)action threw the status of Michigan's sodomy laws into confusion. The trial court's ruling applied to only one county; the other eighty-two counties fell outside the court's jurisdiction. Lambda maintained, however, that since the attorney general did not challenge *MOHR*, the ruling bound all prosecutors throughout the state of Michigan. A series of subsequent criminal cases (none involving any organized gay rights litigators) failed to resolve the confusion.[3]

Lambda took a different tack in its second post-*Bowers* sodomy case but was frustrated in this approach as well. Mica England was a lesbian who had applied for a job with the Dallas police department. During the interview process she was asked about her sexual orientation and replied truthfully. Because Texas had a sodomy law, the police department determined that she was a criminal and, citing department regulations precluding the hiring of criminals, refused to consider her application further. In 1990, Lambda sued the city of Dallas, its police chief, and the state of Texas on England's behalf, arguing that the police department's employment policy was predicated on an unconstitutional law. Texas's sodomy law, it said, violated the right of privacy and equal protection under the state's constitution.

The trial court agreed with Lambda's argument, finding Texas's sodomy law unconstitutional and enjoining the city of Dallas and its police chief from enforcing the law or making employment decisions based on it. Frustratingly, though, the court ruled that Texas's sovereign immunity precluded it from being sued given the procedural posture of the case. Both sides appealed the trial court's ruling, Lambda arguing that the dismissal of the state as a party to the suit was incorrect and the city of Dallas and its police chief arguing, among other things, that England lacked standing to challenge the sodomy law and that the law itself was constitutional under *Bowers*.

A three-judge appellate court unanimously upheld the trial court's ruling. Texas's sodomy law, it said, violated the right of privacy under Texas's constitution. Unfortunately for Lambda, it also agreed that the state itself was not an appropriate party to the suit (*City of Dallas v. England*, 1993). Both sides appealed to the Texas Supreme Court, which declined to hear the case, citing a procedural irregularity in the appeals process. Ultimately, Lambda's inability to include the state as a party in *England* greatly limited the case's reach. *England* carved out a sort of "free" zone in Dallas but did not apply to the rest of the state.

While *MOHR* and *England* ultimately failed to overturn the sodomy laws of Michigan and Texas, respectively, they revealed great judicial openness to sodomy reform claims. All five judges in the two cases had agreed that their state's sodomy law violated state constitutional rights of privacy, notwithstanding *Bowers*.

The state-by-state strategy was finally vindicated in Lambda's third post-*Bowers* effort. While Lambda was developing its own cases, *Kentucky v. Wasson* had been winding its way through the courts. In 1990, the state's intermediate court of appeals partially affirmed and partially overturned the trial court's decision. It agreed with the lower court that the statute violated the right of privacy guaranteed by the Kentucky Constitution, notwithstanding *Bowers*. But it also found that the statute violated state constitutional guarantees of equal protection, a claim the trial court had denied. The state of Kentucky immediately appealed to the state's supreme court. Recognizing the opportunity offered by the case, Lambda offered its assistance to Wasson's private attorneys. It penned an amicus brief presenting psychological and sociological information about lgb people on behalf of the American Psychological Association. More important is the fact that it helped coordinate strategy for organizations submitting amici curiae briefs on Wasson's behalf.[4] Lambda's actions were designed to ensure that the judges on the Kentucky Supreme Court were presented with a panoply of information about the value of lgb people and the harms caused by sodomy laws.

In 1992, Kentucky became the first post-*Bowers* state in the nation to void its sodomy law. By a bare 4–3 majority, the high court ruled that the statute violated both Wasson's right to privacy and his right to equal protection under the state constitution. The court explicitly rejected *Bowers*'s conclusion that majoritarian morality justified laws prohibiting consensual, private acts of sodomy.

> We view the United States Supreme Court decision in Bowers v. Hardwick as a misdirected application of the theory of original intent. To illustrate: as a theory of majoritarian morality, miscegenation was an offense with ancient roots. It is highly unlikely that protecting the rights of persons of different races to copulate was one of the considerations behind the Fourteenth Amendment.

Nevertheless, in Loving v. Virginia (1967), the United States Supreme Court recognized that a contemporary, enlightened interpretation of the liberty interest involved in the sexual act made its punishment constitutionally impermissible. (*Wasson*, 498)

Ultimately, the court concluded that Kentucky's sodomy law lacked any rational basis at all, dismissing as "simply outrageous" Kentucky's suggestion that the law was a rational effort to limit promiscuity, pedophilia, and public sex (*Wasson*, 501). Two dissenting opinions were filed, each emphasizing the immorality of homosexuality and the long history of prohibitions against sodomy.

Armed with the victory in *Wasson*, gay rights litigators turned their attention to other states with sodomy laws. In the eleven years between *Wasson* and the U.S. Supreme Court's decision in *Lawrence*, Lambda, the ACLU, and a handful of smaller gay rights groups challenged the constitutionality of sodomy laws in thirteen states and Puerto Rico.[5] Every challenge raised a state constitutional privacy claim. In states where sodomy laws applied only to same-sex situations litigators also raised equal protection claims, usually based on state constitutional guarantees but sometimes based on federal constitutional guarantees as well.[6] Occasionally they made cruel and unusual punishment claims as well.

As table 9 shows, these challenges were not uniformly successful. Indeed, appellate courts in four states deflected constitutional attacks against sodomy laws before gay rights litigators garnered their next legal victory. Of the four, only the Rhode Island Supreme Court actually considered the merits of the arguments for and against the constitutionality of sodomy laws before issuing its ruling (*State of Rhode Island v. Lopes*, 1995). The other three ducked the issue, invoking procedural hurdles in two cases (*State of Texas v. Morales*, 1994, and *State of Louisiana v. Baxley*, 1994) and deciding the case on alternate grounds in the third (*Sawatzky v. City of Oklahoma City*, 1995). It is intriguing that the Rhode Island legislature voted to eradicate its sodomy law in 1998, partly in response to the court's decision in *Lopes*.

It took sodomy law reformers four years after *Wasson* to secure their next judicial victory. *Campbell v. Sundquist* (1996) involved five lgb plaintiffs who claimed that Tennessee's Homosexual Practices Act violated their state constitutional rights of privacy and equal protection. The case was litigated by former Lambda legal director Abby Rubenfeld. Lambda and the ACLU filed amici curiae briefs. In 1995, the trial court did something that had never before happened in a sodomy law challenge. It granted the plaintiffs' petition for summary judgment. *Summary judgment* means that the court found that there was no material question of fact at issue and that the law clearly supported the plaintiffs' claims. Basically, it meant that the court found the Homosexual Practices Act to be so patently unconstitutional that it saw no need for a trial. Same-sex sexual activity between consenting adults, said the court, clearly fell within the state constitution's right of privacy. The state appealed, but the Tennessee Court of Appeals upheld the lower court's decision. The Tennessee Supreme Court refused to hear the state's appeal, thereby ending litigation in the case.

The pace of sodomy law eradication quickened after *Campbell.* Although courts in three states—Kansas, Louisiana, and Virginia—deflected constitutional challenges in the years between *Campbell* and *Lawrence,* courts in five states—Montana, Maryland, Minnesota, Arkansas, and Massachusetts—held that statutes criminalizing private

TABLE 9. Breakdown of Post-*Bowers* Sodomy Law Challenges

	Case (state)	Basis	Sodomy Law
1992	*Kentucky v. Wasson* (KY)	Arrest for solicitation	Struck down
1993	*Dallas v. England* (TX)	Police department refusal to hire lesbian	Struck down but limited to Dallas
1994	*State v. Morales* (TX)	Facial challenge	Upheld
1994	*Louisiana v. Baxley*	Arrest for solicitation	Upheld
1995	*Sawatzky v. Oklahoma City*	Arrest for solicitation	Upheld
1996	*State v. Lopes* (RI)	Heterosexual	Upheld
1996	*Campbell v. Sundquist* (TN)	Facial challenge	Struck down
1996	*Christensen v. Georgia*	Arrest for solicitation	Upheld
1997	*Gryczan v. State* (MT)	Facial challenge	Struck down
1998	*Topeka v. Movsovitz* (KS)	Arrest for solicitation	Upheld
1998	*Powell v. State* (GA)	Heterosexual	Struck down
1999	*Williams v. Glendening* (MD)	Combination: facial challenge and arrest for solicitation	Struck down
2000	*State v. Smith*	Combination: arrests for sodomy and heterosexual	Upheld
2000	*DePriest v. Virginia*	Arrests for solicitation	Upheld
2001	*Fishers v. Virgina*	Heterosexual	Upheld
2001	*Doe v. Ventura* (MN)	Facial challenge	Struck down
2002	*Jegley v. Picado* (AR)	Facial challenge	Struck down
2002	*Doe v. Reilly*	Facial challenge	Struck down[a]
2002	*LEGAL v. State* (LA)	Facial challenge	Upheld
2002	*Sanchez v. Puerto Rico*	Facial challenge	Upheld
2003	*Lawrence v. Texas*	Arrests for sodomy	Struck down

[a]The Massachusetts Supreme Judicial Court dismissed the case for lack of standing. However, it clarified that the state's two sodomy laws could not be applied to private, consensual acts.

consensual sodomy violated state constitutional guarantees of privacy and/or equal protection (see table 9). The supreme court of a sixth state, Georgia, initially ruled that the right of privacy did not preclude sodomy laws (*Christensen v. Georgia,* 1996) but two years later reversed course and ruled that the right of privacy did preclude such laws (*State v. Powell,* 1998).

What accounts for the varied ability of sodomy reform litigators to mobilize the law successfully in these states? Why the increasing willingness of courts to strike down sodomy laws as the twentieth century segued into the twenty-first? In the following pages, I suggest that shifts in several aspects of the structure of legal opportunities contributed to the increased ability of Lambda and its allies to litigate successfully in the context of sodomy reform. These shifts included changes in the legal frames surrounding privacy and homosexuality, changes in the cultural framing of homosexuality and AIDS, a reduction in access-related constraints, and shifting elite alignments.

Privacy and Standing

Just as each state has its own constitution, with language diverging to a greater or lesser extent from the U.S. Constitution, so does each state have its own unique body of case law concerning privacy. Task force members compiled a database of constitutional provisions and pertinent case law for the twenty-four states with sodomy laws after *Bowers* failed because they recognized that the law in some states would be more favorable to sodomy law reform claims than would the law in others. And indeed, the Kentucky Supreme Court supported its decision in *Wasson* in part by noting that "Kentucky cases recognized a legally protected right of privacy based on our own constitution and common law tradition long before the United States Supreme Court first took notice of whether there were any rights of privacy inherent in the Federal Bill of Rights" (493). It seems reasonable to suggest that the extant body of state law concerning privacy rights played at least some role in shaping judicial outcomes.

It is clear, however, that the existence of constitutional provisions and case law, standing alone, did not entirely structure the ability of gay rights litigators to mobilize the law successfully on behalf of sodomy law reform. For one thing, the articulation of privacy rights in the Louisiana Constitution is among the broadest in the nation. (Kentucky, in contrast, has no explicit constitutional guarantee of privacy.) Article I, Section 5 of the Louisiana Constitution of 1974 expressly guarantees security against unreasonable invasions of privacy to every individual. Yet the Louisiana courts repelled three different privacy-based challenges to the state's sodomy law in the years between *Wasson* and *Lawrence*.

The contradictory decisions issued by the Georgia Supreme Court in *Christensen* and *Powell* provide more evidence that the legal frames surrounding privacy rights do not suffice to explain the divergent outcomes of sodomy law challenges. *Christensen* involved a gay man who had been arrested for soliciting sodomy in a police sting. More specifically, Christensen and an undercover officer struck up a conversation in a rest area. During that conversation, Christensen indicated that he desired to engage in oral sex and agreed to follow the officer to a nearby motel. En route to the motel in his car, Christensen was pulled over and arrested. The ACLU, which represented Christensen, argued that Georgia's sodomy law was an unconstitutional violation of the right of privacy under the state constitution and that consequently laws against soliciting sodomy were also unconstitutional.[7] The state supreme court rejected this analysis by a vote of 5-2. The majority construed the right of privacy in the following way.

When a privacy interest is implicated, the state must show that the legislation has a "reasonable relation to a legitimate state purpose." In the exercise of its police power the state has a right to enact laws to promote the public health, safety, morals, and welfare of its citizens. There is also a concomitant interest in curtailing criminal activities wherever they may be committed. As was acknowledged in Bowers v. Hardwick the law "is constantly based on notions of morality, and if all laws representing essentially moral choices are to be invalidated under the Due Process Clause, the courts will be very busy indeed." We hold that the proscription against sodomy is a legitimate and valid exercise of state police power in furtherance of the moral welfare of the public. Our constitution does not deny the legislative branch the right to prohibit such conduct. Accordingly, O.C.G.A. § 16–6–2 does not violate the right to privacy under the Georgia Constitution. (*Christensen*, 190, footnotes and citations omitted)

Powell involved a heterosexual man who had been convicted of engaging in consensual oral sex with his wife's niece. He had been originally charged both with rape and with aggravated sodomy but at trial had been acquitted of the former charges. He appealed his conviction, claiming that the statute violated his right to privacy under the Georgia Constitution. The Georgia Supreme Court agreed, by a vote of 6–1. This time they construed the right of privacy in the following fashion.

> Today, we are faced with whether the constitutional right of privacy screens from governmental interference a non-commercial sexual act that occurs without force in a private home between persons legally capable of consenting to the act. . . . We cannot think of any other activity that reasonable persons would rank as more private and more deserving of protection from governmental interference than unforced, private, adult sexual activity. We conclude that such activity is at the heart of the Georgia Constitution's protection of the right of privacy.
>   Having determined that appellant's behavior falls within the area protected by the right of privacy, we next examine whether the government's infringement upon that right is constitutionally sanctioned. As judicial consideration of the right to privacy has developed, this Court has concluded that the right of privacy is a fundamental right and that a government-imposed limitation on the right to privacy will pass constitutional muster if the limitation is shown to serve a compelling state interest and to be narrowly tailored to effectuate only that compelling interest. (*Powell*, 332–33, footnotes and citations omitted)

The court then went on to conclude that the only purpose of the sodomy statute was to regulate the private sexual conduct of consenting adults, a purpose that exceeded the permissible police powers of the state because it provided no benefit to the public while unduly oppressing individuals (334).

The divergence of *Christensen* and *Powell* is notable because no significant changes in privacy law occurred between the two cases. If anything, the precedent established by *Christensen* should have weighed against the court's ruling in *Powell*. Yet the Georgia Supreme Court utilized a much more stringent legal standard for reviewing the constitutionality of Georgia's sodomy law in the latter case than in the former. Under the standard utilized in *Christensen*, Georgia needed only to show a reasonable relation to a legitimate state purpose. The presumption was that the law was constitutional. Under the standard utilized in *Powell*, Georgia needed to show that the law was narrowly tailored to further a compelling interest. The presumption here was that the law was unconstitutional.

The high court did make a half-hearted effort to distinguish *Christensen* from *Powell* by noting that the state's police powers legitimately extended to "shielding the public from inadvertent exposure to the intimacies of others, . . . protecting minors and others legally incapable of consent from sexual abuse, and . . . preventing people from being forced to submit to sex acts against their will" (*Powell*, 333). Yet none of these circumstances matched *Christensen*. Although the solicitation occurred in a public place (with no showing that anyone but Christensen and the police officer was privy to the conversation), consummation was designed to take place in private.

Clearly something other than the application of black-letter law was at play in the two cases. One obvious possibility, a shift in the membership of the court, cannot account for the divergent outcomes of *Christensen* and *Powell*. The same seven-member court heard both cases. In the absence of additional information, it seems most likely that the justices were influenced by the different facts of the two cases. Christensen was a gay man who had approached another man he believed was gay (but probably was not) and propositioned him. Powell was a straight man convicted of having consensual oral sex. The justices may simply have seen the privacy interests at stake more clearly in the latter instance than in the former.

The symbolic insult the two cases posed to lgb people should not go unremarked. The activity for which Christensen had been arrested bore no tint of coercion. Powell, on the other hand, had originally been charged with rape as well as aggravated sodomy and had been convicted of the latter only because consent is not a defense. Thus a gay man involved in a clearly consensual activity with another man found that his actions did not fall within the right to privacy, while the same act when performed by a heterosexual man with a possibly nonconsenting partner was encompassed by the right to privacy.

Lambda was well aware of this irony but saw in *Powell* both a promise and a threat. It might serve as the mechanism to eradicate a particularly despised sodomy statute. At the same time, even if the Georgia courts threw out the sodomy statute, they might limit the ruling only to heterosexual sodomy, leaving the law intact with respect to same-sex sodomy. Faced with these possibilities, Lambda became involved with the case, submitting an amicus brief arguing that the sodomy law should be struck in toto. Its argument was evidently persuasive; the Georgia Supreme Court decision closely paralleled Lambda's analysis.

The different outcomes of *Christensen* and *Powell* underscore the importance of finding litigants with stories that judges "get." As we saw in chapter 4, though, a major problem facing Lambda and other sodomy law reformers was that arrests for private, consensual same-sex sodomy were exceedingly rare.[8] In an effort to jump the standing hurdle some litigators used arrests and/or convictions for noncommercial solicitation (that is, where money was not involved) as a means to attack the constitutionality of sodomy laws. The legal argument was straightforward. It is generally not illegal to discuss, advocate, or solicit a legal activity.[9] If same-sex sodomy is permissible, then asking another adult to engage in it must also be permissible.

Lambda never developed a sodomy law challenge centered on solicitation, although on a few occasions it filed an amicus brief in a case already in progress. The ACLU, on the other hand, brought several such challenges.[10] To a one, they failed. *Sawatzky v. City of Oklahoma City* (1995) is instructive here. The facts of *Sawatzky* basically paralleled *Christensen,* except that Sawatzky's challenge was based on his conviction for solicitation, while Christensen's was based on his arrest. The ACLU of Oklahoma used Sawatzky's conviction to challenge Oklahoma's same-sex-only sodomy law, arguing that it violated state constitutional guarantees of privacy and equal protection and also violated federal constitutional guarantees of equal protection—the first post-*Bowers* sodomy challenge to raise a federal equal protection claim. Ultimately, though, the Oklahoma Court of Criminal Appeals ducked the issue, upholding Sawatzky's conviction on the basis of the state's ability to regulate speech in public spaces. Said the court,

> In our view, reasonable prohibitions against soliciting sexual acts do not violate the First Amendment whether the underlying conduct is lawful or unlawful. Our view is based upon the unique status of sexual conduct in our culture. In our community, some forms of overt sexual conduct, including the solicitation of some sexual acts, is simply not appropriate in public places. To suggest that government cannot prohibit such solicitation is unfathomable. (*Sawatzky,* 787)

Rather than building cases around arrests and/or convictions for solicitation, Lambda chose to assemble cases utilizing multiple plaintiffs asserting real, but indirect, harm from the existence of sodomy statutes. For example, in *Jegley v. Picado* (2002) Lambda attacked the constitutionality of Arkansas's sodomy law on behalf of seven lgb people, none of whom had ever been arrested for violating the law. Nevertheless, Lambda contended, they suffered real harm because of the law's existence. One plaintiff, illustratively, was the mother of two children. Because Arkansas courts had previously relied on the law's prohibition of same-sex sexual conduct to deny lesbian mothers custody, she lived in fear of losing her children. Another plaintiff was a nurse. Under Arkansas law, any violation of criminal law could result in the loss of his nursing license.

Other litigators assembled similar cases. The ACLU's *Williams v. Glendening* (1998) involved five plaintiffs. One, a federal employee, had been arrested for solicitation in the past; his arrest record made it difficult for him to obtain a security clearance when he was promoted. None of the others had arrest records, but they could potentially lose their occupation licenses and/or jobs because of their violation of the state's sodomy laws. The Texas Human Rights Foundation's *State of Texas v. Morales* (1994) had five plaintiffs. *Gryczan v. State of Montana* (1997)—litigated by the Women's Law Center with amicus support from Lambda, the ACLU, and several other organizations—boasted six plaintiffs.

Unlike the solicitation-based challenges, these kinds of multiparty facial challenges were generally successful. Of the eight such cases decided between *Wasson* and *Lawrence*, six resulted in the eradication of the state's sodomy law.[11] What is particularly interesting is that these cases by and large did not stumble over the standing hurdle that had bedeviled many earlier sodomy challenges.[12] Part of the reason for this has to do with the difference between state and federal law. State standing requirements are often more relaxed than their federal counterpart. But the legal concept of standing also has a subjective element to it. For example, under Minnesota law a litigant has standing when "he or she has suffered an actual injury or otherwise has a sufficient stake in a justiciable controversy to seek relief from a court."[13] Just what constitutes an "actual" injury or a "sufficient" stake? Existing case law and statutes may offer guidance, but judges often have a fair amount of discretion in construing the parameters of standing. It seems clear that in the years since *Bowers*, judges—even in states not traditionally known for their liberal bent—had become more sensitive to the impact of sodomy laws on the lives of lgb people. The reason for this, I suggest, is that judges were responding to shifts in the larger cultural framing of both homosexuality and AIDS.

The "Normalization" of AIDS

As we saw in chapter 4, emergence of the AIDS epidemic in the early 1980s radically shifted the LOS surrounding sodomy reform by giving opponents of such reform a documented public health issue to support their long-standing "homosexual danger" claims. As the 1980s turned into the 1990s, AIDS began to lose much of its patina of homosexual threat, becoming both medically and legally normalized.

Congress, for example, passed a number of bills designed to protect people with AIDS from discrimination. The first major bill to do so was the federal Fair Housing Act, which was amended in 1988 to include disability among the list "protected" characteristics; the regulations governing the implementation of the act specified HIV disease as a condition included within the definition of disability. A more important legislative enactment—the Americans with Disabilities Act (ADA)—followed in 1990. When the ADA took effect in the summer of 1992, it changed the legal frames surrounding AIDS in significant ways. Among its myriad provisions, the ADA prohibited discriminatory treatment of employees based on HIV disease (unless such workers posed a significant risk to others), required employers to take reasonable steps to accommodate employees with AIDS, and also prohibited discriminatory treatment of employees who associated with HIV-positive individuals.

As AIDS became normalized its utility as a signifier of the dangers of homosexuality for opponents of sodomy reform decreased. In 1992, AIDS was still threatening enough that one of the dissents in *Wasson* invoked it.

> The record in this case contains undisputed testimony by experts presented by [the State of Kentucky] that homosexuals are more promiscuous than heterosexuals; that infectious diseases are more readily transmitted by anal sodomy than by any other form of sexual copulation; and that homosexuals account for 73 percent of all AIDS cases in this country. Clearly the interests of all Kentuckians in protecting public health, safety and morals are at issue. The necessity for controlling such behavior prevails over any equal protection challenge. (*Wasson,* dissent by Justice Wintersheimer, 511)

The majority, however, flatly rejected this justification for Kentucky's sodomy law.

The Commonwealth has tried hard to demonstrate a legitimate governmental interest justifying a distinction [between criminalizing same-sex sodomy but permitting opposite-sex sodomy], but has failed. Many of the claimed justifications are simply outrageous: that "homosexuals are more promiscuous than heterosexuals . . . that homosexuals enjoy the company of children, and that homosexuals are more prone to engage in sex acts in public." The only proffered justification with superficial validity is that "infectious diseases are more readily transmitted by anal sodomy than by other forms of sexual copulation." But this statute is not limited to anal copulation, and this reasoning would apply to male-female anal intercourse the same as it applies to male-male intercourse. The growing number of females to whom AIDS . . . has been transmitted is stark evidence that AIDS is not only a male homosexual disease. The only medical evidence in the record before us rules out any distinction between male-male and male-female anal intercourse as a method of preventing AIDS. The act of sexual contact is not implicated, per se, whether the contact is homosexual or heterosexual. In any event, this statute was enacted in 1974 before the AIDS nightmare was upon us. (*Wasson*, 501)

States continued to invoke AIDS as a justification for their sodomy statutes, but Wintersheimer's dissent in *Wasson* marks the last time a judge found the claim persuasive. The court in *Campbell v. Sundquist* (1996) found Tennessee's asserted interest in preventing the spread of infectious disease to be compelling but concluded that the Homosexual Practices Act was not narrowly tailored to advance that interest because it prohibited all sexual contact between people of the same sex, including contact incapable of spreading disease (263). The *Gryczan* court was equally unpersuaded by Montana's AIDS argument.

The State's assertion that the statute protects public health by containing the spread of AIDS relies on faulty logic and invalid assumptions about the disease. To begin with, § 45-5-505, MCA, was enacted in 1973, almost ten years before the first AIDS case was detected in Montana. . . . Moreover, the State's rationale assumes that all same-gender sexual conduct contributes to the spread of the disease. This is grossly inaccurate. . . . Sexual contact between women has an extremely low risk of HIV transmission.

On the other hand, heterosexual contact is now the leading mode of HIV transmission in this country. . . . [T]he inclusion of behavior not associated with the spread of AIDS and HIV and the exclusion of high-risk behavior among those other than homosexuals indicate the absence of any clear relationship between the statute and any public health goals. (*Gryczan*, 123–24)

By the time *Lawrence v. Texas* was litigated the specter of "homosexual threat" surrounding AIDS had receded so much that the state made no reference to it as a justification for the constitutionality of its sodomy statute. Only one of the myriad amici supporting Texas even mentioned it.[14] The AIDS fear that had so dominated the cultural framing of (male) homosexuality during the latter part of the 1980s had all but entirely lost its persuasive power.

The Cultural Framing of Homosexuality

Just as the cultural framing of AIDS shifted in the 1990s, so did the cultural framing of homosexuality. Trends in public opinion data show that beliefs about homosexuality and gay rights grew significantly more supportive. The American National Election Study (ANES) traditionally asks respondents to rate individuals and groups on a "feeling thermometer" running from 0 to 100, where 0 indicates great coldness of feeling and 100 indicates great warmth. Figure 3 shows that feeling thermometer scores for lesbian and gay men rose by 19 degrees between 1988 and 2000. Moreover, the percentage of respondents awarding lesbians and gay men the lowest possible score (0) dropped dramatically, from 35 percent in 1988 to 12 percent in 2000.

It should be noted here that lesbians and gay men continue to rank among the least liked social groups. By way of illustration, blacks (68 degrees), Hispanics (64), feminists (55), people on welfare (52), and Christian fundamentalists (51) all had higher mean feeling thermometer ratings in 2000. (They also had smaller percentages of respondents scoring them at 0.) Yet it is clear that public chilliness toward lgb people thawed considerably as the 1980s turned into the 1990s and the 1990s into the new millennium.

Shifts in public opinion can also be seen in longitudinal data from the General Social Survey. The public became far more tolerant of sexual intimacy between members of the same sex as the 1990s progressed (fig. 4). Some three-fourths of the American public maintained that same-sex

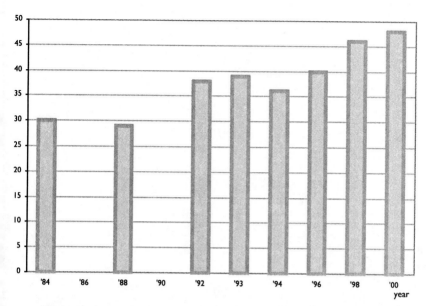

Question: "Still using the feeling thermometer (where 50–100 means you feel favorable and warm, between 0–50 means you don't feel favorable and don't care too much for), how would you rate the following groups . . . gay men and lesbians, i.e., . . . homosexuals?" Scores represent mean responses by year.

Fig. 3. Feeling thermometer ratings for lesbians and gay men, 1984–2000. (Data comes from the National Election Study and were provided for analysis by the Inter-University Consortium for Political and Social Research.)

sexual relations were "always wrong" up through 1991. At that point, attitudes began to shift. By 1993, only about two-thirds believed such conduct was always wrong. By 2002, the number had dropped to slightly more than one-half. These numbers indicate a persistent discomfort with issues of same-sex sexuality, of course. At the same time, they show a very real attitude change about homosexuality.

Other survey data bolster the contention that cultural frames surrounding homosexuality became more favorable in the 1990s than they had been in the 1980s. In 1988, the ANES first asked the following question: Do you favor or oppose laws to protect homosexuals against job discrimination? Forty-seven percent of the respondents said they favored such laws (fig. 5). By 1992, support had shot up by fourteen points, to 61 percent. By the mid-1990s, the number crept up to 64 percent, where it leveled off.[15] Support for the right of lgb people to serve in the military

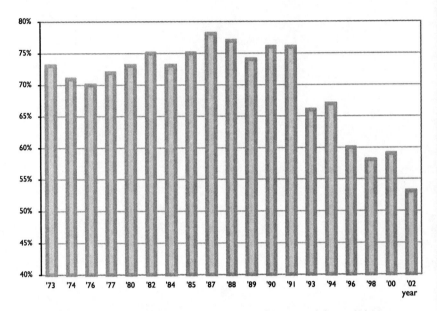

Question: "What about sexual relations between two adults of the same sex? Do you think it is always wrong, almost always wrong, wrong only sometimes, or not wrong at all?" Percentages represent those respondents choosing "always wrong."

Fig. 4.   Attitudes about same-sex sexual relations, 1973–2002. (Data comes from NORC General Social Survey and were provided for analysis by the Inter-University Consortium for Political and Social Research.)

increased during this time period as well. By 2000, 71 percent of ANES respondents agreed that lgb people should be allowed to serve in the military, up from 58 percent in 1993.[16]

Attitudes about homosexuality in the context of familial relationships also eased significantly. Twenty-nine percent of respondents believed that same-sex couples should be legally permitted to adopt children when the ANES first asked the question in 1993. By 2000, the percentage supporting legal adoption rights had risen to 41.[17] Willingness to accord legal recognition to same-sex couples likewise increased. In 1996, when the Gallup Organization first began polling on the subject, only 28 percent of respondents favored laws allowing same-sex couples to entered into legal relationships that would give them some of the rights traditionally associated with marriage. By May 2003, support for such rights had increased to 49 percent (fig. 6). It is worth noting that, although support for same-sex marriage also grew during this time period, respondents appeared to

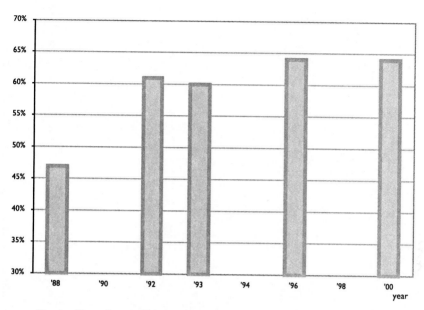

Question: "Do you favor or oppose laws to protect homosexuals against job discrimination?"
Scores represent percentage favoring such laws.

Fig. 5.   Support for employment rights, 1988–2000. (Data comes from the American National Election Study and were provided for analysis by the Inter-University Consortium for Political and Social Research.)

be more comfortable with the concept of civil unions than they did with the concept of same-sex marriage. That is, survey respondents were more willing to grant same-sex couples the substantive rights that come with being married than they were to grant them the social status of being married. Once again, these findings suggest a persistent discomfort with issues of same-sex sexuality while simultaneously they show a significant increase in support for gay rights.

It is difficult to say for certain why the cultural framing of homosexuality became more positive as the twentieth century drew to a close. It is clear, though, that the subject of gay rights became much more visible in the early 1990s than it had been previously, a subject discussed at some length in chapter 3. Among the most prominent and fractious topics were whether openly lgb people should be allowed to serve in the military, whether laws designed to discriminate against lgb people were constitutional, whether the Boy Scouts should be required to accept gay scout-

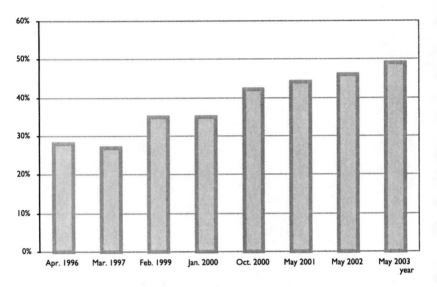

Question for April 1996, October 2000, May 2002, and May 2003 surveys: "Would you vote . . . for or against a law that would allow homosexual couples to legally form civil unions, giving them some of the legal rights of married couples?"

Question for May 2001 survey: "Would you favor or oppose a law that would allow homosexual couples to legally form civil unions, giving them some of the legal rights of married couples?"

Question for March 1997, February 1999, and January 2000 surveys: "Do you think marriages between homosexuals should or should not be recognized by the law as valid, with the same rights as traditional marriages?"

Fig. 6.   Support for legal recognition of same-sex couples, 1996–2003. (Data comes from Gallup polls administered between April 1996 and May 2003.)

masters, and whether same-sex couples should be allowed to marry.[18] While all these disputes show the increasing centrality of gay rights in public discourse, the battle over same-sex marriage most symbolizes the shifting cultural frames surrounding same-sex sexuality.

Consider this: when the Supreme Court decided *Bowers*, the notion of same-sex marriage was not even a blip on the public radar screen. By the time it decided *Lawrence*, same-sex marriage was at the center of the debate over gay rights, so much so that all three opinions made specific reference to it. Justice Kennedy's majority decision specifically noted that *Lawrence* did not involve the question of "whether the government must give formal recognition to any relationship that homosexual persons seek to enter" (2478). Justice O'Connor's concurring opinion specifically cited the preservation of marriage as a legitimate state interest while concluding that Texas had no legitimate interest in criminalizing same-sex sexual activity between consenting adults. Justice Scalia's dissent opined that the decision in *Lawrence* opened the door to same-sex marriage.

> The Court says that the present case "does not involve whether the government must give formal recognition to any relationship that homosexual persons seek to enter." Do not believe it. . . . Today's opinion dismantles the structure of constitutional law that has permitted a distinction to be made between hetero-sexual and homo-sexual unions, insofar as formal recognition in marriage is concerned. (*Lawrence,* 2498)

Chapter 7 details the reasons why same-sex marriage came to assume such a prominent role in the cultural conversation about gay rights. For the purpose at hand, let me simply highlight the enormity of the shift in the cultural frames surrounding same-sex sexuality. In 1986, when the Supreme Court decided *Bowers,* the prevailing public conversation about same-sex sexuality concerned fears of AIDS contagion. The notion of a right to same-sex marriage would have been laughable. By 1992, when the Kentucky Supreme Court decided *Wasson,* the public terror over AIDS had begun to recede and new conversations about the sociopolitical implications of homosexuality (e.g., gays in the military) were emerging. By 1997, when *Gryczan* disabled Montana's sodomy law, the public debate over same-sex marriage had become prominent enough to warrant Congress's attention: the 1996 Defense of Marriage Act (DOMA) specifically limited marriage to opposite-sex couples for all federal purposes and also permitted states to refuse recognition to same-sex marriages performed by other states.[19] By 2003, when the Supreme Court decided *Lawrence,* the cultural panic over AIDS had long since subsided. Thirty-seven states had passed legislation banning same-sex marriage within their borders. Vermont, however, recognized same-sex couples as spouses for all state-level purposes. And in Canada, Ontario had just begun to permit same-sex marriage; its lack of residency requirements meant that American couples could cross the border to marry if they wished, although the validity of those marriages in the United States had yet to be determined.

In short, the cultural framing of homosexuality in the *Bowers* era emphasized lgb people, especially gay men, as "others"—promiscuous vectors of contagion existing in opposition to the sphere of hearth, home, and family. By the time *Lawrence* was decided the notion of homosexuality as existing in opposition to family was collapsing. Emerging in its place was an awareness of the families that same-sex couples created.

That this shift in the cultural framing of homosexuality entered the courtroom can be seen in a new judicial willingness to treat same-sex marriage claims respectfully in the 1990s (see chap. 7). It can also be seen in the increased judicial willingness of judges to consider lgb people as fit and proper parents (see chap. 3).

The increased willingness of the American public in general, and the judiciary in particular, to see same-sex relationships as constituting families rather than threatening them altered the context of sodomy reform litigation. Modern privacy jurisprudence developed in the context of familial decision making. As discussed in chapter 2, *Griswold v. Connecticut* (1965) established that the state could not prohibit the use of contraceptives by married couples because such laws impermissibly interfered with the "intimate relationship of husband and wife" (482) and the "notions of privacy surrounding the marriage relationship" (486). *Eisenstadt v. Baird* (1972) extended *Griswold* to unmarried people: "If the right to privacy means anything, it is the right of the *individual,* married or single, to be free from unwarranted governmental intrusion into matters so fundamentally affecting a person as the decision whether to bear or beget a child" (453).

The majority in *Bowers* had been able to dismiss Michael Hardwick's privacy claim in part because they framed his sexual activity as existing outside the bounds of familial decision making. As Justice White wrote, "No connection between family, marriage, or procreation on the one hand and homosexual activity on the other has been demonstrated, either by the Court of Appeals or by [Hardwick]" (*Bowers,* 190–91). The reframing of same-sex sexuality that occurred in the 1990s undermined White's assertion and made the privacy claims raised by gay rights litigators more compelling, both in a cultural and in a legal sense.

In sum, the public conversation about same-sex sexuality changed markedly in the years after *Bowers v. Hardwick* was decided. Fears about AIDS contagion receded, and new conversations about the sociopolitical implications of homosexuality emerged. Support for gay rights increased in a wide range of contexts. Most notably, Americans became more tolerant of same-sex relationships and more willing to treat same-sex couples as legitimate families. This shift in the cultural framing of homosexuality in turn made the privacy claims raised by gay rights litigators more resonant to judges.

Challenging *Bowers*

Lambda made a series of consequential choices around the dawn of the new millennium. First, it decided to alter its post-*Bowers* strategy for attacking sodomy laws; both Arkansas's *Jegley v. Picado* and Texas's *Lawrence v. Texas* included federal as well as state constitutional claims. By making this change, Lambda signaled that it was contemplating a return to the U.S. Supreme Court. Second, Lambda decided to pursue a writ of certiorari to the Supreme Court when presented with the opportunity in *Lawrence*. And third, it decided to make two different arguments before the Court. It asked the Supreme Court to find that sodomy laws violated the guarantee of equal protection of the laws. It also asked the Court to overturn *Bowers v. Hardwick* and to find that sodomy laws violated the right of privacy. This latter decision was audacious; the Supreme Court has rarely overturned a precedent less than twenty years old. It was also, in retrospect, wise. The Supreme Court's ruling in *Lawrence* was everything Lambda could have hoped for and more. Not only did it explicitly overrule *Bowers,* but it did so in sweeping terms that recognized the dignity and worth of lgb people. Lambda gambled in *Lawrence,* just as the ACLU had gambled in *Bowers.* This time, though, the gamble paid off.

In the following pages, I show that the choices Lambda made were influenced by several factors, including litigator preferences, the mechanics of the judicial process, and changes in the underlying structure of legal opportunities surrounding sodomy reform.

The Reemergence of Federal Constitutional Claims

Lambda's decision to incorporate federal constitutional claims into its sodomy cases was the product of years of discussion, both within the organization and with gay rights litigators across the nation. The Litigators' Roundtable, successor to the Ad-Hoc Task Force, played an important role in facilitating this discussion and establishing an eventual consensus around the "new federal" strategy.

Lambda's underlying motivation in returning to federal constitutional arguments was simple enough. It wanted to dismantle—or at least defang—the legacy of *Bowers v. Hardwick,* a goal it could only partially accomplish via the state-by-state strategy. The problem was that lower courts were relying on *Bowers* to permit discrimination against lgb people in a plethora of different contexts, employing the rationale articulated by the U.S. Court of Appeals for the Federal Circuit in *Woodward v. United States* (1989): "After [*Bowers v.*] *Hardwick* it cannot logically be asserted that discrimination against homosexuals is constitutionally infirm" (*Woodward,* 1076). The specter of *Bowers* thus hung over every gay rights case Lambda litigated. One Lambda attorney analogized the case to a "hammer opponents used in court" over and over again, no matter what the specific legal issue at hand.

On a more emotional level, Lambda wanted to erase a decision it viewed as profoundly insulting and homophobic. Noted gay rights attorney Mary Dunlap (1994, 7) encapsulated the feelings of many when she wrote about *Bowers:* "we 'came out' legally at a highly visible level, and we got bashed legally at a highly visible level." In the words of one Lambda litigator, "we wanted vindication."

There were also resource-based reasons for returning to federal constitutional claims. Litigating state by state is more time-consuming and more expensive than litigating at the federal level, all things being equal. The right federal constitutional challenge could conceivably knock out all remaining sodomy laws with one blow. Moreover, some litigators thought that the only way to bring down sodomy laws in a few states was through a federal constitutional ruling.

Whether to return to federal constitutional claims was never really a matter of debate. *When* to return was. A Lambda staffer posed the question this way: "How long do you have to wait before you can ask the Court to revisit a terrible decision? Every constitutional lawyer in America would have a different answer." And in fact, the ACLU's Lesbian and Gay Rights Project and the Boston-based GLAD both decided to wade back into federal constitutional waters before Lambda did.[20]

In 1996, Lambda came to an internal consensus that the time was right to begin looking for a sodomy case to bring before the Supreme Court. Its decision reflected its sense that the legal and political context surrounding sodomy and homosexuality had changed to such an extent that the logic governing *Bowers* might no longer be persuasive to the Court. It had a number of reasons for drawing this conclusion.

First, the worst-case scenario had not come to pass. No state legislature had reinstituted sodomy laws in response to *Bowers.* In fact, Nevada and the District of Columbia had both legislatively repealed their sodomy laws. In addition, public attitudes about homosexuality and gay rights were far less negative than they had been in 1986. These events led Lambda to posit that, in the words of one litigator, "the world was ready for this."

The wide criticism of the majority's analysis in *Bowers* also helped to persuade Lambda that the precedent might be vulnerable to attack. The great majority of law review articles found the dissenters' arguments in *Bowers* more persuasive than the majority or concurring opinions (see especially Goldstein 1988; Halley 1993; Thomas 1993). The *Bowers* majority had been roundly taken to task for its cramped reading of the right to privacy, its framing of the issue as concerning "a fundamental right to engage in homosexual sodomy," and its uncritical reliance on majoritarian morality as a sufficient rationale for legitimating sodomy laws. Justice Powell's public announcement that he had erred in voting with the majority in *Bowers* likewise seemed to make the precedent more vulnerable. Moreover, in early 1996 Tennessee had become the second state to judicially void its sodomy statute post-*Bowers*. As had the Kentucky Supreme Court in *Wasson*, the Tennessee court had construed the right of privacy much more expansively than had the *Bowers* majority. While both cases were based on state rather than federal constitutional guarantees, they clearly rejected the *Bowers* analysis.

The most important single factor in Lambda's decision to seek Supreme Court review of another sodomy case, however, was a signal from the Supreme Court itself. The membership of the Supreme Court had changed substantially in the years since *Bowers*. By 1994, only three members of the *Bowers* Court remained—Justices Rehnquist and O'Connor, who had voted to uphold Georgia's sodomy law, and Justice Stevens, who had voted to strike it down. The key question for Lambda and its allies was whether the Court's turnover would produce a corresponding shift in its views on the constitutionality of sodomy laws.

The first gay rights case to reach the newly constituted Supreme Court provided few answers. In 1995, the Court decided *Hurley v. Irish-American Gay, Lesbian, and Bisexual Group* (GLIB), otherwise known as the St. Patrick's Day Parade case. *Hurley* offered scant information about the justices' attitudes about gay rights, because the question it posed was whether the organizers of the parade could be compelled to include an expressive message they did not wish to include. The Court decided unanimously that the parade was a private event rather than a public one, that it included an expressive message, and that the state could not constitutionally compel the organizers to permit GLIB to march.

Although the opinion did not speak directly to the sociolegal implications of homosexuality, it did differ markedly in tone from the majority and concurring opinions in *Bowers*. Unlike the authors of those opinions, Justice Souter gave no sense that he found homosexuality distasteful or worthy of condemnation. The language he used when discussing GLIB and its purpose was respectful. For example, he referred to GLIB's members as "openly gay, lesbian, and bisexual descendents of the Irish immigrants" (*Hurley*, 570) rather than depicting them as "avowed" or "militant" homosexuals. Gay rights advocates hoped that the rhetorical differences between *Bowers* and *Hurley* presaged a new judicial openness to gay rights claims.

This hope was realized one year later. In *Romer v. Evans* (1996), a six-justice majority struck down Colorado's infamous antigay constitutional amendment. Passed in 1992, Amendment 2 invalidated all existing state and local provisions barring discrimination on the basis of sexual orientation and prohibited the future enactment of such legislation anywhere in the state. The *Romer* majority concluded that Amendment 2 bore no rational relationship to any legitimate government purpose. They found it instead to be "born of animosity" toward lgb people and designed to make them unequal to everyone else. "This government cannot do. A State cannot so deem a class of persons a stranger to its laws" (*Romer*, 635). The Court struck down the amendment as a violation of the federal equal protection rights of lesbian and gay Coloradoans.

Romer v. Evans will be discussed at length in chapter 6. For the moment, the important point is that Lambda saw *Romer* as what one litigator called a "huge new tool" for attacking state sodomy laws on the federal level. Six justices had rejected Colorado's argument that, among other things, Amendment 2 was a permissible expression of majoritarian morality, designed to protect children, (heterosexual) families, and (heterosexual) marriage. They had recognized the animus toward lgb people underlying Amendment 2 and had explicitly repudiated it. Those same six justices might recognize the animus at the heart of same-sex sodomy laws as well.

Ironically, *Romer*'s potential impact on *Bowers* was articulated by Justice Scalia, a dissenter in the case who argued that, under *Bowers*, Colorado's Amendment 2 must pass constitutional muster.

In *Bowers v. Hardwick*, we held that the Constitution does not prohibit what virtually all States had done from the founding of the Republic until very recent years—making homosexual conduct a crime. . . . If it is constitutionally permissible for a State to make homosexual conduct criminal, surely it is constitutionally permissible for a State to enact other laws merely *disfavoring* homosexual conduct. (As the Court of Appeals for the District of Columbia Circuit had aptly put it: "If the Court [in *Bowers*] was unwilling to object to state laws that criminalize the behavior that defines the class, it is hardly open . . . to conclude that state sponsored discrimination against the class is invidious. After all, there can hardly be more palpable discrimination against a class than making the conduct that defines the class criminal.") And *a fortiori* it is constitutionally permissible for a State to adopt a provision *not even* disfavoring homosexual conduct, but merely prohibiting all levels of state government from bestowing special protections upon homosexual conduct. (*Romer*, 641, citations omitted; emphasis in original)

Scalia's logic chain was reversible. If, under *Romer*, Colorado's Amendment 2 could not pass constitutional muster, then surely sodomy laws were unconstitutional as well.

Lambda's 1996 decision to seek Supreme Court review of another sodomy case was, in summary, based on a combination of litigator preferences, long-term trends, and critical events. The desire to reverse or at least contain *Bowers* was always present. Favorable trends in the cultural framing of homosexuality made this goal seem more attainable, as did waning legislative and judicial support for sodomy laws combined with widespread criticism of the majority's reasoning in *Bowers*. The Supreme Court's decision in *Romer* provided the final push by giving Lambda a new tool with which to fight sodomy laws and signaling the Court's potential openness to gay rights claims.

Developing Test Cases

Having decided to wade back into federal constitutional waters, Lambda set about developing potential test cases. Its decision making here was once again facilitated by extensive discussions with other organized and individual litigators as well as constitutional law professors. Topics of conversation included possible legal theories, fact scenarios, and laws to attack. As the two biggest organized sodomy law litigators, Lambda and the ACLU Lesbian and Gay Rights Project consulted especially closely with one another and ultimately settled on a common strategy. They decided to focus their litigation efforts on the six states that had laws criminalizing same-sex but not opposite-sex sodomy[21] and to raise a fourfold argument: such laws violated privacy and equal protection guarantees under both state and federal constitutions.

Their decision to continue raising state constitutional claims reflected the continued value of the state-by-state strategy. While Lambda and the ACLU wanted to bring a case back up to the U.S. Supreme Court, they also wanted to win at the state level. State constitutional claims allowed them to litigate around *Bowers* even as they were actively seeking to dismantle it.

Consensus about bringing both federal equal protection and privacy claims was more difficult to achieve. The general feeling among the litigators at Lambda and the ACLU was that the equal protection argument had a better chance of succeeding at the Supreme Court than did the privacy argument. *Romer* was an equal protection case, and the litigators saw a strong possibility that all six justices in the *Romer* majority would extend its logic to strike down sodomy laws as well.

Finding at least five votes for the privacy claim was more problematic (table 10). As litigators at Lambda and the ACLU "read" the Court, Rehnquist, Scalia, and Thomas would certainly vote to sustain sodomy laws against a privacy challenge as well as an equal protection challenge. Based on his vote in *Bowers*, Stevens seemed likely to strike such laws down on either constitutional ground, and based on their voting records in earlier privacy and equal protection claims, it seemed at least reason-

TABLE 10. Lambda/ACLU Predictions about Supreme Court Voting Patterns in Hypothetical Sodomy Challenge

Justice	Equal Protection	Privacy	Prior Decisions[a]	Ranking[b]
Breyer	Y	Y	Romer, Dale	1
Stevens	Y	Y	Bowers, Romer, Dale	2
Ginsburg	Y	Y	Romer, Dale	3
Souter	Y	Y	Romer, Dale	4
Kennedy	Y	?	Romer, _Dale_	5
O'Connor	Y	N	Romer, _Bowers, Dale_	6
Scalia	N	N	_Romer, Dale_	7
Thomas	N	N	_Romer, Dale_	8
Rehnquist	N	N	_Bowers, Romer, Dale_	9

[a]Case names without underlining are votes that are considered pro-gay.

[b]Rankings reflect the justices's relative support for the liberal position in civil liberties cases from their arrival on the Supreme Court through 1995, where 1 equals the most liberal justice and 9 equals the most conservative justice. Source for data is Epstein and Knight 1998.

ably likely that Breyer, Ginsburg, and Souter would do so as well. O'Connor and Kennedy were the question marks.

O'Connor's vote in *Romer* suggested she might be open to striking down sodomy laws on the basis of equal protection, but her vote in *Bowers* and in other right of privacy cases intimated that she would not be amenable to a privacy argument. Kennedy's vote in *Romer* likewise implied that he would be amenable to an equal protection argument. Whether he would go for a privacy argument was anyone's guess. On the one hand, his majority opinion in *Romer* revealed that he recognized the animus directed at lgb people and would likely be suspicious of any invocation of morality as a justification for the constitutionality of sodomy laws. On the other hand, his prior voting record in privacy cases closely matched O'Connor's.

Some litigators felt that the cause would be best served by raising only an equal protection claim. It seemed a safer bet. Moreover, they felt that a Supreme Court decision striking down sodomy laws on equal protection grounds might actually be more useful to other gay rights litigation than a decision striking down such laws on privacy grounds. Outside of sodomy law reform, very little gay rights litigation centered on privacy-based arguments by the mid-1990s. Equal protection arguments, though, were at the heart of a wide assortment of cases. The core idea behind the notion of equal protection is that the government must treat similarly situated groups in a similar fashion. If the Supreme Court ruled that lgb people were similarly situated to straight people with respect to their sexual relationships, litigators might be able to wield the ruling to dismantle other forms of discrimination of lgb people, including their exclusion from marriage and from openly serving in the military.

Other litigators thought it was important to raise a privacy claim as well as an equal protection claim. (It bears noting here that everyone appears to have agreed on the merits of an equal protection claim.) An equal protection ruling would only strike down sodomy laws in those states that drew distinctions between homosexuality and heterosexuality. The laws in "equal opportunity" states would survive, requiring yet more litigation. Perhaps even more important is the fact that it would leave the essential holding of *Bowers* intact.

In the end, the mechanics of the legal process helped convince Lambda and ACLU litigators to bring a privacy claim as well as an equal protection claim. Making a federal privacy claim in the lower courts would only commit them to arguing it before the Supreme Court *if* they won at the state level *and if* the basis for the state victory was the federal privacy claim (as opposed to a state claim or a federal equal protection claim) *and if* the state appealed the decision to the Supreme Court *and if* the Supreme Court agreed to hear the case. However, failing to raise the issue in the lower courts would preclude them from arguing it before the Supreme Court when and if they managed to get a case onto the Court's docket. In other words, including a federal privacy claim at the start of a sodomy law challenge would likely not commit Lambda and/or the ACLU to arguing it before the Supreme Court. They would have time to reevaluate their wisdom of this legal argument as the case progressed.

As Lambda and the ACLU were considering legal arguments, they were also contending with the tension between finding litigants who could meet the federal standing requirements and finding litigants whose stories of harm the justices would "get." The core problem, once again, was the general lack of enforcement of sodomy laws. Given the paucity of lgb people who had actually been arrested for private, consensual sodomy, Lambda and the ACLU had two realistic options. The first was to challenge sodomy laws on behalf of gay men who had been convicted of soliciting sodomy. Such litigants would be most likely to jump the standing hurdle. The drawback to this plan was described by one litigator this way: "We didn't want the specter of gay men cruising for sex in public parks" to be raised in the justices' minds. "We didn't want to raise red flags any more than absolutely necessary."

Their other realistic option was to assemble cases with multiple plaintiffs asserting real but indirect harm from the existence of sodomy laws. This approach would allow Lambda and the ACLU to present the Supreme Court with an array of sympathetic litigants who could illustrate the myriad ways petty and profound that sodomy laws were harmful to lgb people. The drawback here was that the lack of criminal prosecution might convince the Supreme Court that the plaintiffs lacked standing.

The desire to avoid what one litigator called the "ick factor" led Lambda and the ACLU to choose the multiple plaintiff option. Lambda set about locating litigants to challenge Arkansas's same-sex-only sodomy law; the ACLU developed a parallel case in Maryland. The cases were launched within a few days of each other in early 1998. A few months later, the ACLU initiated a second case in Puerto Rico; Lambda became cocounsel when Michael Adams, the lawyer in charge of the case, left the ACLU for Lambda.[22]

Then, on September 17, 1998, an event occurred that eerily paralleled the facts in *Bowers*. Police in Houston, Texas, burst into John

Lawrence's apartment based on what turned out to be a false report of an armed gunman on the premises. They surprised Lawrence, who was having sex with Tyrone Garner, and arrested both men for violating the state's sodomy law. Lawrence and Garner were held in jail for over twenty-four hours and subsequently released on bond. They pleaded "no contest" to the charges in criminal court and were each fined two hundred dollars.

In a surreal sense, the arrest of Lawrence and Garner was a gift to sodomy law reformers. Their conviction clearly gave them standing to challenge Texas's law. The location of their arrest (Lawrence's bedroom) made the privacy interest at stake clear. And the fact that Texas's law prohibited only same-sex sodomy meant that federal equal protection arguments could be raised as well. Lambda was called in shortly after the arrest and quickly added the new case to its docket.

In sum, the test cases Lambda and the ACLU developed were shaped by a number of forces, including litigator preferences, the mechanics of the legal process, judicial alignments on the Supreme Court, and a confluence of unlikely events.

Litigating in the Lower Courts

Lambda and the ACLU spent the next several years shepherding these four cases through the courts. The cases progressed quite differently. *Williams v. Glendening,* the ACLU's Maryland case, ended shortly after it began, with a favorable ruling at the trial court level; in a subsequent settlement with the ACLU, the state of Maryland agreed that private, consensual sexual conduct fell outside the scope of the criminal law. This was a clear victory for the ACLU, although it obviously meant that *Glendening* was not headed to the U.S. Supreme Court.

In contrast to Maryland, Arkansas fought to preserve its sodomy law all the way up to the state's supreme court—twice. The first time, it argued that the seven plaintiffs in Lambda's *Jegley v. Picado* lacked standing to challenge the law because they had not been directly harmed by it. The Arkansas Supreme Court unanimously rejected the state's claim and remanded the case for trial. The case then worked its way up to the Arkansas Supreme Court again, this time on a consideration of the merits of Lambda's equal protection and privacy arguments. By a 3–2 vote, the high court struck down the law, ruling that it ran afoul of state constitutional guarantees of privacy and equal protection. Lambda was thrilled to win the case, yet its victory meant that *Jegley* would not be headed to the U.S. Supreme Court either. Because the ruling was based on the state constitution, Arkansas did not have the option of petitioning the U.S. Supreme Court for review.

Puerto Rico's reaction was similar to Arkansas's. It argued in *Sanchez v. Puerto Rico* that the plaintiffs lacked standing to challenge the sodomy law's constitutionality because none of them had been charged with violating it.[23] The trial court rejected this argument and ordered the case to proceed to trial, but the court's ruling was reversed by the court of appeals, which determined that the plaintiffs could not show that they were directly harmed by the law and so lacked standing to challenge it. The ACLU appealed this ruling to the Puerto Rico Supreme Court, which initially declined to accept the case but then reversed itself. The high court ultimately concluded that the plaintiffs were in fact without standing.

With a loss in the Puerto Rico Supreme Court, the ACLU and Lambda (which had become cocounsel in the case) were in a position to ask the U.S. Supreme Court to review the case. There was a clear consensus among the two organizations, however, that *Sanchez* was not a good candidate for Supreme Court review. The merits of the case had never been reached; the legal record focused entirely on questions of justiciability. Lambda and the ACLU knew that the Supreme Court was highly unlikely to consider the merits of a constitutional challenge to Puerto Rico's sodomy law when the courts below had not addressed them; expending additional resources on a case that seemed destined to be denied certiorari seemed unwarranted. Moreover, because the merits of *Sanchez* had not been litigated, Lambda and the ACLU had been unable to build the kind of factual record they thought they would need to bolster their legal arguments.

Lawrence encountered none of the barriers that made *Glendening, Jegley,* and *Sanchez* ineligible or inappropriate for Supreme Court review. Because of their conviction, John Lawrence and Tyrone Garner clearly had standing to challenge the constitutionality of Texas's "Homosexual Conduct" law. The merits of both the privacy and the equal protection arguments had been addressed, first by a panel of Texas's Fourteenth District Court of Appeals in Houston, which struck down the law by a vote of 2–1 as violating state constitutional guarantees of equal protection, and then by the Fourteenth District Court of Appeals sitting en banc, which overturned the panel's ruling by a vote of 7–2. The Texas Court of Criminal Appeals' refusal to hear an appeal in *Lawrence* gave Lambda its second opportunity to file a writ of certiorari before the Supreme Court. This time Lambda went forward.

When Lambda and the ACLU were in the process of developing and litigating *Glendening, Jegley, Sanchez,* and *Lawrence,* they had no idea which one, if any, would make it up to the Supreme Court. As it turned out, *Glendening* and *Jegley* were both derailed, in a manner of speaking, by victory at the state level. The development of *Sanchez* made it technically eligible for Supreme Court review but realistically inappropriate. Only *Lawrence* developed in a fashion that made it not only eligible for review but also a reasonable candidate.

It might have been different. *Jegley,* for example, was decided in Lambda's favor by a 3–2 vote. A one-vote switch would have made it eligible for Supreme Court review as well. Whether Lambda would have asked for a writ of certiorari, whether they would have raised both privacy and equal protection claims, whether the Supreme Court would have taken the case, and, if so, what the Court would have ruled are questions we can only speculate about. The point for the purposes at hand is that litigation strategies are inevitably constrained by events outside the control of the litigators. The most they can do is plan for contingencies. Lambda's executive director Kevin Cathcart referred to this feature of the litigation process when he described Lambda's sodomy reform strategy thus: "Our plan really looks more like an old computer-programming flowchart: if this, then that. We have to have multiple irons in the fire because we just don't know what's going to happen" in any particular case.

Petitioning for a Writ of Certiorari

With *Lawrence* at the certiorari stage, Lambda needed to revisit the issue of whether to ask the Supreme Court to overturn *Bowers v. Hardwick* or to proceed solely with an equal protection claim. The organization solicited input from the Litigators' Roundtable as well as a range of constitutional law scholars. The question was the subject of lengthy and impassioned debate. Unanimity as to the best approach was never achieved. Much of the conversation trod well-worn ground concerning the relative risks and rewards of arguing equal protection versus privacy. The recent Supreme Court decision in *Boy Scouts of America v. Dale* (2000) added fuel to the conversational fire.

Dale, another Lambda case, concerned the question of whether the First Amendment right of expressive association permitted the Boy Scouts to prohibit James Dale from serving as an assistant scoutmaster, despite a New Jersey law prohibiting discrimination on the basis of sexual orientation in public accommodations. *Dale* required the Court to resolve a number of factual disputes, including whether the group's expressive message included a coherent policy of disapproval of homosexuality and, if so, whether the inclusion of an openly gay scoutmaster would significantly burden that message.

The New Jersey Supreme Court had ruled unanimously that the publicly articulated policies of the Boy Scouts did not include any coherent antigay message or purpose and thus that its right of expressive association would not be burdened by Dale's presence. It ordered the organization to reinstate him.

On appeal, the Supreme Court reversed the New Jersey court's ruling, by a vote of 5–4. The majority and dissenting opinions construed the facts at issue in diametrically opposed fashions. Rehnquist's majority opinion accepted the Boy Scouts' assertion that their expressive message included disapproval of homosexuality. It also concluded that, as an openly gay man and "gay rights activist," "Dale's presence in the Boy Scouts would, at the very least, force the organization to send a message, both to the youth members and the world, that the Boy Scouts accepts homosexual conduct as a legitimate form of behavior" (*Dale*, 652).

Stevens's dissenting opinion rejected the Boy Scouts' assertion that their expressive message included disapproval of homosexuality. It also rejected the majority's conclusion that Dale's mere presence as a scoutmaster constituted an expressive message.

> Indeed, if merely joining a group did constitute symbolic speech; and such speech were attributable to the group being joined; and that group has the right to exclude that speech (and hence, the right to exclude that person from joining), then the right of free speech effectively becomes a limitless right to exclude for every organization, whether or not it engages in any expressive activities. That cannot be, and never has been, the law.
>
> The only apparent explanation for the majority's holding, then, is that homosexuals are simply so different from the rest of society that their presence alone—unlike any other individual's—should be singled out for special First Amendment treatment. Under the majority's reasoning, an openly gay male is irreversibly affixed with the label "homosexual." That label, even though unseen, communicates a message that permits his exclusion wherever he goes. His openness is the sole and sufficient justification for his

ostracism. Though unintended, reliance on such a justification is tantamount to a constitutionally prescribed symbol of inferiority. (*Dale,* 695–96)

The worrisome aspect of *Dale* vis-à-vis the certiorari decision in *Lawrence* was that Justices O'Connor and Kennedy had both signed onto Rehnquist's majority opinion rather than Stevens's dissent. *Dale* did not speak directly to either the rights of privacy or equal protection. It did, however, expose a fault line in the Court over the social meaning of homosexuality, captured in the quotes given previously, and also emphasized the crucial swing role played by Kennedy and O'Connor. To some litigators, *Dale* sounded a worrisome note about the more ambitious right of privacy claim.

Ultimately, Lambda had to make a decision, and it chose to include both an equal protection argument and a privacy argument in its writ of certiorari. Its decision was based on a number of factors, including the mechanics of the Supreme Court decision-making process, an anticipated shift in the membership of the Court, and the unusual confluence of events that produced *Lawrence.*

The Supreme Court has virtually unfettered discretion not only in choosing what cases it wants to hear but also in choosing what elements of those cases it wishes to address. Lambda believed (*hoped* may be the better word here) that the Supreme Court would not agree to hear a privacy claim merely to reiterate *Bowers.* The Court was more likely, Lambda thought, to decline to accept the question for review and instead limit the scope of its inquiry to the equal protection claim. Moreover, even if the Supreme Court chose to hear the privacy claim and ultimately upheld *Bowers,* so long as it ruled favorably on the equal protection claim, same-sex-only sodomy statutes would fall.

Lambda was also spurred to include a privacy argument because it anticipated that judicial alignments on the Supreme Court might well become less favorable to gay rights claims in the near future. George W. Bush had won the 2000 presidential election; he had expressed his admiration for the jurisprudence of Justices Scalia and Thomas on a number of occasions. Together with Chief Justice Rehnquist, Scalia and Thomas anchored the conservative wing of the high court; from Lambda's perspective, their track record on gay rights, privacy, and equal protection was dreadful. Were Bush given the opportunity to nominate a Supreme Court justice, Lambda anticipated that he would choose someone cast from the same mold. Worse, court watchers were widely expecting at least one and possibly as many as three justices to retire in the near future. Among the names floated as a likely candidate for retirement was Justice Stevens, the oldest member on the Court. Stevens, who had voted for *Romer* and against *Bowers* and *Dale,* anchored the liberal wing of the Supreme Court. Replacing him with a conservative justice would dramatically shift the Court to the right, making it difficult if not impossible for gay rights claims to prevail.

Finally, Lambda was very cognizant that the events that precipitated *Lawrence* were unlikely to occur again anytime in the foreseeable future. While neither Lawrence nor Garner had led the sort of impeccable lives that Justice Douglas in that long-ago forum on Staten Island had mentioned would be a useful complement to a sodomy law challenge, the fact that they had been arrested in Lawrence's bedroom threw the privacy issue into stark relief. The odds of Lambda finding a future case that more vividly illustrated the privacy interests at stake seemed vanishingly small.

In sum, Lambda rolled the dice in filing its petition for a writ of certiorari in *Lawrence,* but it had real reasons for thinking that the time was right to challenge *Bowers.* The cultural framings surrounding homosexuality had changed considerably since 1986. The number of states with sodomy laws had dropped from twenty-four to fifteen. The membership of the Supreme Court had likewise changed; *Romer* in particular indicated that a majority of the justices might now look favorably on a challenge to the constitutionality of sodomy laws. The facts in *Lawrence* offered a compelling illustration of the privacy issues at stake, and Texas's same-sex-only sodomy law allowed an equal protection claim to be made as well. Waiting to take on *Bowers* at a future point in time seemed problematic. New judicial appointments would probably push the Court further to the right, and another *Lawrence* was not likely to arise, leaving gay rights litigators with the option of bringing solicitation-based cases (and risk triggering the "ick factor") or bringing multiparty facial challenges (and risk stumbling over the standing hurdle).

In retrospect, its decision was wise. The Supreme Court accepted *Lawrence* and agreed to consider both whether same-sex-only sodomy laws violated the federal guarantee of equal protection and whether *Bowers* was correctly decided. On June 26, 2003, the Supreme Court struck down Texas's sodomy law, finding that it impermissibly infringed on the right of privacy. *Bowers* was overruled, just four days shy of its seventeenth anniversary.

Winning Lawrence

The facts behind *Bowers* and *Lawrence* were remarkably similar. In both
cases police had literally looked into the bedroom of a gay man and witnessed him having sex with another man. In both cases, the men had been
arrested in their own bedrooms, handcuffed, and brought to holding
cells, where they were forced to wait a lengthy period of time before their
paperwork was processed.[24] In both cases, gay rights litigators argued
that sodomy law under which the men had been arrested violated their
right of privacy under the federal Constitution.

The similarities between *Bowers* and *Lawrence* extended into the
Supreme Court. In both cases, the privacy question was resolved on a 5–4
vote. But here the similarities ended. In *Bowers,* swing vote Justice Powell had decided that the case was, in his words, "frivolous" and "brought
just to see what the Court would do" (Marcus 1990). He signed onto Justice White's majority opinion upholding Georgia's sodomy law. In
Lawrence, swing vote Justice Kennedy authored the majority opinion
striking down Texas's law. He construed the privacy interest at stake
quite differently.

> The Court began its substantive discussion in *Bowers* as follows:
> "The issue presented is whether the Federal Constitution confers
> a fundamental right upon homosexuals to engage in sodomy and
> hence invalidates the laws of the many States that still make such
> conduct illegal and have done so for a very long time." That state-
> ment, we now conclude, discloses the Court's own failure to
> appreciate the extent of the liberty at stake. To say that the issue
> in *Bowers* was simply the right to engage in certain sexual con-
> duct demeans the claim the individual put forward, just as it
> would demean a married couple were it to be said marriage is sim-
> ply about the right to have sexual intercourse. The laws involved
> in *Bowers* and here are, to be sure, statutes that purport to do no
> more than prohibit a particular sexual act. Their penalties and
> purposes, though, have more far-reaching consequences, touching
> upon the most private human conduct, sexual behavior, and in
> the most private of places, the home. The statutes do seek to con-
> trol a personal relationship that, whether or not entitled to formal
> recognition in the law, is within the liberty of persons to choose
> without being punished as criminals. (*Lawrence,* 2478, citations
> omitted)

Why were gay rights litigators able to mobilize the law successfully in *Lawrence* when they had failed in *Bowers*? Justice Scalia's blistering dissent, which was joined by Rehnquist and Thomas, reiterated an accusation he had initially proffered in his *Romer* dissent: that the decision reflected the majority's political preferences rather than the dictates of the law.

> Today's opinion is the product of a Court, which is the product of a law-profession culture, that has largely signed on to the so-called homosexual agenda, by which I mean the agenda promoted by some homosexual activists directed at eliminating the moral opprobrium that has traditionally attached to homosexual conduct. . . . [T]he Court has taken sides in the culture war, departing from its role of assuring, as neutral observer, that the democratic rules of engagement are observed. (*Lawrence*, 2497)

Rhetoric about the "so-called homosexual agenda" aside, it is clear that Kennedy understood the harms posed by sodomy laws in a way that Powell had not.[25] The significant changes in the cultural frames surrounding homosexuality in the seventeen years since *Bowers* undoubtedly played a role in Kennedy's awareness of the liberty interests at stake. In fact, changes in the cultural framing of homosexuality apparently had an impact on the wider court. Even Justice Scalia felt it necessary to announce that he had "nothing against homosexuals, or any other group, promoting their agenda through normal democratic means" in his dissent (*Lawrence*, 2496). Justice Thomas joined Scalia's dissent but also wrote separately to underscore his distaste for Texas's law. Invoking Justice Stewart's famous critique of a Connecticut law banning contraceptive use in *Griswold v. Connecticut* (1965), Thomas wrote: "I write separately to note that the law before the Court today is . . . uncommonly silly.' If I were a member of the Texas Legislature, I would vote to repeal it. Punishing someone for expressing his sexual preference through non-commercial consensual conduct with another adult does not appear to be a worthy way to expend valuable law enforcement resources" (2498).

Thomas's dissent went on to conclude that he was "not empowered to help petitioners and others similarly situated" (2498) because, as he read it, the Constitution did not encompass a generalized right of privacy. His argument suggests that the political values of justices are tempered by their understanding of what the law requires. Justice O'Connor's concurrence in *Lawrence* suggests this as well. O'Connor provided the sixth vote to strike down Texas's sodomy law, but on a different ground. She rejected the majority's conclusion that the law violated the right of privacy but did find that the law violated the guarantee of equal protection.

It is interesting to note, however, that despite her unwillingness to strike down *Bowers,* O'Connor rejected a central element of *Bowers's* holding: that Georgia's interest in promoting morality constituted a legitimate basis for its sodomy law. Texas asserted the same interest in *Lawrence.* Indeed, it was the *only* rationale Texas advanced for its sodomy law. O'Connor rejected it flatly, analogizing Texas's sodomy law to Colorado's Amendment 2 and concluding that its intent and effect were actually to single out homosexuals and brand them as legally and socially inferior. "Moral disapproval" of homosexuals, she wrote, "like a bare desire to harm the group, is an interest that is insufficient to satisfy rational basis review under the Equal Protection Clause" (2486).

O'Connor's concurrence opens the door to an interesting hypothetical: would she have voted to strike down Georgia's sodomy law in 1986 had the law prohibited only same-sex sodomy? Were the members of the Ad-Hoc Task Force who argued that *Bowers* should be withdrawn and/or consolidated with *Baker v. Wade* correct? The answer is obviously unknowable, but the question is useful because it gets to the heart of the relationship between legal frames and cultural frames. Legal and cultural frames do not exist in isolation from one another. In both *Bowers* and *Lawrence,* cultural symbols and discourses shaped the legal understandings of the presiding justices. Had the ACLU been able to frame the legal issue in *Bowers* as one of equal protection, would O'Connor's vote have changed? Or would the dominant cultural frames surrounding homosexuality at the time have convinced her that people who committed "homosexual sodomy" were sufficiently different from people who committed heterosexual sodomy that states were justified in criminalizing one but not the other?

For what it's worth, my sense is that O'Connor's vote would *not* have changed and that gay rights litigators would have found themselves facing bad precedent on both privacy and equal protection fronts in the alternative universe I've postulated. Both the cultural and the legal context of homosexuality changed significantly in the years between *Bowers* and *Lawrence* in ways that increased the resonance of Lambda's claims and decreased the persuasiveness of "morality" as a basis for distinguishing between homosexuals and heterosexuals. This is not to say that I believe O'Connor switched sides in the "culture war" (to use Scalia's phrase). It is to say that I believe O'Connor had come to more fully understand the constitutional implications of sodomy laws and to more clearly see that laws directed at lgb people were motivated by animus.

The Impact of Lawrence

On June 25, 2003, thirteen states in addition to Texas had operational sodomy laws.[26] On June 26, 2003, all of those laws fell. That *Lawrence* constituted a landmark legal victory for sodomy law reformers is beyond debate. Whether and to what extent *Lawrence* will have an impact on the course of gay rights litigation more generally, however, remains to be seen. In the words of Lambda litigator Pat Logue, *Lawrence* "reshaped the landscape in a way that is clearly profound, and we don't pretend to know all its implications yet" (Coyle 2003). As this book went to press, Lambda was contemplating a number of areas in which *Lawrence* might prove useful. In October 2003 it took a first step in testing the limits of *Lawrence:* together with the ACLU and the Servicemembers Legal Defense Fund, it filed an amicus brief arguing that *Lawrence* required the military to overturn its ban on consensual sodomy.[27] An article posted on Lambda's web site discussed several additional possible lines of argument.

> When gay parents in committed relationships are told that they must choose between living with their partner or their children, we will use the momentum from this great victory on their behalf. We now have a powerful new tool to roll back anti-gay discrimination against public employees, including teachers and law enforcement officials. When public schools refuse to step in and protect lesbian and gay students from violence and harassment, this decision will help us secure their safety. And if any legislature in the country— from the State House in Austin, Texas to a city council in Oregon to the U.S. Congress—passes a law to express disapproval of gay people, we'll use this ruling to fight back. (Lambda Legal Defense and Education Fund 2004)

Lambda's rhetoric notwithstanding, early judicial responses to attempts to use *Lawrence* to leverage further gay rights victories have been decidedly mixed. The Massachusetts Supreme Judicial Court cited *Lawrence* repeatedly in a decision striking down the state's prohibition of same-sex marriage (*Goodridge v. Dept. of Public Health,* 2003) as well as in a related ruling holding that civil unions were a constitutionally inadequate substitute for marriage (*Opinions of the Justices to the Senate*, 2004).[28] The Eleventh Circuit Court of Appeals, in contrast, explicitly rejected the argument that *Lawrence* had any salience to a case challenging Florida's refusal to allow lgb people to adopt children (*Lofton v. Secretary of the Department of Children and Family Services*, 2004). *Lawrence*, said the Eleventh Circuit, concerned itself with criminal penalties for actions involving consenting adults while Florida's adoption law involved a legal privilege involving both adults and children.

The Kansas Court of Appeals likewise minimized *Lawrence*'s reach (*State v. Limon*, 2004). Matthew Limon had been sentenced to seventeen years in prison for having sex with a fourteen-year-old boy when Limon himself was eighteen. Had Limon had sex with a girl rather than a boy, he would have served only fifteen months. The day after the Supreme Court decided *Lawrence*, it remanded *Limon* for reconsideration in light of *Lawrence*, a clear indication that the Supreme Court felt that *Lawrence* controlled *Limon*. The Kansas Court of Appeals rejected the high court's implied direction. The cases, it ruled, were both factually and legally distinct from one another. Unlike *Lawrence*, *Limon* involved a minor.[29] Moreover, *Limon* raised an equal protection challenge while *Lawrence* was decided on a privacy basis.

The Kansas court's differentiation of *Lawrence* as a privacy case is especially notable because it spoke to a concern expressed by a number of gay rights litigators. As noted earlier in this chapter, the universe of gay rights litigators involved in planning the development of *Lawrence* and other potential test cases had been divided over whether to challenge sodomy laws based on privacy, equal protection, or some combination of the two. A sizable number felt that a decision striking down sodomy laws on the basis of privacy might actually be less useful to future gay rights litigation than a decision grounded in the jurisprudence of equal protection. *Limon* suggests the possibility that this view is correct, and that for all its soaring rhetoric, *Lawrence* may have somewhat limited utility as a tool for advancing gay rights claims through litigation.[30]

Only time will tell. At a minimum, *Lawrence* has ensured that *Bowers* can no longer be used as a basis for denying gay rights claims. Whether gay rights litigators can wield it effectively as a weapon for advancing gay rights more broadly is unclear. *Lawrence*, like *Bowers* before it, has shifted the LOS, but the value of this shift—both for advocates and opponents of gay rights—is but a wave of probabilities at the moment. Lambda and its allies will wield their considerable expertise to leverage additional gains just as opponents of gay rights will seek to minimize those gains and, if possible, use *Lawrence* to further their attacks on gay rights.[31] *Lawrence* is, at the moment, an opportunity awaiting action.

Conclusion

Why did gay rights litigators lose *Bowers* but win *Lawrence*? I have argued in this chapter that the key difference between the two cases is that the structure of legal opportunities changed significantly in the intervening years. Turnover in the membership of the Supreme Court, the widespread disparagement of the reasoning in *Bowers* in the legal community, the new legal frame provided by *Romer v. Evans,* the "normalization" of AIDS, and shifts in the cultural framing of homosexuality all combined to make the claims raised by Lambda in *Lawrence* more compelling to the Supreme Court than were similar claims raised by the ACLU in *Bowers.*

It is important to recognize that some of these changes (e.g., turnover on the Court) were beyond the control of Lambda and its compatriots but that others were affected by their actions. Lambda and the ACLU, for example, litigated *Romer v. Evans.* Lambda used multiple techniques to work toward the normalization of AIDS, including litigation, congressional testimony, and the convening of a National AIDS Policy Roundtable to attempt to influence the development of public policy related to HIV disease. Lambda and ACLU staffers wrote law review articles detailing what they saw as the legal defects in *Bowers.* And litigation brought by the two organizations—as well as by GLAD, the National Center for Lesbian Rights (NCLR), and other gay rights groups—helped to change the cultural frames surrounding homosexuality; the emergence of a widespread cultural conversation about same-sex marriage in the 1990s is only the most obvious example of the impact of this litigation.

As I noted in chapter 4, studying legal change from a legal opportunity perspective means more than examining the external environment confronting social movement actors. It also means relating a movement's litigation strategies and outcomes to that external environment. In the context of post-*Bowers* sodomy reform litigation, one particularly important feature of the external environment was the federal structure of the legal system. Gay rights litigators were able to litigate around *Bowers* because of the existence of parallel court systems with independent sources of authority. By turning to state constitutional claims,

Lambda and its colleagues were able to continue chipping away at state sodomy laws. The reduction in the number of states with sodomy laws in turn undermined the "majoritarian morality" claim that served as a basis for the ruling in *Bowers*.

Another important feature of the external environment was the standing requirement. Although Lambda and its fellow litigators encountered fewer standing-related barriers post-*Bowers* than they did pre-*Bowers*, the issue of standing continued to influence their litigation choices. Part of what made *Lawrence* such an obvious vehicle to challenge the constitutionality of Texas's sodomy law is that the plaintiffs in the case clearly met the standing requirement. In this, the motivation for pursuing *Lawrence* and *Bowers* was exactly the same.

Of course, the dramatically different outcomes of the two cases lead to a perhaps inevitable inference that litigating the former case was a "bad" idea while litigating the latter was a "good" one. Here I would like to reiterate a point I made in chapter 4: there is no Rosetta stone to aid in decoding the structure of legal opportunities. The litigators of both cases made a set of choices based on their reading of the legal and political context surrounding gay rights. In both cases, these choices were disputed by other litigators who were arguably equally as expert in their knowledge of gay rights, constitutional law, and the Supreme Court. The closeness of the vote in both cases—5–4 on the privacy claim—makes it clear that there wasn't an obviously right answer either time.

This is not to say that there are never any obviously right or wrong choices about what, where, when, and how to litigate. Legal claims must draw on the existing legal and cultural stock in order to be persuasive. Bringing a federal privacy claim in a sodomy case within a few years of *Bowers* would have been foolish by anyone's estimation, for example. Lower courts, whether federal or state, would have been constrained by *Bowers* to deny the claim, and the Supreme Court would not have granted certiorari in an appeal. Such a case would only have added to the body of precedent construing sodomy as existing outside the realm of protected privacy interests. Organized litigators such as Lambda are all well aware of the "obviously wrong" and "obviously right" litigation choices. The difficulty is in determining the appropriate course of action when the choices are nonobvious.

A final note: The story of sodomy reform efforts reveals that LOS often operates in conjunction with POS. In all four stages of sodomy reform, legal and legislative trends moved in roughly the same direction. This should not be surprising, given that LOS and POS look to many of the same factors to explain the origins, progress, and outcomes of social movements. The critical event of AIDS, for example, closed down both political and legal spaces for the gay rights movement to push for sodomy reform. Shifts in the cultural framing of homosexuality, in turn, opened both the political and legal spaces for the gay rights movement to push for sodomy reform.

This is not to suggest that the two concepts are interchangeable, merely that they overlap. The problem of standing, for instance, narrowed access to the courts but not to the legislative arena. The Model Penal Code, conversely, facilitated legislative sodomy reform but had virtually no effect on judicial reform. In the next chapter, we shall look more intently at the ways in which legal and political opportunity structures differ.

The Law and Politics of Antigay Initiatives

L esbian, gay, and bisexual people have had their civil rights put to a popular vote more than any other group of citizens. As Gamble (1997, 257) has shown, nearly 60 percent of the initiatives and popular referenda that appeared on statewide ballots in the years between 1959 and 1993 focused on the civil rights of lgb people. As a rule, these ballot measures were attempts to repeal newly enacted laws that prohibited discrimination on the basis of sexual orientation.[1] Some ballot measures also sought to prohibit jurisdictions from passing any gay rights laws in the future.

The most famous example of an antigay rights ballot measure is, of course, Colorado's Amendment 2. In 1992, Colorado voters approved the following amendment to their state constitution.

> NO PROTECTED STATUS BASED ON HOMOSEXUAL, LESBIAN, OR BISEXUAL ORIENTATION. Neither the State of Colorado, through any of its branches or departments, nor any of its agencies, political subdivisions, municipalities or school districts, shall enact, adopt or enforce any statute, regulation, ordinance or policy whereby homosexual, lesbian, or bisexual orientation, conduct, practices, or relationships shall constitute or otherwise be the basis of or entitle any person or class of persons to have or claim any minority status, quota preferences, protected status or claim of discrimination. This Section of the Constitution shall be in all respects self-executing.

Table 11 itemizes the major ballot measures designed to stem the progress of gay rights.[2] As it indicates, antigay ballot measures have not always been successful. The same year that Coloradoans approved Amendment 2—the measure at the heart of *Romer v. Evans*—voters in Oregon rejected a similar measure known as Measure 9. And in 1994, although antigay rights activists attempted to place initiatives on the ballot in ten states, only two of the proposed initiatives actually made it to a

TABLE 11. Breakdown of Antigay Initiatives and Referenda

Year	Location[a]	Type[b]	Outcome	For (%)	Case Name (if applicable)
1974	Boulder, CO	R	passed	83	
1977	Dade Cty, FL	R	passed	69	
1978	CALIFORNIA	I	failed	42	
	Wichita, KS	R	passed	83	
	St. Paul, MN	R	passed	63	
	Eugene, OR	R	passed	64	
	Seattle, WA	R	failed	37	
1980	Santa Clara Cty, CA	R	passed	70	
	San Jose, CA	R	passed	75	
1982	Austin, TX		failed	37	
1984	Duluth, MN		passed	76	
1985	Houston, TX		passed	82	
	Kings Cty, WA	R	dnq[c]		
1986	Davis, CA		failed	42	
1988	St. Paul, MN		failed	44	
	OREGON	R	passed[d]	57	
1989	Irvine, CA	R	passed		
	Athens, OH		passed	53	
	Tacoma, WA	R	passed		
1990	MASSACHUSETTS	R	blocked		*Collins v. Commonwealth*[e]
	Wooster, OH		passed	63	
	Seattle, WA	R	failed	45	
1991	Concord, CA	I	passed	50.2[f]	
1991	Riverside, CA	I	blocked		*Citizens for Responsible Behavior*
	San Francisco, CA	R	failed	40	
	Denver, CO		failed	45	
	St. Paul, MN	R	failed	46	
1992	ARIZONA	I	dnq		
	COLORADO	I	passed[g]	53	
	FLORIDA	I	dnq		
	Tampa, FL	R	passed[h]	59	
	Portland, ME	R	failed	43	
	OREGON	I	failed	43	
	Corvallis, OR	I	failed	34	
	Springfield, OR	I	passed	56	
1993	Anchorage, AK	R	blocked		*Faipeas v. Anchorage*
	Tampa, FL	R	passed[h]	56	
	Lewiston, ME	R	passed	68	
	Cincinnati, OH	I	passed[i]	62	
	Canby, OR	I	passed	56	
	Cornelius, OR	I	passed	62	
	Creswell, OR	I	passed	58	
	Douglas Cty, OR	I	passed	72	
	Estacada, OR	I	passed	54	
	Jackson Cty, OR	I	passed	59	
	Junction City, OR	I	passed[j]	50.1	
	Josephine Cty, OR	I	passed	64	
	Keizer, OR	I	passed	53	
	Klamath Cty, OR	I	passed	64	
	Lebanon, OR	I	passed	65	

SIX

TABLE 11. *Continued*

Year	Location[a]	Type[b]	Outcome	For (%)	Case Name (if applicable)
	Linn Cty, OR	I	passed	68	
	Medford, OR	I	passed	58	
	Molalla, OR	I	passed	55	
	Oregon City, OR	I	passed	53	
	Sweet Home, OR	I	passed	69	
1994	ARIZONA	I	dnq		
	FLORIDA	I	blocked		*In re Advisory Opinion to the Attorney General*
	Alachua Cty, FL	I	passed[k]	57	
	IDAHO	I	failed	49.9	
	MAINE	I	dnq		
	MICHIGAN	I	dnq		
	MISSOURI	I	dnq		
	Springfield, MO	R	passed	71	
	NEVADA	I	dnq		
	OHIO	I	withdrawn		
	OREGON	I	blocked		
	OREGON	I	failed	44	
	Albany, OR	I	passed	59	
	Cottage Grove, OR	I	passed	57	
	Grants Pass, OR	I	passed	60	
	Gresham, OR	I	failed[l]	50.5	
	Junction City, OR	I	passed[j]	57	
	Lake Cty, OR	I	passed	58	
	Marion Cty, OR	I	passed	61	
	Oakridge, OR	I	passed	51	
	Roseburg, OR	I	passed	65	
	Turner, OR	I	passed	79	
	Venetta, OR	I	passed	55	
	Austin, TX	R	passed	62	
	WASHINGTON	I (2)	dnq		
1995	West Palm Beach, FL	R	fail	44	
1995	MAINE	I	failed	47	
	WASHINGTON	I (2)	dnq		
1996	Broward Cty., FL	R	dnq		
	IDAHO	I	dnq		
	MAINE	R	passed		
	Lansing, MI	R	passed	52	

[a]Names in capital letters signify statewide ballot measures. Local measures are identified by city/ county name.

[b]R = referendum; I = initiative.

[c]DNQ = did not qualify for the ballot.

[d]The measure was subsequently overturned in *Merrick v. Bd. of Higher Ed.*

[e]Full case citations are contained in the chapter text and in the table of cases.

[f]The initiative was subsequently overturned in *Bay Area Network of Gay & Lesbian Educators v. City of Concord.*

[g]The initiative was subsequently overturned in *Romer.*

[h]The 1992 referendum was voided; it passed again in 1993.

[i]The initiative was appealed but ultimately upheld in *Equality.*

[j]The 1993 initiative was thrown out by a court because of voting irregularities; it passed again in 1994.

[k]The initiative was subsequently overturned in *Morris v. Hill.*

[l]Gresham City Charter requires supermajority to pass ballot initiative.

vote, and they failed, albeit by small margins. Nevertheless, citizen law-making on issues concerning gay rights has generally produced results counter to the interests of lgb people. Of the fifty-seven ballot measures ultimately submitted to a popular vote, forty-five passed, for a success rate of 77 percent.[3]

The generally strong ability of antigay rights activists to roll back gay rights through citizen lawmaking suggests that they possess an advantage over gay rights activists in the electoral arena. Gay rights activists have sought to mitigate this disadvantage in several ways, most notably through the legal system. By turning to the courts, gay rights activists have been able to stave off numerous antigay measures by convincing judges that the measures are legally defective. For example, Lambda challenged the legality of antigay ballot measures in California, Colorado, Florida, Ohio, and Oregon, successfully derailing almost all of them.[4]

Romer v. Evans ranks as the most consequential of the legal challenges to antigay ballot measures. Nine days after Colorado voters passed Amendment 2 at the ballot box, Lambda, the ACLU, and the newly formed Colorado Legal Initiatives Project (CLIP) asked Colorado's district court to enjoin Amendment 2 from taking effect.

It took *Romer* three and a half years to work its way up to the U.S. Supreme Court. During that time, it went to trial twice, once to determine whether Amendment 2 would be enjoined before it took effect (yes) and once to determine whether it served a compelling governmental interest (no). In each instance, the state appealed the unfavorable outcome to the Colorado Supreme Court. Both times, the state high court upheld the lower court decision. By the time *Romer* finally reached the U.S. Supreme Court, four different courts had reacted unfavorably to the constitutionality of Amendment 2.

The Supreme Court responded in the same fashion. By a 6–3 majority, the Court struck down Amendment 2, ruling that it was "born of animosity" toward lgb people and denied their right to equal protection under the U.S. Constitution. Amendment 2, it said, "classifies homosexuals not to further a proper legislative end but to make them unequal to everyone else. This Colorado cannot do. A State cannot so deem a class of persons a stranger to its laws" (635).

In this chapter, I examine the divergence of the electoral and legal outcomes of antigay initiatives. My analysis is centered on the political and legal progress of Amendment 2 but also touches on the many other initiatives designed to retard the progress of the gay rights movement. My core argument is that the differences in the electoral and legal outcomes of antigay initiatives are largely attributable to differences between the *political* and *legal* structures of opportunity within which pro- and antigay rights activists operated. These differences include the mechanics of the decision-making process, the decision makers themselves, the alliance and conflict system, and the frames available to pro- and antigay rights activists. I begin by sketching out the various forms of antigay ballot measures.

The Form and Scope of Antigay Ballot Measures

Antigay ballot measures take two basic forms. Popular referenda seek to repeal existing laws. In the context of gay rights, popular referenda virtually always address laws that have been enacted quite recently. Before the late 1980s, all but one gay rights law (Wisconsin) was the product of local decision making, and so repeal efforts were also locally based. But as the scope of gay rights laws increased, so did the scope of antigay repeal efforts. For instance, early in 1988 Oregon's governor implemented an executive order protecting state employees from discrimination based on sexual orientation. Antigay activists mobilized in opposition to the executive order and by the end of the year had succeeded in engineering its repeal through a popular referendum called Measure 8.

Initiatives seek to make new law, although they may also attempt to repeal existing law. Like referenda, ballot initiatives generally arise in the immediate aftermath of perceived gains by the gay rights movement. Although statewide initiatives have received the lion's share of publicity, table 11 shows that the large majority of antigay initiatives have taken place at the city or county level. There are three primary types of antigay initiatives. Adams (1994) refers to them as *specifically targeted, overtly hostile,* and *stealth* initiatives.

Specifically targeted initiatives seek to remove power from governmental decision makers to prohibit discrimination based on sexual orientation. Colorado's Amendment 2 was a specifically targeted initiative. It prohibited state and local governments in Colorado from enacting, enforcing, or adopting any law that prohibited discrimination based on "homosexual, lesbian, or bisexual orientation, conduct, practices, or relationships" or gave lgb people any claim to "minority status, quota preferences, [or] protected status" based on their sexual orientation. The phrasing of Amendment 2 was subsequently copied by antigay activists in several other locales, including Cincinnati (1993), Arizona (1994), and Missouri (1994).

Overtly hostile initiatives also seek to limit governmental ability to remedy discrimination based on sexual orientation. In addition, they seek to ensure that public agencies officially condemn homosexuality. Oregon's Measure 9, voted on the same day as Amendment 2, is the paradigmatic example of an overtly hostile initiative. The proposed constitutional amendment provided that

> All governments in Oregon may not use their monies or properties to promote, encourage, or facilitate homosexuality, pedophilia, sadism, or masochism. All levels of government, including public educational systems, must assist in setting a standard for Oregon's youth which recognizes that these "behaviors" are "abnormal, wrong, unnatural, and perverse," and that they are to be discouraged and avoided. State may not recognize this conduct under sexual orientation or sexual preference levels, or through quotas, minority status, affirmative action, or similar concepts.

Other overtly hostile initiatives have been less explicit than Oregon's Measure 9 but are nevertheless designed to ensure governmental condemnation of homosexuality. An initiative on Idaho's 1994 ballot forbade all public school employees from sanctioning homosexuality as a "healthy, approved, or acceptable behavior" (Proposition One), language mirrored by a proposed Washington initiative that same year (Initiative 608).

Stealth initiatives take the opposite tack from overtly hostile proposals. They never explicitly mention homosexuality or sexual orientation, instead proposing to limit the scope of civil rights laws to certain specified classifications, usually including race, sex, ethnicity, religion, national origin, age, disability, and marital status. These initiatives appear neutral on their face but are nonetheless designed to repeal existing gay rights laws and prevent the passage of future ones. The letter accompanying a 1994 petition to place a stealth initiative on Florida's ballot offers a clear illustration of the initiative's underlying purpose: "This petition is designed to stop homosexual activists and other special interest groups from improper inclusion in discrimination laws. . . . Therefore, this amendment would prevent homosexuality and other lifestyles from gaining special protection in discrimination laws" (quoted in Adams 1994, 590).

The three different kinds of antigay initiatives reflect shifting assessments among antigay activists of the best approach to fighting the so-called homosexual agenda. For example, antigay activists in Idaho originally proposed an overtly hostile initiative that was similar to Oregon's Measure 9 in tone. An opinion by Idaho's attorney general that the initiative was unconstitutional combined with the electoral defeat of Oregon's Measure 9 and the simultaneous success of Colorado's Amendment 2 convinced them to amend their measure to soften (but not eliminate) the overt hostility toward lgb people. Likewise, the legal problems faced by Amendment 2 and its clone Cincinnati's Issue 3 (passed in 1993) prompted antigay activists to try stealth initiatives as an alternative to specifically targeted proposals.[5]

Despite variations in the scope and content of antigay initiatives and referenda, they share a number of structural features in common. At the most basic level, they are attempts by opponents of gay rights to expand the scope of conflict from the legislative and/or executive branches to the larger voting public, seeking thereby to appeal to a set of decision makers potentially more aligned against the concept of gay rights.[6] We turn now to the mechanics of citizen lawmaking, examining both the citizen lawmaking process and the ways in which gay rights advocates such as Lambda have been able to turn to the courts to keep antigay measures off the ballot.

The Mechanics of Citizen Lawmaking

Although the great majority of antigay ballot measures arise in response to recently enacted gay rights laws, most gay rights laws have not given rise to antigay ballot measures. A major reason for this involves the mechanics of citizen lawmaking. Fewer than half of the states in the nation allow voters to initiate ballot measures to check the state legislative process.[7] In the years between 1975 and 1992, statewide gay rights policies were enacted in sixteen states, either through legislative action or executive order.[8] Only five of those states—California, Massachusetts, Ohio, Oregon, and Washington—permit popularly initiated ballot measures. In each state but California, the enactment of gay rights policies was closely followed by popularly generated attempts at repeal.[9] In other words, in almost all the states where people could use the citizen lawmaking process to counter legislative actions to protect gay rights, they attempted to do so.

The requirements for putting proposed measures onto the ballot vary from state to state and locality to locality, but at a minimum qualifying a proposed referendum or initiative requires the signatures of a certain percentage of the voting population. These percentages vary. In order to qualify for the ballot in Colorado, a proposed initiative must garner the signatures of at least 5 percent of the voters who cast ballots for the secretary of state in the last election. In order to qualify in Arizona, however, a proposed constitutional initiative must be signed by at least 15 percent of the voters who cast ballots in the last gubernatorial election. Some states require as well that the signatures be geographically disbursed. Nevada, for instance, requires that 10 percent of the eligible voters in three-quarters of the counties sign onto a proposed initiative to qualify it for the ballot. The more stringent the signature requirements the fewer the initiatives that qualify for the ballot.[10]

In addition to signature requirements, some states have textual requirements for proposed ballot initiatives. A common requirement is that the proposed measure be limited in scope to a single subject.[11] A second common requirement is that the proposed ballot measure contain a title or summary that explains the measure's substance.[12] Finally, some states and localities limit the substantive areas open to citizen lawmaking. In states such as Idaho, Maine, and Washington, voters may propose statutory laws but not constitutional amendments, while the reverse holds true in Florida, Illinois, and Mississippi. Likewise, many localities do not permit voters to utilize citizen lawmaking to amend charters but do allow popularly generated measures on statutory matters.

The mechanics of citizen lawmaking offer several opportunities for gay rights activists and other interested parties to prevent proposed antigay measures from qualifying for the ballot. For example, Lambda and the ACLU raised both constitutional and procedural arguments in their successful effort to prevent one of the nation's earliest antigay initiatives from coming to a vote. In 1991, a California group called Riverside Citizens for Responsible Behavior developed a ballot initiative designed to repeal two protective ordinances recently enacted by the Riverside City Council and to remove all power to remedy discrimination based on sexual orientation from the legislative body. The "Citizens' Ordinance Pertaining to Homosexuality and AIDS" specifically sought to forbid the Riverside City Council from enacting any law or policy that

(a) defines homosexuality, bisexuality, sexual orientation, sexual preference, affectional preference, or gay or lesbian conduct as a fundamental human right;
(b) classifies homosexuality or AIDS as the basis for determining an unlawful discriminatory practice and/or establishes a penalty or civil remedy for such practice;

(c) provides preferential treatment or affirmative action for any person on the basis of sexual orientation or AIDS; or

(d) "promotes, encourages, endorses, legitimizes or justifies homosexuality.

The proposed ordinance also forbade the city of Riverside from spending any city monies, either directly or indirectly, to fund any individual, activity, or organization that promoted, encouraged, endorsed, legitimized, or justified homosexual conduct.

Although the "Citizens' Ordinance" received a sufficient number of signatures to be placed on the ballot, the city council refused to do so, believing it to be unconstitutional. Riverside Citizens for Responsible Behavior subsequently filed suit in the Superior Court of Riverside County, seeking to have the city council ordered to place the initiative on the ballot. The city of Riverside, represented by Lambda and the ACLU, in turn asked the court to declare that the city's decision was proper.

After consideration of the issues involved, the superior court agreed with the Riverside City Council, finding that the proposed ballot measure was both procedurally and constitutionally impermissible. Procedurally, the city of Riverside's charter did not permit the electorate to enact a measure as broad as the "Citizens' Ordinance." Constitutionally, the proposed measure ran afoul of the Fourteenth Amendment, said the court, because it was "designed to permit and encourage private discrimination against homosexuals and persons with AIDS" (*Citizens for Responsible Behavior v. Riverside City Council,* 1991). Riverside Citizens for Responsible Behavior promptly appealed the lower court ruling to the California Court of Appeals, which refused to grant them relief, thus blocking the attempt by antigay rights activists to use citizen lawmaking to stem the progress of gay rights.

Lambda has also used procedural arguments to derail a number of other ballot measures. In a 1994 case, Lambda invoked subject-matter requirements in a successful bid to block a proposed constitutional amendment from appearing on Florida's ballot. The language of the stealth initiative stated, in relevant part, that

The state, political subdivisions of the state, municipalities or any other governmental entity shall not enact or adopt any law regarding discrimination against persons which creates, establishes, or recognizes any right, privilege or protection for any person based on any characteristic, trait, status or condition other than race,

color, religion, sex, national origin, age, handicap, ethnic background, marital status or familial status. (Proposed Initiative §
1(b))

"All laws inconsistent with this amendment," the measure continued,
would be repealed.

Among the objections raised by Lambda was that the proposed measure violated Florida's single-subject requirement because it enumerated
ten different classes of people who would be protected under civil rights
laws and thus really raised ten different questions. The Florida Supreme
Court agreed and knocked the antigay initiative off the ballot.[13]

Although procedural challenges have prevented several antigay ballot
measures from coming to a vote, they have not been uniformly successful. For example, the ACLU failed in its attempt to derail Idaho's antigay
initiative through a preelection challenge. In *ACLU v. Echohawk* (1993),
the ACLU claimed that Idaho's Proposition One was unconstitutionally
vague because it failed to define ambiguous terms such as *homosexual
behavior* and employed terms such as *minority status* and *special rights*
that had no specific legal meaning. The Idaho Supreme Court rejected the
ACLU's contention without itself specifically defining the terms at issue.
The measure was subsequently brought to a vote and defeated by a razor-
thin margin.[14]

The Politics of Antigay Initiatives

Campaigns to stem the progress of gay rights through citizen lawmaking
have shared a number of features. All have been responses to (perceived)
gains by the gay rights movement. All have been driven largely by religious conservatives with ties to the New Right. All have been conducted
largely via sound bite, and all have employed two major frames: morality and "special rights." In the following pages, I use the campaign over
Amendment 2 to illustrate the ways in which the mechanics of the political process, the availability of resource networks, the configuration of
decision makers vis-à-vis gay rights, and the existing cultural stock all
combined to facilitate the passage of antigay ballot measures.

The Origin of Amendment 2

The immediate impetus of Amendment 2 was the Colorado Springs
Human Rights Ordinance. In the spring of 1991, the Human Rights Com-

mission of Colorado Springs held hearings on a proposed human rights ordinance that would prohibit discrimination based on a person's "race and color, their religion and creed, their national origin and ethnicity, their age, marital status, their sexual orientation, or their disabled condition" in employment, public accommodations, sales and services, and the transfer or financing of property.[15] This proposed ordinance followed on the heels of a similar ordinance passed in Denver in 1990 as well as a proposed statewide human rights bill that would, among other things, add sexual orientation to a list of grounds upon which "ethnic intimidation" was prohibited.

The Colorado Springs proposal engendered immediate and vociferous opposition. Colorado Springs was home to a large number of fundamentalist Christian organizations, including Focus on the Family, the country's largest Christian radio ministry. Members of these organizations spearheaded the assault on the proposed ordinance, and the city council ultimately defeated it by an 8–1 vote.[16]

An unintended consequence of the proposed Human Rights Ordinance is that it sparked a coordinated effort to repeal gay rights laws across the state. The majority of the key players in the push for Amendment 2 came from Colorado Springs and had lobbied against the proposed ordinance. In the spring of 1991, Tony Marco, one of the local activists who was working against the ordinance, contacted David Noebel. Noebel was the head of Summit Ministries, a anticommunist organization with ties to the Christian Crusade; he had written a book in 1977 titled the *Homosexual Revolution,* in which he linked tolerance of homosexuality with pedophilia, atheism, totalitarianism, and nihilism. Noebel in turn contacted Kevin Tebedo, the son of state senator Maryanne Tebedo. Noebel recounted the meeting that led to the notion of Amendment 2 in a 1993 article.

> So the three of us got together—Tony Marco, Kevin Tebedo and myself. . . . And we said, no further. This is not going any further. I mean it was so obvious what was going on. [The homosexuals] were going to pick us apart, piece by piece. They were just going to go city by city, county by county. And there was only one way to stop it, and that was to do something statewide, at least. (Quoted in Harkavy 1993, 28)

Colorado for Family Values (CFV) was formed to do just that. The people involved in its formation comprised a who's who list of conservative Christian activists. Aside from Marco, Noebel, and Tebedo, the group included Bill McCartney, coach of the University of Colorado's football team and founder of Promise Keepers; Barbara Sheldon of the Traditional Family Values Coalition; Randy Hicks of Focus on the Family; Jayne Schindler of Eagle Forum; and Senator Bill Armstrong.[17] Will Perkins, a man whose television commercials for used cars made him widely known in Colorado Springs, became the voice of CFV during the Amendment 2 campaign.

CFV's links to national New Right organizations gave it access to resources gathered from earlier anti–gay rights efforts. The text of Amendment 2 was drafted by the National Legal Foundation (a conservative litigation organization founded by Pat Robertson) and drew heavily on the principles articulated in the Riverside "Citizens' Ordinance." The campaign to promote Amendment 2 likewise drew heavily on a handbook published by an attorney for Concerned Women for America entitled *How to Defeat Gay Rights Legislation*. CFV's connection to conservative Christian churches and New Right organizations also gave it access to populations of Colorado citizens likely to support Amendment 2.

Amendment 2 and the Mechanics of Citizen Lawmaking

As noted previously, Colorado has relatively lax signature requirements for placing a proposed measure on the ballot. CFV easily garnered enough signatures to qualify Amendment 2 for the ballot. Although Lambda was well aware of Amendment 2's existence, its hands were tied. In Colorado, courts do not have the power to pass on the constitutionality of a proposed initiative until and unless it is passed into law. The state does not have a single-subject requirement for popularly initiated ballot measures, nor does it limit the permissible subjects for ballot measures. Amendment 2 was thus less viable for a preelection challenge than ballot proposals in other jurisdictions.

Framing Amendment 2, Part I: The Politics of Morality

Haider-Markel and Meier have noted that the politics surrounding antigay initiatives resembles the kinds of "morality politics" surrounding issues such as abortion. Morality politics, in their terms, tend to be "partisan, seek non-incremental solutions, [and] focus on deeply-held values" (1996, 334). Oregon's antigay initiative campaign is a paradigmatic example of this invocation of morality politics: virtually all of the campaign rhetoric produced by the Oregon Citizen's Alliance (OCA), the rough counterpart to CFV, emphasized the "deceitful, grasping, and immoral nature of homosexuals" (Douglass 1997, 26).

For example, a key tool of the OCA was a video it produced called "No Special Rights." The video purported to expose the underlying agenda of the gay rights movement. The bulk of it was simply spliced-together footage of a handful of gay pride parades, with an emphasis on drag queens, scantily clothed men, leather-clad women, and displays of sexual conduct such as kissing. A few interviews with purported "participants" were interspersed; they focused on sadomasochistic and pedophilic practices. In short, the video attempted to equate homosexuality with moral deviance and to engender a visceral reaction in its viewers.

The framing of Amendment 2 by CFV likewise incorporated the rhetoric of morality. In the final days of the campaign, CFV distributed literature highlighting what it referred to as "astonishing, fully-documented reports of the actual goals of homosexual extremists," as well as "graphic, disgusting facts" that "will shock and repel."[18] In particular, CFV worked to paint homosexuals as pedophiles. A tabloid distributed by CFV contained the following bulletin.[19]

TARGET: CHILDREN

Lately, America has been hearing a lot about the subject of childhood sexual abuse. This terrible epidemic has scarred countless young lives and destroyed thousands of families. But what militant homosexuals don't want you to know is the large role they play in this epidemic. In fact, pedophilia (the sexual molestation of children) is actually an accepted part of the homosexual community!

CFV also argued that legalized same-sex marriage was the ultimate goal of the gay rights movement, a goal that would harm children in still other ways: "Homosexual 'marriages' will only erode traditional family structures, sap resources from legitimate, traditional families (by increasing disease-driven insurance rates, etc.) and cause measureless misery to helpless children, who would be the most wretched victims of such 'marriages.'"[20]

In addition, CFV also painted homosexuals as endangering the public's health. Lesbians and gay men, CFV claimed, were society's "most persistent and change-resistant communicators of sexually transmitted diseases." Their ability to transmit "a host of highly communicable, even incurable, diseases" was augmented in "occupations like health care, child care and food care." Homosexuals were such prolific breeders of disease, CFV argued, that caring for them would tax available resources to the breaking point. Its campaign literature claimed that, "by the mid-1990's, it will be difficult for sick persons to get hospital beds because of overcrowding by AIDS-infected homosexuals."[21]

In making these homosexual danger claims, CFV was seeking to motivate the significant minority of Colorado voters with deep-seated objections to homosexuality to go to the polls on election day. As noted in chapter 4, about three-fourths of Americans surveyed in 1991 by the General Social Survey agreed that "homosexuality is always wrong." It is interesting to note that a similarly worded question asked of Coloradoans in 1992 suggested that Coloradoans were somewhat *more* tolerant of homosexuality than was the nation as a whole. During the campaign over Amendment 2, the *Denver Post* commissioned a polling firm to survey attitudes about homosexuality. Among other things, respondents were asked to respond to the statement "Homosexuality is morally wrong." Forty-six percent agreed with the premise of the statement, while 40 percent disagreed; the remaining 14 percent either said they were neutral or did not know (Gerstmann 1999, 99–100). Despite the seemingly greater tolerance of Coloradoans about the moral legitimacy of homosexuality, however, a plurality still believed that homosexuality was immoral. This population offered potentially fertile ground for CFV's homosexual threat claims.

Framing Amendment 2, Part II: Special Rights

Although CFV invoked the politics of morality, its primary rhetorical strategy was the invocation of "special rights." In its campaign to enact Amendment 2 CFV consistently argued that the initiative was not designed to deprive homosexuals of equal rights but simply to ensure that homosexuals were unable to get special rights based on their "life-style choice." CFV framed homosexuals as different from "legitimate" minorities. The baseline comparison group it invoked was African Americans. Lgb people, it argued, were not sufficiently "like" African Americans to warrant protections under civil rights laws.

Campaign materials disseminated by CFV were designed to highlight the differences between the two groups. In one widely distributed tabloid, CFV asked voters to compare the hardships faced by homosexuals to those faced by African Americans. Only the latter group, it argued, had been barred from voting and denied access by law to drinking fountains, bathrooms, businesses, and restaurants. The clear implication was that African Americans merited legal protections in a way that lgb people did not.

Schacter (1994) refers to this framing as the "discourse of equivalents." The crux of this discourse of equivalents is the notion that some groups in society receive rights that are unavailable to others and, hence, are "special." In another widely disseminated tabloid, CFV laid out the criteria for deciding which groups should receive "special rights."

> Amendment 2 upholds common sense civil rights laws and Supreme Court decisions, which say that people who want protected class status have to show they need it in three fair, logical ways:
>
>   1. A group wanting true minority rights must show that it's discriminated against to the point that its members cannot earn average income, get an adequate education, or enjoy a fulfilling cultural life.
>   2. The group must be clearly identifiable by unchangeable physical characteristics like skin color, gender, handicap, etc. (not behavior).
>   3. The group must clearly show that it is politically powerless.

Homosexuals, CFV claimed, met none of these criteria. For one thing, homosexuality was a "life-style choice" rather than an unchangeable physical characteristic. Moreover, homosexuals were advantaged rather than disadvantaged. According to one of CFV's principal spokesmen, homosexuals were "affluent, well-educated, sexually deviant political power brokers" who "sport[ed] average annual household incomes over $55,000" (Perkins 1992). Their undue political power, in fact, was the reason why a citizen-initiated amendment to Colorado's constitution was needed. As Tony Marco testified at Amendment 2's trial, the amendment was necessary because other voters "simply could not compete with gay militants' ability to lobby, to influence legislation, [and] to promulgate its views through print and other media."

> It was obvious that the aggression of gay militants through the legislature was not going to cease. . . . The legislature is very vulnerable to all kinds of lobbying and other activity without citizens'

direct representation on that activity—lobbying for which I discovered gay militants were very, very well equipped and were very well experienced. And so the only way to insure that this kind of activity would stop would be through passage of [a] constitutional amendment. (Quoted in Keen and Goldberg 1998, 109)

Without Amendment 2, CFV argued, heterosexuals would fall yet another rung further down the economic ladder as homosexuals got "their" jobs through "quota preferences"; they would also lose the "right to live out their beliefs" to the extent those beliefs diverged from homosexual orthodoxy (see Perkins 1992).

In depicting Amendment 2 as a necessary corrective to the disproportionate influence of lgb people on the legislative process, CFV was seeking to tap into public antipathy toward *civil rights laws* as much as public antipathy toward lgb people.[22] This approach fell on fertile ground. Several surveys conducted early in 1993 found that a significant percentage of people who opposed discrimination based on sexual orientation also opposed the extension of existing civil rights laws to include lgb people.

A Gallup poll undertaken in April 1993 found that 80 percent of respondents surveyed believed that "homosexuals should . . . have equal rights in terms of job opportunities" but also found that only 52 percent favored "extending civil rights laws to include homosexuals." A *New York Times* poll undertaken a month later found that 78 percent of respondents favored equal rights for homosexuals in terms of job opportunities but only 42 percent supported the enactment of civil rights protections for lgb people (Schmalz 1993). A *U.S. News and World Report* poll undertaken in June 1993 similarly found that 65 percent of respondents opposed discrimination against gay men and lesbians but only 50 percent supported the enactment of civil rights protections for lgb people (Shapiro, Cook, and Krackov 1993).

Gerstmann's interviews with several key figures in the political struggle over Amendment 2 indicate that the "special rights" framing was a major component in Amendment 2's electoral success. Both proponents and opponents of the measure felt that the general public distinguished between discrimination and civil rights laws, disavowing the former but finding the latter untenable as a solution. As Jean Dubofsky, the lead attorney for the plaintiffs in *Romer v. Evans,* explained:

The "no special rights" slogan was very clever, particularly given a time when at least white males don't like affirmative action. The

Amendment 2 people spent a lot of time talking about [how] you don't want gays and lesbians getting in front of you in line for jobs or scholarship or college. Of course, that wasn't what Amendment 2 was about overall, but that's the way it was sold. . . . People I talked with voted for it because they felt gays and lesbians should not get affirmative action. (Quoted in Gerstmann 1999, 103–4)

The efficacy of CFV's "special rights" framing was highlighted by one of the polls commissioned by the *Denver Post* before the 1992 election. Respondents were asked to respond to the following statement: "When homosexuals talk about gay rights, what they really mean is that they want special rights." Nearly three out of every five respondents noted agreement with the statement.

Amendment 2 and the Campaign Process

Opponents of Amendment 2 were well aware of the cultural resonance of the "special rights" framing employed by CFV. The form of modern campaigns, however, hobbled their efforts to reframe the central question at issue. Three major tools of modern campaigning are pamphleteering, direct mail, and media advertising. Each of these tools engages in "sound bite" politics, where the quick and repeated invocation of political symbols plays a major role.[23] Opponents of Amendment 2 found themselves on the rhetorical defensive with respect to "special rights" from the outset, because they could not find an equally resonant sound bite with which to counter CFV's framing. As one of the antiamendment activists Gerstmann interviewed observed, "there is no one good phrase or slogan to counter 'special rights.' It takes fifteen minutes of real discussion to undo the damage that phrase does" (1999, 105).

These fifteen minutes were not generally available to Amendment 2's opponents during the political battle over the ballot measure. They *did* become available to Amendment 2's opponents in the legal battle that followed the passage of the amendment. We turn to that legal battle now.

The Litigation of Amendment 2

Nine days after Colorado voters passed Amendment 2 at the ballot box, opponents of the amendment filed a constitutional challenge in federal district court. The complaint was filed in the name of Richard Evans (an

openly gay man who worked for Denver's mayor and who served on the
Mayor's Gay and Lesbian Advisory Committee), five other openly lgb
people, a heterosexual man with AIDS, and the cities of Boulder, Aspen,
and Denver—each of which had gay rights ordinances that would be
nullified if Amendment 2 went into effect.[24]

Filing a legal challenge was not a spur-of-the-moment decision. CLIP
had organized some six months earlier to explore legal strategies in the
event that Amendment 2 passed. The moving force behind CLIP was
Richard Evans, the man who would end up becoming the lead plaintiff in
Romer. He solicited Jean Dubofsky, a former justice on the Colorado
Supreme Court, to be the lead attorney in the challenge—if a challenge
was needed. Lambda, the ACLU's Lesbian and Gay Rights Project, and
the Colorado ACLU filled out the preelection team. (For ease of presentation, I shall often refer to this legal team simply as the Lambda team, but
this shorthand should not be read to imply that Lambda was more important than Dubofsky or the ACLU in determining the path of litigation.)

In the days before the elections, the "fallback" legal team considered
a wide range of possible legal claims. The complaint they eventually filed
in Colorado's district court included everything but the kitchen sink.
Among other things, it alleged that Amendment 2 violated the federal
Constitution's guarantees of equal protection, freedom of association
and expression, freedom from establishment of an official religion, due
process, and the right to petition government for a redress of grievances,
as well as the supremacy clause. The complaint also alleged that Amendment 2 violated Colorado's constitution by unlawfully restricting citizens' home-rule authority, violating state limits on voter initiatives, and
overstepping the limitations on state constitutional amendments.[25]

It is intriguing that the pro- and antiframing of Amendment 2's scope
and purpose altered very little when the forum shifted from the ballot
box to the courts. In both forums, the proponents of Amendment 2
argued that it would simply prevent lgb people from seeking special protections based on their sexual "orientation, conduct, practices, or relationships." Proponents of the amendment also argued in both forums
that the ballot measure would enable the state of Colorado to focus its
resources on those groups that truly required extra assistance, to protect
the familial and religious rights of those with deep-seated and profound
beliefs about the immorality of homosexuality, to protect the traditional
family, and to promote the psychological and physical well-being of children. Proponents of Amendment 2 also consistently depicted homosexuality and bisexuality as a "life-style choice," which apparently conferred

some benefits (more money, more education) and some disadvantages (more diseases, less emotional stability, shorter life expectancy). They emphasized the distinctions between sexual orientation and race. They told horror stories of what might happen if Amendment 2 were not enacted.

Opponents of Amendment 2 likewise framed its scope and purpose quite similarly in both the political and the legal campaign. They told horror stories of what would happen if Amendment 2 *were* enacted. They argued that the phrase *special rights* was a red herring, that Amendment 2 would actually deprive lgb people of the kinds of rights and protections that most people took for granted. In both places, they depicted Amendment 2 as motivated by animus toward lgb people. In both places they emphasized that homosexuality was more than simply a "life-style choice." They emphasized the similarity between sexual orientation and race.

Why then did Amendment 2 prevail in the court of public opinion but fail in the court of law? I argue in the following pages that the divergence in the electoral and legal outcomes of Amendment 2 is largely a product of the differences in the political and legal structures of opportunity surrounding Colorado's antigay initiative. When Amendment 2 moved from a political question to a legal question, several key factors shifted, including the configuration of decision makers, the decision-making process, and the resonance of legal and cultural frames.

The Configuration of Elites

The most obvious difference between the political and legal battles over Amendment 2 was the locus of decision making. In the political campaign, the Colorado electorate had the duty and power to decide Amendment 2's fate. In the legal campaign, that responsibility fell to judges. Thirteen judges heard arguments about the constitutionality of Amendment 2 during the course of its litigation: one district court judge, the three justices of the Colorado Supreme Court, and the nine members of the U.S. Supreme Court. Of those thirteen jurists, nine agreed that the amendment was fatally flawed: the district court judge, two of the justices on the Colorado Supreme Court, and six of the justices on the U.S. Supreme Court.

Justice Scalia's blistering dissent from the U.S. Supreme Court's opinion in *Romer* proposed an explanation for why the majority of the jurists deciding *Romer* differed from the majority of Colorado's electorate. As he saw it, striking down Amendment 2 was an act "not of judicial judgment, but of political will" (*Romer*, 653).

> When the Court takes sides in the culture wars, it tends to be with the knights rather than the villeins—and more specifically with the Templars, reflecting the views and the values of the lawyer class from which the Court's Members are drawn. How that class feels about homosexuality will be evidenced to anyone who wishes to interview job applicants at virtually any of the Nation's law schools. The interviewer may refuse to offer a job because the applicant is Republican; because he is an adulterer; . . . or even because he hates the Chicago Cubs. But if the interviewer should wish not to be an associate or partner of an applicant because he disapproves of the applicant's homosexuality, then he will have violated the pledge which the Association of American Law Schools requires all its member-schools to exact from job interviewers: "assurance of the employer's willingness" to hire homosexuals. This law school view of what "prejudices" must be stamped out may be contrasted with the more plebian attitudes that apparently still prevail in the United States Congress, which has been unresponsive to repeated attempts to extend to homosexuals the protections of federal civil rights laws. (652–53)

The question of whether judges make decisions based on law, politics, or some combination of the two is a major one, and one I shall turn to presently. For the moment, the point I wish to make is that, whether the jurists deciding Amendment 2's fate engaged in legal analysis or advanced their elite political agenda, they utilized a different decision-making calculus than did the majority of Colorado's voters in the 1992 election. When Amendment 2 shifted from the ballot box to the courtroom, a major aspect of opportunity structure also shifted.

As it stands, and with all due respect to Justice Scalia, it seems difficult to attribute the Supreme Court's decision in *Romer* solely to the political values of six of its members. Comparing the *Romer* justices to their *Bowers* brethren is useful here.

As discussed in chapter 5, six of the nine seats on the Court changed hand in the ten years between *Bowers* and *Romer*. At first glance, the large turnover in the Court's membership adds fuel to Scalia's contention that *Romer* was the product of individual values rather than "objective" legal analysis. Scholars have demonstrated that major doctrinal changes are often preceded by membership changes on the Court.[26] However, comparing the ideological positions of the *Bowers* justices to their *Romer* replacements suggests that, on the whole, the ideological tenor of the Court remained reasonably stable in the decade between the two cases.

Table 12 arrays the justices of both courts on a liberal-conservative scale ranging from 1 (most liberal justice) to 9 (most conservative justice). As in all winner-takes-all voting schemes, the voters in the middle matter more than the voters anchoring the edges of the ideological spectrum, because they are the ones who will swing the outcome of ideologically charged cases. In order to carry a case, the justices on either end of the ideological spectrum have to convince two of the three justices in the middle (positions 4–6) to vote with them. As table 12 shows, the swing justices on the *Romer* Court were roughly equivalent to the swing justices on the *Bowers* Court with respect to their likelihood to support the liberal position in civil liberties cases. If anything, they were slightly more amenable to conservative arguments than were the *Bowers* justices.

Of course, aggregate measures say nothing about the justices' attitudes about homosexuality. Yet just one year prior to *Romer*, the Court had unanimously upheld the right of the organizers of Boston's St. Patrick's Day Parade to prevent a group from marching under a banner identifying themselves as openly gay (*Hurley v. Irish-American Gay, Les-*

TABLE 12.   Comparative Ranking of Justices in *Bowers* and *Romer*

Rank[a]	*Bowers* Justices	Civil Liberties (%)[b]	*Romer* Justices	Civil Liberties (%)[c]
1	Marshall[d]	80	Breyer	63
2	Brennan	79	Stevens	62
3	Stevens	58	Ginsburg	61
4	White	44	Souter	48
5	Blackmun	43	Kennedy	35
6	Powell	35	O'Connor	34
7	O'Connor	28	Scalia	30
8	Burger	28	Thomas	28
9	Rehnquist	19	Rehnquist	23

[a]1 = most liberal justice; 9 = most conservative justice.

[b]Percentages represent justices' support for the liberal position in civil liberties cases from their arrival on the Supreme Court through 1985. Source for data is Segal and Spaeth 1989.

[c]Percentages represent justices' support for the liberal position in civil liberties cases from their arrival on the Supreme Court through 1995. Source for data is Epstein and Knight 1998.

[d]Underlined names are justices who cast "gay-friendly" votes, that is, justices who voted in the minority in *Bowers* and the majority in *Romer*.

bian, and Bisexual Group, 1995). The parade was a private event with an expressive message, the Court ruled, and the government could not compel the organizers to include GLIB. Were the justices in the *Romer* majority as reflexively pro-gay as Scalia's dissent implied, one suspects they would have supported GLIB's position rather than opposing it.

In sum, it seems unwarranted to reduce the decision-making process in *Romer* solely to the application of elite political preferences. In the aggregate, the *Romer* justices were at least as conservative as their predecessors in *Bowers.* In the specific context of gay rights, the Court had unanimously rejected GLIB's claim just one year prior to *Romer.* It seems more reasonable to posit that the jurists hearing *Romer* were influenced, at least to some extent, by the legal frames undergirding the case.

The Availability of Legal Frames

Although the original complaint filed by the Lambda team listed every conceivable theory under which Amendment 2 might be found wanting, during the course of the actual litigation, the team focused the bulk of its energy on two claims arising from the Equal Protection Clause. First, it claimed that Amendment 2 infringed on the fundamental right to participate equally in the political process. The crux of its argument was that a measure that restricted any identifiable group's ability to bring about change through ordinary political processes warranted strict scrutiny. To support this claim, it relied primarily on a 1969 case called *Hunter v. Erickson.*

In *Hunter,* the Supreme Court struck down an Akron, Ohio, law that prohibited the city council from passing any "fair housing laws" without the approval of the electorate, after finding that the measure was intended to prevent racial minorities from seeking protection against housing discrimination. The Court ruled that Akron could "no more disadvantage any particular group by making it more difficult to enact legislation on its behalf than it may dilute any person's vote or give any group smaller representation than another of comparable size."

In addition to *Hunter,* the legal team attacking Amendment 2 also cited cases dealing with restrictions on the exercise of the franchise, cases concerning reapportionment, and cases concerning the rights of minority parties.[27] The link between these cases was the common concern that animated them, namely, the "special judicial duty to ensure to all persons regardless of their social identity equal access to the day-to-day political process."[28]

The virtue of this equal-participation argument is that it allowed the

Lambda team to sidestep the discourse of equivalents that had worked so effectively in the political context. It did not matter whether lgb people were sufficiently "like" African Americans to warrant heightened protection by the courts. What mattered was whether Amendment 2 prevented lgb people from exercising a fundamental right.

A particularly interesting feature of this fundamental rights argument is that Lambda and its colleagues did not themselves think it was their strongest legal argument. In fact, they thought they were most likely to prevail on the merits by showing that Amendment 2 was motivated by an impermissible purpose (animus) and lacked any rational relationship to legitimate governmental ends (Gerstmann 1999; Keen and Goldberg 1998). But in order to win a preliminary injunction, they needed to convince the court that Amendment 2 would do "irreparable harm" to lgb people were it allowed to take effect, and they were concerned that a showing of animus would not be enough. So they cast about for a suitable fundamental rights argument.

Of the fundamental rights possibilities around them, "equal participation" seemed the strongest. However, it was not without its weaknesses. Chief among them was a case called *James v. Valtierra* (1971), decided only two years after *Hunter.* In *James,* the Supreme Court upheld a California referendum that prohibited state and local governments from creating low-income housing projects without the approval of the electorate. The plaintiffs in *James* had argued that the measure violated the rights of poor people in much the same way as the initiative in *Hunter* violated the rights of racial minorities. The Supreme Court, however, declined to accept this analogy. They noted that, unlike in *Hunter,* the law at issue in *James* did not rest on racial classifications. If *Hunter* were extended beyond suspect classes, the Court reasoned, it would mean that "a State would not be able to require referendums on any subject unless referendums were required on all, because they would always disadvantage some group" (*James,* 142).

Not surprisingly is the fact that the state of Colorado relied on *James* to argue that the fundamental right asserted by Lambda and its colleagues did not exist. The debate over whether people had a fundamental right to participate equally in the political process dogged every step of *Romer*'s litigation. In the end, the U.S. Supreme Court declined to answer the question, basing its ruling solely on the *second* claim raised by Lambda and its colleagues, namely, that Amendment 2 was unconstitutional because it did not meet the minimum requirement that a law be rationally related to a legitimate governmental interest.

Nonetheless, advancing the fundamental rights claim served several purposes. First, it shifted the debate from whether lgb people should receive "special rights" such as "quota preferences" to whether it was constitutional for a majority to fence lgb people out of the political system by preventing them, and them alone, from seeking to improve their lot through the legislative process. This reformulation of the scope and purpose of Amendment 2 convinced both the district and supreme courts of Colorado that Amendment 2 would do "irreparable harm" to lgb people were it allowed to take effect. The preliminary injunctions issued by these courts in turn altered dramatically the balance of power between pro– and anti–Amendment 2 forces by requiring that Amendment 2 be subject to *strict scrutiny* in the trial on the merits.

Judicial review of cases implicating the right to equal protection proceed along one of three different tiers (see *Frontiero v. Richardson*, 1973). Most laws need only be *rationally* related to a *permissible* governmental objective (rational-basis review). Laws that infringe on fundamental rights or make suspect classifications, however, are subject to strict scrutiny; in order to pass constitutional muster, such laws must be *narrowly drawn* to advance *compelling* governmental interests. Laws that make quasi-suspect classifications are subject to intermediate scrutiny; they must be *substantially related* to *important* governmental interests. In practical effect, the determination that Amendment 2 would be subject to strict scrutiny in the trial on its merits ended the lower court phase of *Romer,* because legislation rarely ever meets the compelling interest standard.

Despite the height of the legal hurdle facing it, the state of Colorado chose not to exit the litigation process. Instead, it advanced a set of interests that it alleged were compelling and argued that Amendment 2 was tailored as narrowly as possible to advance those interests. As the main litigator for the state has since admitted, the state was aware that several of its asserted purposes were not "compelling" under existing law (Tymkovich, Dailey, and Farley 1997, 299–300). Its strategy was really to establish the rational basis of Amendment 2, preparatory to requesting review by the U.S. Supreme Court. The state hoped that the U.S. Supreme Court would reject the fundamental rights analysis adopted by the Colorado Supreme Court and instead decide *Romer* via rational-basis analysis.

The Lambda team was well aware of Colorado's strategy. It was concerned that the state might be right—that the U.S. Supreme Court might be unwilling to accept that the right to participate equally in the political process constituted a fundamental right. As a result, although *Romer* was judged under the strict scrutiny standard in both the district and supreme courts of Colorado, the goal of both sides was to win on rational-basis grounds. In a way, the Colorado judges hearing the case became incidental to the real audience: the nine justices on the U.S. Supreme Court.

Amendment 2 and the Legal Process

Opponents of Amendment 2 were disadvantaged in the political battle over the measure, because they were unable to find a sound bite with which to counter CFV's "special rights" framing. As one of the activists involved in the Amendment 2 campaign noted earlier, "It takes fifteen minutes of real discussion to undo the damage that phrase does." During the litigation of Amendment 2, opponents got those "fifteen minutes of real discussion," because the mechanisms of persuasion altered. Unlike the political campaign over Amendment 2, the legal struggle did not proceed via sound bite. It proceeded via legal brief. Opponents of the amendment were able to leverage the process of litigating to their advantage by articulating the myriad petty and profound harms that would accrue to lgb people were the amendment to take effect. Over the course of the litigation, the Lambda team and numerous friendly amici detailed a veritable laundry list of harms that would result to lgb people, often illustrating these harms with hypothetical and real-life examples of discrimination. Among other things, they argued, Amendment 2 would

- Fence lgb people out of the political system by preventing them, and them alone, from seeking to improve their lot through the legislative process;
- Prevent elected officials from responding to the concerns of their constituents;
- Prevent lgb people from turning to Colorado's courts for a redress of injuries relating in some fashion to their sexual orientation. "Suppose, for example, that a Colorado municipality passed an ordinance that required any gay person entering the town to register with the local police department. Or suppose that a community college with an otherwise open enrollment refused to allow lesbians to take any classes in its automotive mechanics department. Such treatment would almost certainly violate the Equal Protection Clause. . . . Nonetheless, on its face,

Amendment 2 would require the Colorado courts to dismiss lawsuits brought under [federal civil rights law] since the gravamen of each lawsuit would be a claim of discrimination' on the basis' of sexual orientation";[29]

- Open lgb people to arbitrary and capricious actions by judges. "Suppose, for example, that a lesbian plaintiff were to bring a garden-variety personal-injury lawsuit. At a bench trial, the judge rules against her on the grounds that because she is a lesbian her testimony is inherently incredible and he believes that lesbians 'deserve' whatever misfortunes come their way";[30]
- Open lgb people to arbitrary and capricious actions by police;
- Eliminate programs allowing voluntary protective custody in prisons around the state for lgb persons who preferred not to live with the jail's populations;
- Prevent county and school district programs designed to deter teen suicide from counseling students about sexual orientation;
- Prevent county and school district programs from training employees to recognize and respond to the harassment of lgb students;
- Interfere with collective bargaining agreements, even in private contexts, because unions would be unable to turn to administrative and judicial forums to enforce existing grievance and arbitration agreements;
- Prevent local and state HIV-prevention programs from discussing homosexuality; and
- Open lgb people to arbitrary and capricious actions by libraries and other public facilities.

The Lambda team also described all the existing statutes, regulations, ordinances, and policies that would be repealed should Amendment 2 take effect, among them

- Residents of Aspen, Boulder, and Denver would lose their protections from discrimination on the basis of sexual orientation in employment, housing, and accommodations;
- Governor Roy Romer's executive order protecting state employees from discrimination based on sexual orientation would be rescinded;
- Health insurance providers would no longer be prohibited from

using sexual orientation as a criterion for insurability or premiums;

- The canons of conduct for judges and lawyers forbidding them from discriminating based on sexual orientation in the performance of their professional duties would be rescinded; and
- Antidiscrimination policies at state universities would be rescinded.

Even more important than giving the *Romer* plaintiffs a forum to detail the dangers to lgb people posed by Amendment 2, the legal process also forced the state of Colorado to articulate the purposes advanced by Amendment 2. To survive strict scrutiny, the state needed to show that the scope of Amendment 2 was narrowly tailored so as to advance a compelling governmental interest in the least restrictive manner possible. Even under rational basis analysis (which the state hoped and the Lambda team feared the Supreme Court would apply in place of strict scrutiny), the state needed to show that Amendment 2 was rationally related to a legitimate governmental purpose. Much of the power of CFV's framing during the political campaign had come from evoking the specter of the homosexual threat to "legitimate" minorities, to children, to heterosexuals, and to the rights of all those who believed homosexuality to be immoral. When these "homosexual threat" arguments were examined systematically, they collapsed.

For example, the state of Colorado argued that Amendment 2 served the compelling purpose of deterring discrimination, because it forced the state to focus its limited resources on those circumstances, such as racial and sexual discrimination, that most warranted attention. The Lambda team made several responses to this argument. It drew on the experiences of Wisconsin, the state with the oldest gay rights law, to debunk the notion that protecting lgb people from discrimination would hinder the enforcement of other civil rights laws; Wisconsin's records showed that the enactment of a statewide gay rights law did not reduce the state's ability to handle other civil rights claim and only marginally increased costs. Lambda and its litigation partners also detailed the many state and local laws prohibiting discrimination based on nonsuspect classifications, including marital status, veteran's status, and *any* legal off-duty conduct, including smoking. As the Lambda team phrased it: "Nothing in the state's proffered purpose explains why the preservation of state resources required that gay people be denied all protection from discrimination on the basis of their sexual orientation, while everyone else—from smokers to heterosexuals to divorcees—may continue to be protected."[31] Moreover, Lambda emphasized, requiring government to *refrain* from invidious discrimination did not in and of itself consume *any* resources.

The state of Colorado also argued that Amendment 2 served the compelling purpose of protecting religious liberty, by ensuring that the government could not coerce, either explicitly or implicitly, a belief about the morality of homosexuality. Without Amendment 2, it noted, landlords with deep-seated religious objections to homosexuality might be compelled to compromise them under threat of governmental sanctions. Amendment 2 prevented governments from entering "the political marketplace by forcing private persons to subscribe to or advance particular political beliefs."[32] In response to this argument, the Lambda team argued that the "means" of Amendment 2 were such a poor fit to the "ends" of religious liberty that they failed even the most lenient standards of rational review. Amendment 2 targeted lgb people even when other people's individual freedoms were not at issue, such as in the context of health insurance. However, it left in place laws prohibiting discrimination on the basis of characteristics such as marital status and legal off-duty conduct that implicated religious freedom just as much as any law excluded by Amendment 2. To the extent that the purpose of Amendment 2 was to protect religious liberty, the rational approach would be to craft a religious exception to antidiscrimination ordinances.[33]

CFV's framing of the threat that lgb people posed to traditional families and children likewise collapsed when it was fully articulated. The state of Colorado contended that Amendment 2 served the compelling purposes of protecting children, traditional families, and the institution of (heterosexual) marriage. Without Amendment 2, the state argued, there would be nothing to prevent the state or a local government from endorsing, at least implicitly, the view that homosexuality and heterosexuality were morally equivalent. Such an implicit endorsement would undermine the traditional family in several ways. For one, it would interfere with the efforts of parents to teach their children moral values, because if "a child hears one thing from his parents and the exact opposite message from the government, parental authority will inevitably be undermined. While some may think it is desirable for children to find homosexuality acceptable, the Constitution 'excludes any general power of the State to standardize its children.'"[34]

Moreover, a state's implicit endorsement that homosexuality and heterosexuality are morally equivalent would also undermine the norm of heterosexual marriage, because "married heterosexuals might choose to become homosexual." In addition, Amendment 2 fostered the state's compelling interest in protecting the morals of its children and steering them toward healthy individual and societal life-styles. Homosexuals had lesser life expectancies and suffered greater morbidity, the state argued. It also submitted evidence indicating that lgb teenagers accounted for 50 percent of suicide attempts although they constituted only a small percentage of the population. "Amendment 2 helps to avert unnecessary suffering for those who may be influenced relative to their sexual preference by not lending government's voice to the debate," concluded the state.[35]

Lambda and its colleagues made several responses to these contentions. They attacked the state's premise that forbidding discrimination on the basis of sexual orientation was the equivalent of endorsing homosexuality: "By the State's reasoning, when government forbids private employers from discriminating against Buddhists on the basis of their Buddhism, it endorses Buddhism and prevents parents from inculcating their children with non-Buddhist religious principles."[36]

They used a two-pronged approach to attack the state's contention that gay rights laws threatened families. First, they presented statistical evidence showing that the divorce rates in states that had instituted statewide gay rights laws had actually *declined* after the enactment of these laws. Second, they ridiculed the state's notion that heterosexuals might just wake up one morning and "choose" to become homosexuals if the state did not actively discourage such behavior.

Finally, they marshaled extensive sociological evidence showing that lgb people posed neither physical nor psychological harm to children. It was Amendment 2, they countered, that posed a threat to children. Scientific research on sexual orientation showed that it was fixed long before puberty and was highly resistant to change. Amendment 2 would only harm lgb youth by further legitimating discrimination against lgb people, preventing schools from counseling teenagers about their sexual orientation, and prohibiting HIV-prevention programs from discussing same-sex sexuality.

In sum, the requirements of the legal process both gave the Lambda team space to articulate the ways in which Amendment 2 threatened the civil rights of lgb people and forced the state to explicitly articulate the governmental purposes advanced by the ballot measure. When pushed into the open and examined dispassionately, the "homosexual threat" that had allegedly necessitated Amendment 2 dissolved. Some of it looked downright silly. Amendment 2's impact on the rights of lgb people, conversely, became much clearer.

The Difference between Legal and Cultural Frames

A final difference between the political and the legal battles over Amendment 2 concerned the meaning of key terms such as *special rights, minority status, protected class status,* and *quota preferences.* Although these terms *sounded* as though they were legal standards, they had no real legal meaning. They were the legal equivalent of psycho-babble (legal-babble, if you will).[37] The National Legal Foundation, which helped CFV draft Amendment 2, recognized the difference between the legal and cultural meanings of these terms. In a letter to Tony Marco dated June 13, 1991, the National Legal Foundation coached CFV about the strategies for framing Amendment 2. "[W]hile homosexuals do not get far by asking the electorate for special privileges, they do get a good deal of sympathy by asking to be 'treated just like everyone else'" (quoted in Keen and Goldberg 1998, 11). CFV, the letter advised, should frame the issue as one of special rights in the political campaign but should avoid it in the actual text.

> If language of denying special privileges to homosexuals is in the amendment, it could possibly allow homosexuals to argue that they are not asking for any special privileges, just those granted to everyone else. I believe that "No Special Privileges" is a good motto for the amendment's public campaign, but I fear the possible legal ramification if it is included in the amendment itself. (Quoted in Keen and Goldberg 1998, 11)

As a result of the disjoint between the cultural and legal meanings of terms such as *special rights,* they lost much of their persuasive power when they were invoked in the legal rather than the electoral context. For instance, part of the political debate over Amendment 2 was whether granting "protected class status" on the basis of sexual orientation would lead to affirmative action for homosexuals and bisexuals. Proponents of Amendment 2 argued that laws prohibiting discrimination on the basis of sexual orientation would inevitably lead to "quota preferences," which would disadvantage both "legitimate" minorities such as African Americans (who were socially disadvantaged for reasons beyond their control) and the larger heterosexual population (who would then be losing jobs not only to less qualified minorities but also to homosexuals).

This framing of Amendment 2 was quite successful in the political campaign over gay rights because of the popular conflation of laws prohibiting discrimination and laws mandating affirmative action. Leanna Ware, the director of Wisconsin's Civil Rights Bureau, addressed this perception for the Lambda team during Amendment 2's trial. Employers, she explained, were often confused about whether Wisconsin's law prohibiting discrimination on the basis of sexual orientation required them to institute affirmative action policies for lgb people. The results of focus group research conducted during the Amendment 2 campaign echoed this sense.

> The public is wary of anything that hints of "affirmative action." [Opponents of Amendment 2] would be well advised, in discussing discrimination in the workplace or housing, to place emphasis on *retaining* one's job or one's residence after the employer or landlord learns that the person is homosexual. When the subject turns to *hiring* homosexuals or *accepting* them as tenants, the specter of quota arises in many people's minds. (Quoted in Gerstmann 1999, 105)

This logic chain was severed when the battle over Amendment 2 shifted to the courts. Legally, the institution of civil rights protections on the basis of a certain characteristic is not at all the same as requiring affirmative action based on that characteristic. Civil rights protections have been seen as a way to *stop* state-sanctioned disadvantaging of disfavored groups. Affirmative action has been seen as a way to *ameliorate* the effects of past discrimination. Although the two are not completely unrelated, they are not equivalent, and the one does not ineluctably lead to the other.

Conclusion

The structure of *legal* opportunities often operates in conjunction with the structure of *political* opportunities. However, the two are not interchangeable. In this chapter, I have utilized a case study of antigay initiatives to illustrate the ways in which legal opportunity structure and political opportunity structure differ. Specifically, I have argued that the differential ability of gay rights activists to stop antigay initiatives at the ballot box and in the courtroom is largely a function of differences in the structures of opportunity within which the activists operated. Several aspects of the political opportunity structure (the configuration of decision makers, the mechanics of the decision-making process, and the availability of cultural frames) regularly combined to disadvantage gay rights advocates vis-à-vis their opponents. In the legal system, the allocation of advantage and disadvantage reversed. The configuration of decision makers, the decision-making process, and the existing legal frames generally operated to advantage gay rights advocates vis-à-vis their opponents.

Although my examination has focused on how gay rights advocates have used the legal system to mitigate political defeats, I do not wish to leave the impression that turning to the courts always operates to the advantage of gay rights advocates. Do not forget *Bowers*.[38] Consider also the case of employment. The major gains of the gay rights movement in the employment context have come through the passage of gay rights laws and through collective bargaining, *not* through the courts. A major reason for this is that legal frames do not lend themselves to gay rights claims concerning employment *except* in those jurisdictions with gay rights laws on the books.[39]

I also do not wish to leave the impression that turning to the courts is an unproblematic endeavor for social movements. Scholars of legal mobilization have examined the ways in which legal arguments can both empower and disempower groups in their attempts to effect social change (e.g., Kairys 1982; McCann 1994; Smart 1989). Merry (1985, 60) notes that legal frames "provide symbols which can be manipulated by their members for strategic goals, but they also establish constraints on that manipulation."

In this chapter I have simply endeavored to show that legal and political opportunity do not always operate in tandem with respect to a given movement claim and that disadvantages in one system do not necessarily translate into disadvantages in the other. In some ways, this is not a novel claim. Scholars have commonly argued that groups litigate at least in part because they are disadvantaged in the political process (see Scheppele and Walker 1991).[40] What my examination of antigay initiatives adds to this body of scholarship is an articulation of several of the key factors conditioning the differential outcomes of political and legal activism on a particular issue. In the following chapter, I continue my exploration of the relationship between legal and political opportunity by examining the extent to which legal "wins" can effect actual social change.

SEVEN

The Case of Same-Sex Marriage

ame-sex couples masquerading as opposite-sex couples have successfully obtained marriage licenses and married each other
throughout American history.[1] In the 1970s, however, lesbians and
gay men finally began to argue that they had the *right* to marry their
same-sex partners. The first recorded legal challenge occurred in 1970,
when Jack Baker and Mike McConnell sued a Minnesota county clerk
who had refused to grant them a marriage license. The two men argued,
among other things, that the state's refusal to allow them to marry each
other violated their rights to due process and equal protection. In 1971,
the Minnesota Supreme Court became the first appellate court in the
nation to consider the subject of same-sex marriage. It ruled against
Baker and McConnell, holding that the fundamental right to marry did
not apply to same-sex unions, because, by definition, marriage could only
occur between one man and one woman.

Baker v. Nelson was the first in a twenty-three-year-long series of rulings across the nation upholding the right of states to prohibit same-sex
marriage.[2] In the 1990s, however, gay rights activists finally succeeded in
fracturing this judicial consensus. Courts in three different states—
Hawaii, Alaska, and Vermont—ruled that same-sex couples had a constitutional interest in being able to marry.

In no instance did same-sex marriage advocates ultimately get what
they were litigating for: marriage licenses. But the translation of these
decisions into public policy took markedly divergent paths. The Alaskan
plaintiffs in *Brause and Dugan v. Bureau of Vital Statistics* (1998) not
only failed to receive marriage licenses, they precipitated the development and passage of a state constitutional amendment restricting marriage to opposite-sex couples. The Hawaiian plaintiffs in *Baehr v. Lewin*
(1993) saw the institution of a similar constitutional amendment in reaction to their litigation, but they also witnessed the passage of a law (the
Reciprocal Beneficiaries Act) designed to grant unmarried couples many
of the state-level rights and benefits traditionally accorded to married
couples. Moreover, the *Baehr* plaintiffs also saw their litigation spark a

nationwide debate over same-sex marriage, with consequences for the public policies of the federal government and most states. The Vermont plaintiffs in *Baker v. State of Vermont* (1999) had yet another experience. On July 1, 2000, in response to their litigation, they saw Vermont become the only state in the United States to accord same-sex couples the rights and privileges traditionally associated with heterosexual marriage, albeit under the name "civil unions" rather than marriage.

In this chapter, I use the lens of legal opportunity structure to examine the dominoes set into motion by these three court decisions. An LOS perspective lends itself to three propositions. The first is that legal decisions such as *Baehr, Brause,* and *Baker* rarely produce clear wins or losses for advocates of sociopolitical reform. Instead they produce opportunities for action on the part of both reformers and their opponents, opportunities that may or may not be exploited successfully. The second is that the value of any particular opportunity is not just a function of an actor's abilities but is also dependent on the other institutional and sociolegal factors that combine to create the structure of legal opportunities. In other words, similar legal decisions occurring in different states may create dissimilar opportunities for action because of differences in each state's LOS. The third proposition is that changes in the structure of legal opportunities may reverberate in the structure of political opportunities as well. As I showed in chapter 6, LOS and POS are not interchangeable. But neither are they completely independent from one another. Changes in one simultaneously affect and are constrained by the contours of the other.

In the following pages, I lay out the origins, progress, and outcomes of *Baehr, Brause,* and *Baker.* I then argue that the reason why Hawaii, Alaska, and Vermont reacted so differently to the decisions in these cases was largely a function of differences in the LOS and POS in the three states rather than of differences in the strategies of pro- and anti-same-sex marriage activists. I begin by providing some background into why gay rights activists have pursued the right to marry.

Why Marriage?

Legally recognized marriages bring with them a plethora of state- and federal-level rights and responsibilities. In 1997, the Government Accounting Office (GAO) released a report detailing 1,049 separate governmental benefits associated with civil marriage. The lion's share of rights and responsibilities associated with marriage falls under two categories: financial and familial. Even a partial listing of financial benefits is eye-opening. Married couples may file tax returns jointly, inherit from each other automatically in the absence of a will, share income from governmental programs such as Social Security and Medicare, obtain wrongful death benefits for a surviving partner, obtain joint insurance policies, and partake in employer-provided benefits such as access to health insurance and pension protections. The familial benefits are even more significant. A small sampling includes the following: Married couples are treated as each other's automatic next of kin for purposes of medical decision making, hospital visitation, and burial arrangements. They are assumed to have joint rights and responsibilities in parenting, including custody and visitation in the event of divorce. And they may take bereavement or sick leave to care for each other or for their children. It is important to note that couples can obtain relatively few of these benefits for each other in any way *other* than marriage. In short, the institution of marriage is a powerful mechanism for promoting familial and economic stability.

That gay rights litigators would pursue same-sex marriage seems obvious now. But there has been severe intracommunity tension over the value of pursuing marriage as a movement goal. As one Lambda litigator recalled in an interview with me, "There were some issues over which we all fought quite bitterly [in the late 1980s and early 1990s], and there were strong disagreements, marriage being chief among them."

This tension has largely, but not invariably, played out along gender lines, with lesbian activists more critical than their gay male counterparts of marriage as an institution.[3] Lambda was not immune from this tension. In fact, a debate between two of its lawyers helped to ignite it, in what Bill Rubenstein (1997, 1635) called a "marriage announcement of sorts." In 1989, *Out/Look*, a now defunct lesbian and gay journal, published two articles side by side. The first article, written by then–Lambda executive director Tom Stoddard, was entitled "Why Gay People Should Seek the Right to Marry" and set out practical and philosophical reasons why same-sex marriage rights should become a priority for the gay rights movement. The second article, written by then–Lambda legal director Paula Ettelbrick, was called "Since When Is Marriage a Path to Liberation?" and set forth reasons why same-sex marriage should *not* be a priority for the movement.[4]

The practical upshot of this intracommunity fissure was that, until 1993, none of the major gay legal groups treated same-sex marriage as an immediate priority. That all changed when the Hawaii Supreme Court handed down its groundbreaking decision in *Baehr v. Lewin*. We turn to it now.

Baehr v. Lewin and Its Impact

In 1991, three same-sex couples in Hawaii filed suit after being denied marriage licenses, arguing that they had a fundamental right to marry each other under Hawaii's constitution. Their lawyer was Dan Foley, an attorney who had done work for the ACLU in the past but was acting independently with respect to *Baehr*. Foley approached both Lambda and the ACLU for assistance in the case, but they both declined the invitation to become cocounsel. Lambda did decide, however, to submit an amicus curiae brief supporting same-sex marriage.

Like many of the marriage challenges preceding it, *Baehr* was dismissed by the trial court, which ruled that Hawaii's marriage statute did not contemplate marriages between members of the same sex. On appeal, however, the Hawaii Supreme Court made history by becoming the first court in the nation to treat seriously the claim that same-sex couples had a constitutional interest in marrying each other. It is interesting that it rejected the plaintiffs' right-to-marry argument and based its ruling on a claim the plaintiffs had not raised: that the state's ban on same-sex marriage constituted sex discrimination and thus was subject to strict scrutiny under Hawaii's constitution.[5] It reinstated the case and remanded it for a trial to determine whether the state's rationale for banning same-sex marriage was important enough to constitute a compelling governmental interest.

The Hawaii Supreme Court's ruling set many wheels into motion. At the most basic level, it instituted a legal frame that would make it exceptionally difficult for Hawaii to defend its ban on same-sex marriage, just as the Colorado Supreme Court's early ruling in *Evans v. Romer* made it exceptionally difficult for Colorado to defend the constitutionality of Amendment 2.

The 1993 decision also prompted action by the Hawaii legislature. It quickly amended the state's marriage statute to clarify that marriage required a man and a woman.[6] It also created the Commission on Sexual Orientation and the Law to study the legal inequities faced by same-sex couples. Late in 1995 the commission issued its report, recommending that the legislature legalize same-sex marriage or, at the very least, establish domestic partnerships. Legislative responses to this proposal spanned the gamut. Bills were introduced variously to legalize same-sex marriage, to establish domestic partnerships, and to amend Hawaii's constitution to prohibit same-sex marriage. While a domestic partnership bill passed in the senate in 1996, it failed to pass in the house, and the issue of same-sex marriage receded from the legislature's agenda until the trial court handed down its decision in *Baehr* late in 1996 (about which more subsequently).

The 1993 decision in *Baehr* reverberated far beyond Hawaii's shores. It served as the impetus for widespread gay rights mobilization around same-sex marriage rights. Preeminent among the newly mobilized in this area was Lambda. After the decision came down, Lambda reversed its earlier stance of nonaction with respect to same-sex marriage. Part of the reason for this reversal may have been staff turnover. Both Tom Stoddard and Paula Ettelbrick had departed Lambda by the time *Baehr* came down. And Evan Wolfson, one of the remaining Lambda litigators, was a vocal proponent of same-sex marriage. Interviews with present and former staff members, though, indicate that the legal opening provided by *Baehr* was the primary stimulus for Lambda's change of heart.

The organization now took up Dan Foley's invitation to act as cocounsel in the case. Evan Wolfson was tapped to become Lambda's litigator. In addition, Lambda established the Marriage Project in late 1994, also headed up by Wolfson. The Marriage Project's goal was to coordinate and facilitate state-by-state political organizing and public education around the issue of same-sex marriage. Its emphasis on political mobilization reflected Lambda's recognition that the *Baehr* decision was both promising and dangerous for gay rights advocates. The Full Faith and Credit Clause of the U.S. Constitution generally requires that states recognize official acts and proceedings of other states.[7] Should Hawaii sanction same-sex marriages, other states might well be forced to recognize those marriages. However, exceptions to the requirements of the Full Faith and Credit Clause have been granted when recognizing that a marriage violates the "strong public policy" of the state.[8] Lambda recognized that *Baehr* might provoke a backlash and that opponents of same-sex marriages would probably attempt to carve "strong public policy" objections into law across the nation. If they succeeded, lgb people might well find their marriages recognized in some states but not in others. The Marriage Project was designed to forestall this scenario by providing an umbrella organization within which gay rights activists could work to raise public awareness of the discrimination faced by same-sex couples, to file court cases as appropriate, and to lobby public officials. It garnered support and involvement from a wide array of gay rights organizations and non-gay allies, as well as a number of religious groups.[9]

Lambda was right. Concern about the possibility that other states might have to recognize same-sex marriages performed in Hawaii prompted widespread opposition. Conservative groups such as the Family Research Council, Focus on the Family, and the Christian Coalition and religious organizations such as the Mormon, Catholic, and many evangelical churches vigorously lobbied federal and state legislators to pass laws designed to counter *Baehr* (Dunlap 1996; Nagourney 1996).

By and large, opponents of same-sex marriage had more success on the political front than did supporters. Although supporters were able to deflect bills in several states, by the time the trial court issued its decision in *Baehr* late in 1996, sixteen states had passed bills doing one or more of the following: explicitly defining marriage as a union between one man and one woman, prohibiting marriage between members of the same sex, and prohibiting recognition of same-sex marriages performed in other jurisdictions.[10] Most striking is the fact that shortly before the trial on *Baehr* was to begin Congress passed—and President Clinton signed—DOMA, which (a) exempted states from the requirements of the Full Faith and Credit Clause insofar as it pertained to recognizing same-sex marriages performed in other states and (b) defined the words *marriage* and *spouse* to encompass only heterosexual couplings for all federal purposes.[11] *Baehr*'s impact even extended to the 1996 presidential race. On the eve of the Iowa caucuses, a "marriage protection" rally was endorsed by all but one of the five Republican presidential candidates.[12]

When, on December 3, 1996, the trial court assigned to hear *Baehr* ruled that Hawaii had shown *no* rational reason—much less a compelling one—for preventing same-sex couples from marrying, additional reactions were sparked.[13] The state immediately requested and received a stay of the lower court's ruling pending an appeal to the Hawaii Supreme Court. The Hawaii legislature, in turn, revisited the subject of same-sex marriage. It passed two bills in 1997. The first, called the Reciprocal Beneficiaries Act, gave a laundry list of legal and economic protections to couples, both homosexual and heterosexual, who were ineligible to marry.[14] It became effective in the summer of 1997.

At the time, the Reciprocal Beneficiaries law offered the broadest set of protections to same-sex couples anywhere in the nation. Specifically, the law offered about 60 state-level benefits to registered beneficiaries, including hospital visitation, family leave, health coverage, and inheritance. It fell far short, however, of the 160 or so state-level benefits offered by legal marriage in Hawaii. (Moreover, some of the benefits promised by the bill were subsequently chipped away. Within a few months of the law's enactment, Hawaii's attorney general issued an opinion letter stating that private employers were not required to provide health insurance to the reciprocal beneficiaries of their employees.[15] And the provision that reciprocal beneficiaries of state employees be eligible to receive health benefits expired in 1999, when the legislature did not reauthorize it.)

The second bill passed by the legislature in response to the 1996 *Baehr* trial court ruling authorized the people of Hawaii to vote on a constitutional amendment that would grant the legislature the power to restrict marriage to opposite-sex couples.[16] The proposed amendment was placed on the 1998 ballot. Proponents and opponents of same-sex marriage engaged in massive campaigns to sway the vote on the upcoming ballot measure.[17] As in Colorado during the Amendment 2 campaign, opponents of same-sex marriage were more successful in framing their argument in the court of public opinion. Voters in Hawaii ultimately approved the measure by a margin of more than 2–1. The Hawaii Supreme Court subsequently dismissed *Baehr,* ruling that the amendment had taken the marriage statute "out of the ambit of the equal protection clause of the Hawaii Constitution" and that the case was therefore moot.[18]

While the 1996 trial and subsequent ruling in *Baehr* clearly affected the POS and LOS vis-à-vis same-sex marriage in Hawaii, it also affected the POS and LOS on the mainland. As the trial drew closer and the decision came down, legislatures and governors across the nation became more concerned about the Full Faith and Credit implications of legalizing same-sex marriage in Hawaii. The number of states implementing "mini-DOMAs" accelerated sharply (see fig. 7), even though supporters of gay rights managed to deflect several measures. As noted previously, sixteen states had passed such laws by the time the trial court decision in *Baehr* came down; fourteen of those sixteen occurred in 1996. In 1997, nine more states passed mini-DOMAs.[19] By the close of 1998, when Hawaii voters passed their constitutional amendment, the number of states with mini-DOMAs had risen to thirty.[20] The passage of anti-same-sex marriage bills subsequently tapered off after Hawaii's constitution was amended. Only one state, Louisiana, passed such a measure in 1999. In 2000, however, four more states passed mini-DOMAs,[21] largely, I argue subsequently, in reaction to the Vermont high court's decision in *Baker v. State* and the subsequent creation of civil unions.

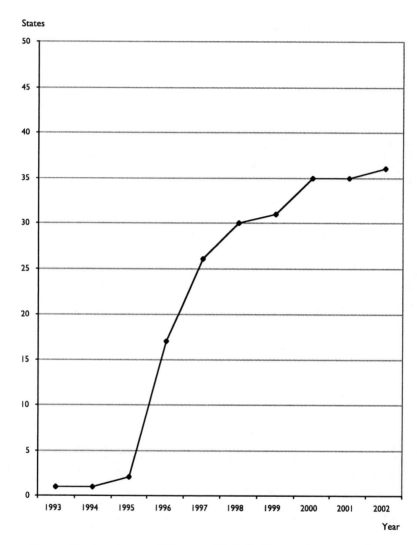

Fig. 7.   Number of states with laws specifically limiting marriage to opposite-sex couples

In sum, *Baehr* was neither a clear win nor a clear loss for gay rights advocates. Instead, the change it made in the structure of legal oportunities created space for action by multiple actors in multiple domains. Allies and opponents of same-sex marriage in Hawaii and on the mainland used *Baehr* as a focal point for mobilization. Legislators in Hawaii responded to *Baehr*'s progress by simultaneously enacting a broad Reciprocal Beneficiaries law and seeking to amend the state's constitution to give itself the sole power to define the parameters of marriage. Hawaiian voters in turn amended their constitution. Legislators in Congress and in thirty-four states across the nation passed laws designed to limit same-sex marriage while legislators in many other states considered, but did not enact, similar laws.

In addition to these events, *Baehr* also inspired a handful of same-sex couples across the nation to contemplate legal challenges to their states' marriage laws. We turn to one such legal challenge now.

Brause and Dugan v. Bureau of Vital Statistics and Its Impact

In 1995 two men, Jay Brause and Gene Dugan, sought a marriage license from the Alaska Bureau of Vital Statistics. It was denied, and together with their private counsel they sued, seeking to force the state to allow them to marry each other. They raised three claims: that the gender-neutral language of Alaska's marriage law permitted same-sex marriage and that refusing to allow them to marry violated their fundamental rights to privacy and equal protection under Alaska's constitution.

They were inspired by two recent legal decisions. The first was the 1993 ruling in *Baehr v. Lewin*. The second was a 1995 decision by a trial court in Fairbanks, Alaska. The case, *Tumeo v. University of Alaska*, involved a challenge to the University of Alaska–Fairbanks's policy of limiting spousal benefits to the "husbands" and "wives" of its married employees. The judge in the case (Meg Greene) ruled that, under Alaska's constitution, the university could not treat same-sex couples in committed relationships differently from heterosexually married couples. In the course of issuing her decision, she also suggested that Alaskan law might require marriage to be extended to same-sex couples (*Tumeo*, slip op. 7, n. 8).

Brause and Dugan were not the only ones inspired by *Tumeo*. In response to the decision, the Alaska legislature enacted a mini-DOMA, revising its marriage statute to explicitly exclude same-sex marriages and to refuse recognition to same-sex marriages performed in other jurisdictions.[22] Brause and Dugan subsequently amended their suit, asking the court to find that the revised statute was unconstitutional as well.

The trial court issued its ruling early in 1998. As did the Hawaii Supreme Court before it, the Alaska court found the ban on same-sex marriage to constitute sex discrimination. In addition, it held that the fundamental right of marriage extended to same-sex couples and that Alaska could not infringe upon that right absent a compelling governmental purpose. The court ordered a trial to determine whether the state could demonstrate such a purpose. The state petitioned the Alaska Supreme Court for review of the decision, but the high court declined to intervene.

The trial never had the chance to occur. Within three months of the decision, the Alaska legislature approved a proposed constitutional amendment that said in relevant part, "To be valid or recognized in this State, a marriage may exist only between one man and one woman."[23] As had occurred in Hawaii, the proposed constitutional amendment was placed on the 1998 ballot for ratification by the citizenry. As had occurred in Hawaii, the amendment passed by a margin of more than 2–1.[24] In light of the newly amended constitution, *Brause* was dismissed.

At the close of 1998, advocates of same-sex marriage seemed outgunned and outmaneuvered. Seemingly favorable changes in the structure of legal opportunities in Hawaii and Alaska created space for activism in both legal and political terrains, but their adversaries were generally able to utilize that space more effectively than they were. Constitutional amendments wiped out judicial gains in both states. Congress passed the DOMA. Another thirty states (not including Hawaii and Alaska) passed mini-DOMAs. But within a year, the landscape would change dramatically.

Baker v. State of Vermont and Its Impact

In 1997, three same-sex couples sued Vermont for denying them marriage licenses. *Baker v. State* differed from its predecessors, *Baehr* and *Brause*, in that organized litigators were involved in the case from the outset. The three couples were represented by Susan Murray and Beth Robinson, two private lawyers with long-standing interest and involvement in gay rights concerns. They were also represented by Mary Bonauto of the Boston-based gay rights law firm GLAD. *Baker* was a product of extended discussions among the legal staffs of all the major gay rights litigation organizations. The Marriage Project and the Litigators' Roundtable, both hosted by Lambda, provided a forum for these discussions.

Much had changed in the six years since *Baehr* was initiated. The dissension about the merits of pursuing same-sex marriage had all but disappeared. The major groups all agreed that the time was right to push the legal envelope still further by bringing a same-sex marriage suit in a state with a relatively friendly attitude toward gay rights.[25] When Robinson and Murray presented them with the opportunity to bring a suit in Vermont, organized gay rights litigators were happy to get on board.[26] Vermont seemed a fine choice. Its courts had a track record of openness to gay rights claims. By way of illustration, its supreme court was the first in the nation to approve a second-parent adoption by a same-sex couple.[27] The court also had a track record of reading Vermont's equal protection clause more expansively than the federal equal protection clause. In addition, the Vermont Constitution contained an unusual provision called the Common Benefits Clause, which the courts had construed to mean that benefits provided by the state had to be made available to all citizens.[28] Organized gay rights litigators hoped that the combination of these three factors would produce a decision upholding the right of same-sex couples to marry.

Baker's initial foray into the courts was unsuccessful. The trial court dismissed the case late in 1997, finding that the state's interest in promoting "the link between procreation and child rearing" constituted a sufficient reason for banning same-sex marriage.[29] On appeal, however, the Vermont Supreme Court disagreed with the lower court's ruling. In its December 20, 1999, decision, the court unanimously ruled that Vermont's differential treatment of same-sex and opposite-sex couples violated the Common Benefits Clause of the state's constitution.

Unlike the Hawaii Supreme Court in *Baehr*, the *Baker* court did not remand the case for a trial to determine whether the state had adequate justification for discriminating against same-sex couples.[30] Instead it drew on oral arguments and the evidence contained in the numerous briefs submitted both by the parties and by a slew of amici curiae[31] to determine that the ban on same-sex marriage was irrational. Said the court, "The extension of the Common Benefits Clause to acknowledge plaintiffs as Vermonters who seek nothing more, nothing less, than legal protection and security for their avowed commitment to an intimate and lasting human relationship is simply, when all is said and done, a recognition of our common humanity" (*Baker*, 889).

Notwithstanding its finding that Vermont's refusal to allow same-sex marriages was unconstitutional, the supreme court did not order the state to start issuing marriage licenses immediately. Instead it ordered the legislature to come up with a way—whether through the extension of marriage or the creation of a different institution—to give same-sex couples all the benefits and protections that Vermont provided to married couples.[32]

The legislature's reaction was swift. The same day the decision came down, the speaker of the Vermont House of Representatives, Michael Obuchowski, polled his colleagues about their reaction to the ruling. Given three real options—extending marriage, creating a new "marriage-like" status, or attempting to circumvent the high court's ruling—the representatives polled that day largely felt that instituting some sort of domestic partnership was the most likely alternative (Lisberg and Remsen 1999). And although legislative proposals ultimately ran the gamut from legalizing same-sex marriage to adding a mini-DOMA provision to the constitution to impeaching the Vermont Supreme Court, initial predictions turned out to be correct. Four months after *Baker* was handed down, the legislature passed the Civil Unions Act[33] and Governor Howard Dean signed it into law. It became effective on July 1, 2000.

The creation of civil unions was in many ways a major victory for gay rights. Under the act, same-sex partners entering into civil union are treated as the functional equivalent of heterosexual spouses insofar as Vermont law is concerned. Nonetheless, civil unions still fall far short of marriage. The Civil Unions Act itself distinguishes civil unions from marriage, which it defines as "the legally recognized union of one man and one woman." More important is the fact that the establishment of a civil union does not entitle a couple to any of the rights and benefits that result from marriage under *federal* law. This has led to some bizarre results. For example, the members of a couple in a civil union are "married" for the purposes of filing state income tax forms in Vermont but are single for the purposes of filing federal income tax forms. Civil unions also fall short of marriage in that they are not transportable from state to state.[34] This too leads to bizarre results, not the least of which is that a couple joined in civil union are each other's legal next of kin in Vermont but are legal strangers in other states.[35]

Like *Baehr*, *Baker*'s impact also extended beyond its state's borders. Supporters of same-sex marriage seized on *Baker* and the civil union law it prompted as mobilizing agents. Every major gay rights organization issued press releases lauding both events. Recognizing that lgb couples might react to Vermont's law by filing same-sex marriage suits in their own states, Lambda, GLAD, the ACLU, and the NCLR also took the unusual action of jointly issuing a pamphlet that explained the requirements, benefits, and limitations of civil unions and attempted to channel the activism of lgb people.

This is a thrilling victory—and undoubtedly the beginning of a new era, but there's a need for patience, planning and strategic thinking in the work ahead for all of us. We are in a long term civil rights struggle. There is no quick fix for the discrimination we will encounter. The struggle to gain acceptance and to dismantle the legal regime erected against our families will take time.

Legal advocates do not recommend that lawsuits be filed in most instances of discrimination. We must proceed collectively and carefully, moving forward the best cases in the best places at the best times. The organizations listed below, in partnership with local lawyers, are happy to talk about the kinds of problems you are facing so that we can position ourselves with those few cases which will best move us forward toward full citizenship and equality.

There are valuable roles to play apart from litigation. The discrimination you face can be turned into a valuable educational tool when you share that experience with your community and with policy makers. We all need to talk with our elected leaders as well as our neighbors to persuade them that recognizing the "common humanity" of gay people (as the Vermont Supreme Court put it) and same-sex families is fair, necessary for strong families, valuable for communities and solid public policy. Join us in our collective work to win the Freedom to Marry, recognition and protection of all families, and full equality under law.[36]

Opponents of same-sex marriage also seized on *Baker* and civil unions as mobilizing agents. As with *Baehr,* opponents were somewhat more successful on the political front than were supporters of same-sex marriage. Four additional states passed mini-DOMAs in 2000; references to *Baker* and/or civil unions were commonly part of legislative debates on the issue. That Vermont played an important role in the passage of these laws is particularly obvious in Nebraska's case. On November 3, 2000, voters in that state amended their constitution to reserve marriage to opposite-sex couples and to prohibit the state from recognizing marriages, civil unions, domestic partnerships, or "other same-sex relationships" contracted in another state.[37]

In sum, *Baker* was similar to *Baehr* in that it was neither a clear win nor a clear loss for gay rights advocates. Consistent with the expectations of an LOS perspective, favorable legal decisions in both states produced opportunities for sociolegal change rather than sociolegal change itself.

Where *Baker* differed from *Baehr*—and from *Brause*—of course, is in the real-world outcome it inspired. Although all three cases produced rulings that favored the expansion of marriage to include same-sex couples, Vermont, Hawaii, and Alaska forged very different public policies in response to those rulings. A separate-but-equal system was put into place in Vermont. A limited set of benefits was extended to same-sex couples in Hawaii, but the power to define marriage was also removed from the state's judiciary and vested in its legislature. A constitutional amendment banning same-sex marriages was implemented in Alaska.

In the following pages I consider the question of why Vermont reacted more favorably than Hawaii or Alaska to the prospect of treating same-sex relationships as equal to opposite-sex ones. My core contention is that, although the decisions in the three states were reasonably similar, they created dissimilar opportunities for action because of differences in each state's LOS and POS.

Differences in the LOS and POS in Hawaii, Alaska, and Vermont

In his seminal article on the radiating impact of courts, Marc Galanter (1983, 136) argued that "the messages disseminated by courts do not carry endowments or produce effects excepts as they are received, interpreted, and used by (potential) actors. Therefore, the meaning of judicial signals is dependent on the information, experience, skill, and resources that disputants bring to them." LOS theory would suggest, however, that the value of any particular opportunity is more than just a function of the actors' information and ability. It is also dependent on other institutional and sociolegal factors, such as access to the formal institutional structure of the law, existing legal and cultural frames, and the configuration of elite alignments. Similar judicial signals, in other words, may create dissimilar opportunities for a particular set of disputants because of systematic differences in the political and legal opportunity structures in which those signals reverberate. As I will show, the signals sent by *Baehr, Brause,* and *Baker* played out in very different contexts.

Configuration of Judicial Elites and Legal Framing of Same-Sex Marriage

I have referred to the decisions in *Baehr, Brause,* and *Baker* as being reasonably similar in that the courts in all three cases ruled that same-sex couples had a constitutional interest in being able to marry one another. It is important to recognize, however, that the three cases were at different stages of completion when the legislatures stepped in.

The Alaska case was at the earliest stage of litigation when it was preempted by the legislature. A lower court judge had denied a motion to dismiss the case, ruling that the litigants had raised a valid legal question and that the state would be required to demonstrate a compelling purpose for its prohibition of same-sex marriage at trial. Because no final decision had been handed down, the Alaska legislature could act without directly challenging the court. Its action was preventative rather than curative. The Hawaii legislature was likewise able to act before a final decision about the constitutionality of prohibiting same-sex marriage was handed down, and so its actions were also preventative rather than curative.

The Vermont legislature, in contrast, was faced with a fait accompli. The Vermont Supreme Court ordered it to develop a mechanism whereby same-sex couples would receive all the state-level benefits and protections already provided to married couples. The court also informed the legislature that it would retain jurisdiction in the case. If the legislature did not enact implementing legislation within "a reasonable period of time," it said, the court might reopen the case, this time mandating the institution of same-sex marriage. By its actions, the Vermont Supreme Court put the legislature in the position of either supporting same-sex partnerships (of some sort) or precipitating a constitutional crisis. In effect, the stakes were much higher for the Vermont legislature than they were for its counterparts in Hawaii and Alaska.

That the cases were at different stages of completion was at least partly a function of the judges deciding them. The Alaska case was just in its initial stages, of course, but the Hawaii and Vermont suits had reached their state courts of last resort. The pace of response to these two suits differed markedly. The Hawaii Supreme Court, for reasons as yet unknown, sat on the case for nearly three years. It received the case early in 1997 and, based on its prior history of handing down decisions, was widely expected to issue a ruling within twelve to eighteen months. Yet the *Baehr* court did not issue its final ruling—vacating the lower court decision in light of the 1998 constitutional amendment—until December 1999. One likely explanation for the high court's actions is that it deliberately chose to await the outcome of the ballot measure before issuing its ruling, perhaps to guard its legitimacy.

In contrast to the slow and measured pace of the Hawaii Supreme

Court—deciding initially that a compelling state purpose was necessary to sustain the ban on same-sex marriage, remanding the case for a trial on the merits, and then holding on to the case for years—the Vermont Supreme Court acted in a relatively quick and decisive manner. Although it deliberated the case for some eighteen months, the ruling it ultimately issued was final. While the Hawaii Supreme Court's actions may have been strategic, the Vermont Supreme Court's actions certainly were. The majority opinion by Chief Justice Amestoy makes the strategic element of the *Baker* ruling clear. In response to Justice Johnson's dissenting opinion, which argued that the Vermont high court should mandate same-sex marriage, Amestoy wrote the following.

> Our colleague greatly underestimates what we decide today and *greatly overestimates the simplicity and effectiveness* of her proposed mandate. First, our opinion provides greater recognition of—and protection for—same sex relationships than has been recognized by any court of final jurisdiction in this country with the instructive exception of the Hawaii Supreme Court in *Baehr.* Second, the dissent's suggestion that her mandate would avoid the "political caldron" of public debate is—even allowing for the welcome lack of political sophistication of the judiciary—*significantly insulated from reality.* (*Baker,* 888, citations omitted; emphasis added)

As evidence for his assertion, Amestoy cited the constitutional amendments in Hawaii and Alaska that overturned court decisions favoring same-sex marriage. Clearly, Amestoy was cognizant of the political backlash that the Vermont decision might provoke and was attempting to defuse it by requiring the extension of marriage rights rather than marriage itself to same-sex couples.

In sum, the decisions in *Baehr, Brause,* and *Baker,* while all recognizing the constitutional interest of same-sex couples in marrying, presented different signals to their respective legislatures. The stakes were higher for the Vermont legislature than for the Hawaii and Alaska legislatures because of the finality of the decision and because of the legal frame established by it. Yet this difference in signaling is insufficient, standing alone, to account for the very different ways in which the three cases were translated into public policy. The Vermont legislature could have started the process of constitutional amendment notwithstanding *Baker.* Indeed, attempts were made. And the legislatures in Hawaii and Alaska were certainly not required to put proposed constitutional amendments on the ballot in their states. Something more was going on. We turn next to an examination of the amendment process.

Access to the Formal Institutional Structure of the Law

Polls conducted in Vermont, Hawaii, and Alaska shortly after the decisions in *Baker, Baehr,* and *Brause* came down indicated a deep split in public opinion about the propriety of same-sex marriage. For example, a poll conducted by the *Rutland Herald, Times Argus,* and WCAX-TV in January 2000 found that only 38 percent of respondents agreed with the decision in *Baker* and that less than 15 percent thought that marriage should be extended to same-sex couples (Graff 2000). A similar poll conducted by the *Honolulu Star-Bulletin* in January 1994 found that nearly three out of five Hawaiians opposed same-sex marriage (Essoyan 1994). A pair of public opinion surveys conducted in Alaska in the immediate aftermath of *Brause* presented somewhat divergent findings: one poll found that about two-thirds of the Alaskans surveyed favored an amendment banning same-sex marriage, while the other found that only about one-half of the surveyed group favored such an amendment (Rinehart 1998).

While the majority of people in all three states apparently favored a continued ban on same-sex marriage, the ability of antigay activists to tap into the process of citizen lawmaking varied across state lines. In both Hawaii and Alaska, opponents of same-sex marriage had relatively easy access to an important institutional mechanism for lawmaking, namely, constitutional amendment. In Vermont, however, access was much more difficult. A comparison of amendment procedures illustrates the differences among the three states.

The amendment process in Alaska and Hawaii is quite similar. In both states, a two-thirds majority vote in both legislative houses authorizes placement of a constitutional amendment on the ballot.[38] In Alaska, the vote occurs at the next regularly scheduled general election.[39] In Hawaii, the vote takes place at the next congressional election (every even year).[40] The procedure for amending Vermont's constitution is more cumbersome. The amendment must first pass the senate with a two-thirds vote. It must then pass the house by a simple majority. At that point, the houses must recommend the constitutional amendment for action by the *next* session of the legislature. Then both houses must approve the amendment again, this time by a simple majority vote. The amendment is then placed on the ballot for ratification by the people. It becomes law if it garners a simple majority of the popular vote.[41]

The relative ease of amending the constitution allowed opponents in Alaska to capitalize on people's initial discomfort with the superior court's ruling in *Brause* to counteract it. The court issued its ruling late in February 1998. Within three months, the legislature had okayed a proposed anti-same-sex marriage amendment, allowing it to be put before voters that same year. Similar action by the Hawaii legislature in 1997 put a proposed amendment on the 1998 ballot (the next congressional election year).

The constitutional amendment strategy was less feasible for same-sex marriage opponents in Vermont because of the length of time and number of hurdles required to change the constitution. An amendment initially proposed by the legislature in 2000 could not make it onto the ballot until 2003 at the earliest, assuming that four different legislative bodies approved it (two votes in the house and two in the senate). This is not to say that opponents could not have chosen to pursue an amendment strategy. Indeed, attempts were made. But in Vermont the onerous amendment procedures, together with factors such as the configuration of political and judicial elites and existing sociolegal frames, made preempting the court's ruling through citizen lawmaking much more difficult than in either Hawaii or Alaska.

This was not accidental. According to my interviews with members of Lambda's staff and other key players in the fight for same-sex marriage, a major reason Vermont was considered a good location in which to file a same-sex marriage suit was the relative difficulty of amending its constitution. Gay rights advocates were cognizant that, just as with antigay initiatives, courts of public opinion were likely to be less favorable to their goals than were courts of law. In the aftermath of the federal DOMA and its state-level counterparts, organized same-sex marriage activists were eager to avoid ballot-box battles on the subject of marriage if they could. The formal institutional structure of Vermont law, they reasoned, would mitigate the chance that favorable courtroom decisions would be erased through constitutional amendment.

Of course, legislators intent on subverting *Baker*'s intent could have started the amendment ball rolling despite the procedural hurdles, just as legislators intent on honoring *Baehr* or *Brause* could have refused to initiate the amendment process. The difference in the ultimate impact of the three court decisions was obviously dependent on the actions of lawmakers as well as the structure of the lawmaking process. We turn to the set of elite political alignments in Alaska, Hawaii, and Vermont next.

Configuration of Political Elites and Cultural Framing of Gay Rights

Differences in the opportunities provided by *Baehr, Brause,* and *Baker* extended to the attitudes of state legislators and governors as well as the process of constitutional amendment. Quite obviously, lawmakers in Vermont were more open to the notion of granting equal marriage rights to same-sex couples than were lawmakers in Hawaii. Hawaiian lawmakers were in turn more open to gay rights claims than were their Alaskan counterparts.

Part of the reason for this difference was the partisan composition of the legislatures in the three states (the governors of all three states were Democrats). Historically, Democrats have been more favorable to gay rights claims than have Republicans (see Button, Rienzo, and Wald 1997; Hertzog 1996; Riggle and Tadlock 1999). Both houses of the relatively hostile Alaska legislature were controlled by Republicans, and the Republicans were much more likely than their Democratic counterparts to support the creation of a constitutional amendment banning same-sex marriage. (In fact, the vote in the senate broke down along strict party lines: the fourteen Republicans voted to authorize the amendment while the six Democrats voted against it.) The relatively more tolerant legislatures of Hawaii and Vermont, in contrast, were controlled by Democrats. Republicans in these states were also more likely than Democrats to oppose extending the rights associated with marriage to same-sex couples, although the relationship between partisan affiliation and support for same-sex marriage was far from perfect.

Moving beyond partisanship per se, the attitudes of the political elites in the legislatures and executive branches of the three states were particularly important in structuring the contours of the opportunities presented by *Brause, Baehr,* and *Baker*. Legislatures are complex, hierarchical structures. Each house is presided over by the leader of whichever party has the most seats. This elite actor, variously referred to as the majority leader or the speaker, has significant agenda-setting capacities, usually including the determination of whether and when a particular bill will be discussed and voted upon. Committee chairs are also elite political actors, albeit with a smaller portfolio. As a rule, bills introduced into a legislature are referred to one or more appropriate committees, which are composed of a subset of the members of the entire body. Bills must make it through committee before they can be voted on by the body of the legislature as a whole (called voting "on the floor"). Like majority leaders, committee chairs have significant agenda-setting functions, which often include the scheduling of committee bills for consideration.

The house and senate majority leaders in Alaska were singularly opposed to the superior court's ruling in *Brause,* as were the relevant committee chairs in both bodies and the governor. By way of illustration, on the first business day after *Brause* was handed down, the senate majority leader, Robin Taylor, announced the introduction of a bill authorizing a constitutional amendment to ban same-sex marriage and issued the following statement.

> [I]t is apparent that our Judiciary needs further clarification on fundamental values. Marriage has been the foundation of civiliza-tion for thousands of years and in cultures around the world. Mar-riage is the most important social institution in our society. The state has a . . . principal interest in preserving and protecting the special status of marriage, regardless of religious beliefs. (Quoted in Clarkson, Coolidge, and Duncan 1999, 227)

Political elites in Hawaii, however, were more mixed in their reactions to the court rulings in *Baehr.* Democratic governor Ben Cayetano announced his opposition to the notion of same-sex marriage early on. Democratic speaker of the house Joe Souki announced that in reaction to the December 1996 trial court ruling in *Baehr* he would push for two measures: a constitutional amendment to circumvent the court's decision and a domestic partnership bill giving same-sex couples some of the rights and responsibilities traditionally associated with marriage (see Eskridge 2002, 23). The judiciary committee and the rank-and-file mem-bers of the house acquiesced to both requests. Within a few weeks the house passed one bill authorizing a constitutional amendment to ban same-sex marriage and another bill providing a limited set of benefits to "reciprocal beneficiaries," which the house defined as including couples who were excluded by law from marriage, whether because they were of the same sex or because, like a mother and son, they were too closely related to each other.

The senate, which had passed a reasonably comprehensive domestic partnership bill the year before only to see it fail to progress in the house, balked at the house's language. As Art Leonard (1997) reported in *Lesbian/Gay Law Notes*, several senators in key committee positions were adamantly opposed to a constitutional amendment banning same-sex marriage and were supportive of a broad array of domestic partnership benefits for same-sex couples. They refused to allow consideration of any proposals to ban same-sex marriage outright. This effectively killed the house's legislation.

The senate then passed a very different pair of bills. One was a "life partnership" bill similar in scope to Vermont's civil union law. The other was a proposed constitutional amendment that allowed the state to reserve marriage to opposite-sex couples, so long as "the application of this reservation does not deprive any person of civil rights on the basis of sex." This measure was clearly symbolic rather than court evading, given that the *Baehr* court had already ruled that banning same-sex marriage constituted sex discrimination under Hawaii's constitution.

In any event, the split in elite alignments between the house and the senate forced the creation of a conference committee to attempt to reconcile the two bills. Lambda and other advocates of same-sex marriage hoped that the divide between the chambers was too great to allow an acceptable compromise to be reached. They were sorely disappointed when, after two months of negotiations, a consensus emerged. First, the committee suggested placing a constitutional measure on the 1998 ballot "to clarify that the legislature has the power to reserve marriage to opposite sex couples." This language was clearly intended to circumvent *Baehr* in a way that the senate's original was not, but it was less harsh than the house's version in that it allowed—but did not require—the prohibition of same-sex marriages. Second, the conference committee suggested the enactment of a "reciprocal beneficiaries" measure, defining it as the house did but expanding the number of benefits its conferred. As noted previously, the final measure accorded reciprocal beneficiaries about 60 of the more than 160 state-level benefits accorded to married couples. These benefits included medical decision-making and inheritance rights as well as access to employee health benefits (although that provision lapsed in 1999) but excluded any benefits related to taxation as well as adoption and custody rights.

As noted in the March 1997 edition of *Lesbian/Gay Law Notes*, the scheduling of the votes on the two measures suggested that senate leaders were holding the proposed constitutional amendment "hostage" to the successful legislative passage of and gubernatorial acquiescence to the reciprocal beneficiaries measure. (This tactic led to some unusual lobbying efforts: some of the most vocal opponents of same-sex marriage found themselves lobbying for passage of the reciprocal beneficiaries measure in order to get the proposed constitutional amendment on the ballot!) In the end, both measures were passed.

The reactions of political elites in Vermont differed in some key respects from the reactions of political elites in Hawaii and Alaska. Most notably, they were more deferential to the judiciary's judgment. All of the major institutional players—the governor, the majority leaders in the house and senate, and the chairs of the house and senate judiciary committees—accepted the *Baker* ruling as a mandate to rectify the unequal treatment of opposite- and same-sex couples. Governor Howard Dean, for example, praised the supreme court for its flexibility in allowing the legislature to craft a solution to the unequal treatment of same-sex couples even though he also stated his opposition to same-sex marriage. He announced that he would favor the establishment of a parallel institution in accord with the supreme court's requirements.[42] Other political elites were even more supportive of the Vermont Supreme Court's decision. Speaker of the House Michael Obuchowski, for instance, argued that the most appropriate response to the logic of *Baker* was to open marriage to same-sex couples. Lieutenant Governor Doug Racine echoed Obuchowski's sentiment.

The attitudes of key legislative actors structured much of the legislative debate over the *Baker* ruling. Most obviously, the chairs of both the house and senate judiciary committees refused to schedule hearings or votes on several bills designed to circumvent the supreme court's decision, including proposals to impeach the members of the high court and proposals to amend the state's constitution to prohibit same-sex marriages. More subtly, the attitudes of legislative leaders influenced the context in which *Baker*'s directive was evaluated. The hearings chaired by Thomas Little, the Republican chair of the house judiciary committee, are illustrative.

In an interview with William Eskridge (2002, 58), Little explained that his preferences about the appropriate legislative reaction to *Baker* were not fully formed when the judiciary committee received the issue to study but that he felt it was important to build consensus and avoid divisiveness on the issue of same-sex marriage. To that end, he scheduled twenty-nine days of hearings on the subject, soliciting a wide range of legal, academic, social, and religious viewpoints. The committee—which was composed of five Republicans, five Democrats, and one Progressive—ultimately decided that the Vermont General Assembly should respond to *Baker*'s mandate by creating a separate-but-equal institution to be known as civil unions. The most striking feature of the 8–3 vote was that not a single member wanted to circumvent the high court's decision. The three dissenters, in fact, felt that the committee had not gone far enough and that it should have pushed for same-sex marriage.[43]

This is not to say that the Vermont legislature was unanimous in its deference to the supreme court's ruling in *Baker*. A number of legislators were staunchly opposed to giving same-sex relationships the imprimatur of official sanction. And ultimately, the house vote was close: the Civil Unions Act was passed by a margin of 76–69.[44] It seems reasonable, though, to suggest that the attitudes and tactics of political elites in Vermont played a significant role in shaping the political system's response to a change in the structure of legal opportunities.

Certainly Beth Robinson and Susan Murray, the Vermont lawyers who initiated *Baker v. State* in conjunction with GLAD, thought so. They spent a full two years lobbying key legislators and engaging in other forms of political activism around same-sex marriage prior to filing a lawsuit. In fact, they turned down the opportunity to bring suit in 1995, believing that the political climate was not yet conducive to extending marriage rights to lesbian and gay couples.[45] Their primary vehicle for activism was the Vermont Freedom to Marry Task Force, which they helped form in 1995. The task force developed in reaction to the 1993 decision in *Baehr* and the early legislative backlash it provoked and explicitly drew on the rubric set forth by Lambda when it established the Marriage Project.

In this respect, the tactics of gay rights activists differed markedly in Vermont, Hawaii, and Alaska. Hawaii's *Baehr* was brought prior to any local political organizing around same-sex marriage. Such organizing only began after the 1993 decision, when the Hawaii legislature moved to amend the marriage statute to explicitly require opposite-sex couples. Recall as well that none of the national legal and political gay rights groups began mobilizing behind same-sex marriage until after the 1993 decision. And although Lambda recognized that *Baehr* was likely to stimulate a political backlash, most pro-same-sex marriage activism in Hawaii and around the nation was defensive in posture, as lgb activists tried to stymie attempts to enact mini-DOMAs.

Political activism in Alaska on behalf of same-sex marriage was likewise defensive. *Brause* was not litigated as part of a holistic effort to effect sociolegal change in Alaska. It was brought by a single gay male couple and a private lawyer. Gay rights activists in Alaska largely became aware of the litigation only after the trial court had issued its decision and they had to scramble to try to deflect a political backlash.

While it seems reasonable to assume that the energy expended by gay rights activists in Vermont to lay the political groundwork for same-sex marriage paid dividends, it is important to recognize that the political terrain was somewhat more fertile in Vermont than in Hawaii or Alaska. Prior to 1998, all three states were considered to have relatively tolerant attitudes toward lgb people. Their legislatures were among the earliest to decriminalize sodomy, Hawaii's in 1972, Vermont's in 1977, and Alaska's in 1978. And none of them had what Bill Eskridge (1999) refers to as "no promo homo" laws, that is, laws designed to ensure that sex and AIDS education did not treat homosexual behavior as acceptable.

On the track of political acceptance of gay rights claims, however, Vermont and Hawaii outpaced Alaska. Alaska had not enacted a statewide gay rights law prior to the filing of a same-sex marriage lawsuit. Vermont and Hawaii had. In fact, they were among the earliest states to do so. Vermont's law was enacted in 1991 and was comprehensive in scope, protecting lesbians and gay men from discrimination in public and private employment, public accommodations, education, housing, credit, and union practices. Hawaii's law, passed in 1991, was more limited than Vermont's, prohibiting antigay discrimination only in public and private employment. These laws reflected different political cultures; they also reflected the varying electoral influence of lgb people. Lgb people have typically played a much smaller role in Alaskan elections than they have in elections in Hawaii and Vermont, where they constitute a not insignificant constituency for Democrats and, in the case of Vermont, Progressives.

In sum, the attitudes of political elites about same-sex marriage and the history of political acceptance of gay rights claims differed quite a bit in Alaska, Hawaii, and Vermont. The Alaska legislature was controlled by Republicans who were staunchly opposed to granting marriage, or any of its attendant rights, to same-sex couples. Even less controversial rights, such as the right to be free from sexual orientation discrimination in employment or public housing, had not yet been enacted in Alaska. Gay rights activists had done no political groundwork to soften up the legislature or the public with respect to same-sex marriage, and the lgb community played only a small role in electoral politics.

The political situation in Hawaii was somewhat more amenable to the notion of treating same-sex relationships as the legal equivalent of opposite-sex ones. The legislature was controlled by Democrats, but there was a fissure between the house and senate leadership concerning the desirability of same-sex marriage and/or domestic partnerships. The house was much more hostile than the senate to extending marriage-like rights to same-sex couples, and this split forced a compromise. Although political groundwork concerning same-sex marriage had not been done prior to *Baehr*, the Hawaii legislature had passed a limited statewide gay rights law already, and the lgb community played a significant role in the Democratic electoral coalition.

The political situation in Vermont was more favorable still to the interests of those seeking to equalize the legal footing of same-sex and opposite-sex relationships. The legislature was, like Hawaii's, controlled by Democrats, but the leadership was much more consistently favorable to the prospect of extending marriage rights to same-sex couples. Activists had been working on this issue for years, building support both at the grassroots level and in the general assembly. And finally, Vermont was among the most progressive states in terms of its gay rights legislation, and the lgb community was actively involved in electoral politics.

Conclusion

This chapter has used the issue of same-sex marriage to explore the effects of legal decisions on the real lives of lgb people.[46] As it has shown, "wins" in court do not translate simplistically into preferred public policy outcomes. In the case of Alaska, victory in the courtroom arguably damaged the sociolegal position of lgb people in the state; a prohibition on same-sex marriages is now enshrined into the state's constitution. Nothing short of a new constitutional amendment or a determination that Alaska's constitution violates the U.S. Constitution will remove it. This is a much higher hurdle to jump than the one same-sex couples faced prior to the litigation of *Brause*. In the case of Vermont, victory in the courtroom appears to have advanced the sociolegal status of lgb people in the state, albeit not as much as gay rights advocates had hoped. While same-sex couples cannot marry, they can enter into a civil union, which gives them all the state-level rights and responsibilities accorded to married couples.

In the case of Hawaii, victory in the courtroom in 1993 and in 1996 seems to have precipitated numerous shifts in public policy, several favorable to the interests of same-sex couples and several unfavorable to those interests. Same-sex Hawaiian couples may now become reciprocal beneficiaries, as may opposite-sex pairs who are not legally permitted to marry. This accords them some important state-level benefits that they did not have prior to *Baehr*, although far fewer than those accorded to married couples. Hawaii's constitution now also contains an amendment allowing the legislature to reserve marriage to opposite-sex couples. Beyond Hawaii, *Baehr* inspired the passage of the federal DOMA and thirty-five state mini-DOMAs, which have placed significant new hurdles in the path of same-sex couples seeking to marry.

The notion that courtroom "wins" do not translate simplistically into favorable public policy is a vein that has been mined by other scholars (see especially McCann 1994; Rosenberg 1991). What I offer in this chapter is a way to conceptualize the relationship between legal decisions and public policy. Specifically, I argue that it is useful to think of legal decisions as creating moments of opportunity for a wide range of legal and political actors operating within specific legal and political contexts. Viewing legal decisions in this way offers a number of benefits. First, it highlights the fact that the process of legal reform is not autonomous but rather contingent on the interaction of a variety of institutional, cultural, and strategic factors. Thus similar legal decisions can be translated into very different public policies because of differences in the strategic choices made by various actors and/or differences in the specific legal and political contexts in which those decisions are interpreted. In the context of same-sex marriage, these differences included the available legal and cultural frames, the configuration of political and legal elites, and access to the formal institutional structure of the law.

Second, viewing legal decisions this way privileges neither structural nor behavioral analyses of legal reform. Instead it encourages us to examine the relationship between actors and the sociopolitical and legal institutions within which they operate. Third, it emphasizes the interdependence of law and politics. Legal decisions, after all, are commonly interpreted and implemented by political actors. This interdependence means that the opportunity created by shifts in the structure of legal opportunities is often mediated by the prevailing structure of political opportunities and vice versa.

Finally, viewing legal decisions as creating moments of opportunity bounded by the specific legal and political contexts in which they occur allows us to comprehend both the promise and the limitations of legal mobilization. The story of same-sex marriage litigation can be told in two different ways. From one perspective, seven people in Hawaii (the six plaintiffs and Dan Foley, their lawyer) started a revolution. By bringing a suit whose legal merits were convincing to the majority of the Hawaii Supreme Court, these seven individuals rocketed same-sex marriage to the center of the movement for gay rights. They fomented widespread change in the legal framing of same-sex marriage and inspired same-sex couples in other states, most notably Vermont, to stand up and assert their "right" to marry each other. They likewise fomented widespread change in the cultural framing of marriage by forcing the issue of same-sex marriage into mainstream consciousness. Prior to *Baehr*, the issue of same-sex marriage remained confined to the gay and lesbian press. Since 1993, however, the subject has been covered by every major U.S. newspaper and newsmagazine, particularly within the past few years. In addition, a number of highly rated television shows have dealt with the topic in recent years.[47] Moreover, these depictions have generally been sympathetic.

That cultural frames have begun to shift is also suggested by public opinion data. Well over half of the American population continues to oppose same-sex marriage, but the numbers are beginning to fall. Polling by Princeton Survey Research Associates, for example, shows about a five-point increase in the percentage of Americans favoring legally sanctioned same-sex marriages in the years between 1994 and 1998. Polling by Yankelovich Partners reveals a six-point increase in the years between 1989 and 1998. Polling by Gallup between 1996 and 2000 shows a seven-point increase. These numbers are not substantial, but they do suggest that attitudes about same-sex marriage are beginning to soften.

Litigation and its aftermath also seem to have provoked religious groups around the nation to seriously consider the subject of same-sex marriage. Although many denominations have issued statements opposing the right of same-sex couples to marry, others have proclaimed their support.[48] Many churches and synagogues across the nation now perform religious ceremonies for same-sex couples, often referred to as holy unions. It is important to note that this movement in religious attitudes toward same-sex marriage followed rather than preceded *Baehr*. It is at least plausible to suggest that these changes are a by-product of same-sex marriage litigation and the public conversation it engendered.

The story of same-sex marriage litigation can also be viewed in a dimmer light. From this perspective, winning legal concessions in a politically hostile environment may be less than useless; it may be actively harmful to a social movement's sociolegal goals. As many scholars have noted, there is often a substantial gap between the promises of legal reform and its actual impact (see especially Canon and Johnson 1999; Horowitz 1977;

Rosenberg 1991). The most common reasons cited for this gap are the lack of enforcement power of the courts and its lack of independence from the other branches. This was certainly the case in Alaska, Hawaii, and Vermont. In all three states, the legislatures were able to take legal decisions and refashion them to their liking. Scholars have also noted the not insubstantial costs of litigating and have suggested that litigation competes with, and diverts resources from, other potentially more useful forms of activism (see McCann 1986; Rosenberg 1991; Scheingold 1974). This has certainly been the case with litigation over same-sex marriage. Gay rights activists across the nation were forced to devote their energies and resources to the struggle for same-sex marriage in the aftermath of *Baehr,* if only to attempt to deflect political backlash. *Baehr,* in effect, forced the larger movement for gay rights to fight a battle it had not chosen and exacted a great political cost: the passage of marriage defense acts in Congress and thirty-five states.

My point here is not to draw conclusions about the wisdom of pursuing same-sex marriage through the courts. It is simply to claim that viewing legal decisions as creating moments of opportunity bounded by the specific legal and political contexts in which they occur allows us to examine both the promise and the limitations of mobilizing the law on behalf of sociolegal goals. In the concluding chapter, I examine this subject further.

EIGHT

LOS and Legal Change

The sociolegal implications of homosexuality have changed enormously in the thirty-five some years since Stonewall. In 1969, every state in the nation but one criminalized same-sex sexual intimacy. Police regularly harassed the patrons of gay bars. Gay rights laws were nonexistent; lgb people had little recourse against discrimination in employment, public accommodations, and other areas of central importance to daily life. Individuals known or suspected to be homosexual were commonly given dishonorable discharges from the military. Openly gay parents lived in constant fear of losing custody of their children. The notion that same-sex couples might have a constitutional interest in marrying each other was not even a blip on the public policy radar.

By the middle of 2003, the legal status of lgb people had radically altered. The U.S. Supreme Court had held sodomy laws to be an unconstitutional invasion of the right of privacy. Thirteen states had implemented reasonably comprehensive gay rights laws, while eight additional states had passed more limited gay rights measures. Hundreds of localities had instituted similar provisions. Lgb people were officially permitted to serve in the military, so long as their sexual orientation was not revealed publicly. Those whose sexuality became known were entitled to honorable, rather than dishonorable, discharges. Judicial reactions to parental homosexuality had become far more tolerant. Although some courts still considered parental homosexuality to be harmful to children, many more considered it to be irrelevant. Joint adoptions by same-sex couples were permitted in a growing handful of states. Courts in three different states had ruled that same-sex couples had a constitutional interest in marrying each other, and courts in four additional states were considering the question.[1] A civil union law had gone into effect in Vermont, giving same-sex couples all the state-level rights and benefits associated with marriage. And following an Ontario court's ruling that same-sex couples had the right to marry, Canada had announced its intention to legalize same-sex marriage throughout the nation. Canada's policy change was of more than theoretical interest to same-sex couples in

America since Canadian law does not limit marriage to Canadian residents; within a few months of the Ontario court ruling dozens of American couples had married in Canada and then returned to the United States, although the status of their marriages under U.S. law remains unclear.

This book has endeavored to understand the role litigation has played in changing the sociolegal implications of homosexuality. More specifically, it has attempted to grapple with a specific puzzle: the varying ability of Lambda and other gay rights litigators to mobilize the law on behalf of gay rights. In this concluding chapter, I draw together some of the major strands of my analysis and consider some of its implications for the study of legal mobilization and legal change.

Litigation and LOS

The core claim of this book has been that the concept of *legal opportunity structure* can help us to understand the emergence, progress, and outcomes of Lambda's gay rights litigation. Specifically, I argued that Lambda's decisions about what kinds of cases to pursue, the tactics it used in pursuing those cases, and their ultimate legal outcomes were dependent in large part on the contours of the legal opportunity structure surrounding gay rights. I articulated several distinct dimensions of legal opportunity structure, namely, Lambda's ability to gain access to the formal apparatus of the law with respect to a specific claim, the configuration of power among decision makers with respect to that claim, the nature of the alliance and conflict systems surrounding that claim, and the availability of relevant legal and cultural frames. Let us take a closer look at each of those dimensions.

Access

Scholars utilizing the concept of political opportunity structure have been unanimous in their estimation of the importance of access to the formal institutional structure of the political system in shaping the emergence, progress, and outcomes of collective action. I have shown that access to the formal institutional structure of the law plays a similarly important role in shaping the emergence, progress, and outcomes of legal action. The primary institutional locus of the law examined in this book has been the courtroom. As have many other social movements, the gay rights movement has encompassed myriad sociolegal claims, and some of those claims have fit more comfortably into the mechanics of the judicial process than have others. Lambda and its colleagues had little problem getting access to the courts to battle antigay ballot measures, for example, but had much greater difficulty getting access to the courts to fight sodomy laws. For the purpose of access, the key difference between the two types of claims involved the nature of the harm alleged. While the harms caused by sodomy laws were very real, they were also largely indirect, and so gay rights litigators encountered persistent problems satisfying the legal requirement of standing, which mandates that someone be "directly harmed" by a law in order to be able to challenge its validity in court. The harms caused by an antigay ballot measure such as Amendment 2, conversely, were direct ones, ranging from the petty (discrimination by public libraries) to the profound (exclusion from the political process). Gay rights litigators thus had little problem meeting the standing requirement when challenging their constitutional validity. I showed that these variations in access had real repercussions for the ability of litigators to mobilize the law on behalf of gay rights claims. In *Bowers*, for example, the limited ability of gay right advocates to surmount the standing hurdle (Michael Hardwick had standing; the Does did not) allowed the Supreme Court to frame the issue before it as "homosexual sodomy" to the exclusion of "heterosexual sodomy." In *Romer*, however, access to the formal apparatus of the legal system allowed Lambda and its allies to reverse losses incurred in the electoral arena.

Access-related constraints vary across time as well as issue area. The primary generator of shifts in access over time is the passage of new ordinances, statutes, and constitutional amendments. A prime example here concerns employment. As a rule, gay rights litigators have been unable to use the courts to contest antigay discrimination in hiring and firing except in those jurisdictions with gay rights laws on the books, because, barring a specific statute to the contrary, it is perfectly legal for private actors to discriminate against lgb people on the basis of their sexuality. But as the number of states and localities with gay rights statutes and ordinances encompassing employment has risen, litigators have been increasingly able to use the courts to give those laws teeth.

The passage of new laws can thus expand access to the courts; it can also limit it. The widespread passage of mini-DOMAs in the aftermath of *Baehr* certainly impeded the ability of Lambda and other gay rights litigators to articulate claims amenable to judicial remedy, which, like the standing requirement, is a prerequisite for bringing suit in a court of law.

Similarly, Amendment 2 was as much about limiting the access of lgb people to the judicial process as it was about limiting access to the political process.

A second generator of shifts in access over time is the establishment of new case law. Chapter 2 detailed how the 1965 Supreme Court decision in *Griswold v. Connecticut* did more than hold that the Constitution embodied a right to privacy that encompassed the procreative decisions of married couples. It also anchored a line of decisions that expanded the right of privacy into other spheres of sex-related decision making, most notably abortion. The articulation of a right to privacy encompassing at least some aspects of sexuality in turn suggested a new legal theory for challenging sodomy laws that litigators could bring into court, namely, that sex between two consenting adults, when undertaken in private, should also properly be encompassed by the right to privacy.

Bowers v. Hardwick (1986) is another example of the ways in which new case law can affect the ability of social movement litigators to access the institutional mechanisms of the law. *Bowers* effectively foreclosed the federal court system as a route through which sodomy laws could be challenged, at least for the time being. Only after years of litigating sodomy laws under state constitutions did Lambda consider bringing another federal case, and its decision to do so was based in large part on the Supreme Court's decision in *Romer v. Evans*, which suggested that the high court might be receptive to another sodomy challenge.

A third generator of shifts in access over time is the evolution of cultural understandings about the relationship between social movement claims and the law. Early attempts to litigate same-sex marriage were all but laughed out of court for failure to state a cognizable legal claim (another prerequisite for bringing suit). Courts in recent years have been far more open to the claim that same-sex couples have a constitutional right to marry, less because the amalgam of laws pertaining to marriage has changed than because of changes in judicial understandings about the meaning and sociolegal implications of homosexuality. Similarly, the willingness of judges to accord lgb people standing to contest sodomy laws under state constitutions in the 1990s was partly a reflection of the different requirements for standing in federal and state courts but also partly a shift in judicial understandings of the ways in which sodomy laws stigmatize lgb people.

While courtrooms have played a major role in my analysis, it is important to recognize that they are not the only formal institutions of the law. The processes that shape the amending of constitutions and other forms of citizen lawmaking are also properly considered to be institutions. So are legislative processes. Issues of access likewise play an important role with respect to these institutions. Chapter 7 examined the ways in which variations in the ease of amending state constitutions shaped the ability of same-sex marriage opponents to use the amendment process to trump disfavored court rulings as well as the ways in which legislative decisions modified court rulings. Chapter 6 discussed how cross-state variations in the mechanics of the citizen lawmaking process sometimes facilitated and other times hampered the ability of antigay advocates to use referenda and initiatives to undermine perceived gay rights gains. The chapter also compared the citizen lawmaking process to the judicial process.

The dance of pro- and antigay advocates depicted in chapters 6 and 7 highlights the fact that access to the formal institutional structure of the law is an important variable for both movement and opposition actors. It also highlights the fact that the institutional structure of the law is decentralized and that its constituent elements are endowed with different entrance requirements. In some instances Lambda was able to use its access to the judicial system to trump or prevent citizen decision making. In others, oppositional forces used their access to citizen lawmaking processes to trump or prevent judicial decision making.

In sum, my examination of Lambda and its gay rights litigation indicates that variations in the organization's ability to access the formal institutional structure of the law played a significant role in shaping the contours and outcomes of its litigation docket and that changes in access-related constraints variously widened and narrowed its ability to mobilize the law on behalf of particular gay rights claims. My analysis also highlights the dialectical relationship between movements and oppositional forces and the ways that access to the formal institutional structure of the law variously privileges one sets of actors over the other. Finally, my examination suggests the importance of decentering courts, of viewing them as one of many potential locations for legal action.

Configuration of Power

Scholars of political opportunity structure have emphasized the importance of elite alignments in shaping the emergence, progress, and outcomes of collective action. I showed that the configuration of elite alignments also plays an important role in shaping the emergence, progress, and outcomes of legal action.

Specifically, I argued that judicial attitudes have colored decision making in gay rights cases and that these attitudes have varied systematically over time. For example, I argued that the increasing conservatism of the federal bench in the 1980s played a role in determining the outcome of sodomy reform litigation. I paid particular attention to the decision of President Reagan to replace the Supreme Court's relatively liberal Potter Stewart with the significantly more conservative Sandra Day O'Connor, who in turn voted to staunch the expansion of sexual privacy rights on numerous occasions and who provided one of the five votes to uphold Georgia's sodomy law in *Bowers v. Hardwick*.

I also showed that the Supreme Court's attitudes toward gay rights changed significantly in the years between *Bowers* and *Lawrence v. Texas*. This change seems to have been in part a product of membership turnover on the Court, although I showed that the general ideological leanings of the justices who decided *Romer* and *Lawrence* were quite similar to—and perhaps even a bit more conservative than—the *Bowers* justices they replaced. The membership turnover argument is also undercut to some extent by the fact that Justice O'Connor voted to uphold Georgia's sodomy law in 1986 but voted to strike down Texas's law in 2003, albeit under different legal theories of the case. I argued instead that the Court's changing attitude marked an evolution in its understanding of the sociopolitical implications of homosexuality. The changing rhetoric of the Supreme Court opinions in *Bowers* and *Lawrence* is only the most obvious marker of this attitude shift. Where the former was dismissive and contemptuous of the privacy interests asserted, the latter was respectful.

I also showed that this attitudinal shift was not confined to the Supreme Court. Lower courts throughout the nation became more open to gay rights claims over time. This shift is seen most clearly in cases involving lgb parents. Twenty-five years ago the great majority of judges deciding parenting cases concluded that homosexuality was a pernicious influence, one that clearly threatened the best interests of children. In more recent years, judges have been increasingly likely to conclude that a parent's homosexuality is irrelevant in the context of custody decisions. Notably, while some of these changes in the tenor of lower court decisions have occurred in the aftermath of appellate court pronouncements on the subject, in no instance has a change in judicial evaluations of parental homosexuality been prompted by new legislative enactments. The changes have all come from internal rather than external shifts in sociopolitical understandings of homosexuality.[2]

Ultimately, my account reiterates the central finding of behavioralist accounts of judicial decision making: that personal values influence case outcomes, at least when those cases have ideological components to them (see especially Segal and Spaeth 1993). (Where it departs from the standard attitudinal account is in its treatment of judicial attitudes as a contributing rather than primary determiner of case outcomes.) In addition, my examination of Lambda and its litigation suggests that gay rights litigators are well aware of the ideological biases of the judges before them and take that knowledge into account when planning and executing their litigation strategies. Perhaps most crucially, it suggests that judges may become more comfortable with social movement claims as those claims percolate throughout society. To the extent this is true, it underscores two common claims about legal change: first, that time is a particularly valuable resource for movement litigators (see especially Galanter 1974) and, second, that courts are responsive to shifts in public opinion, rarely stepping too far into the vanguard or lagging too far behind.

Alliance and Conflict Systems

The literature on political opportunity structure commonly emphasizes the importance of allies in facilitating collective action. I have argued that allies also play an important role in facilitating legal action. The Litigators' Roundtable, for example, provides a forum for gay rights litigators to try out new legal theories, explore rhetorical approaches, forge agreements among the group, and coordinate the processes of litigation. In a related vein, amicus support from religious denominations, medical organizations, and other civil rights groups has signaled the courts about the importance of Lambda's cases and has allowed Lambda to present gay rights claims as within the mainstream of American society rather than on the radical fringe.

My claims about the importance of allies mesh closely with existing scholarship on the courts (e.g., Epstein and Knight 1998; Handler 1978; Segal and Spaeth 1993). Where I differ is in my emphasis on the importance of opposing forces. Oppositional forces, I showed, played a significant role in each of the three case studies that form the heart of this book. Indeed, I believe it is impossible to understand Lambda's varying ability to mobilize the law on behalf of gay rights claims without reference to the conflict system surrounding those claims. The actions of antigay activists, after all, prompted the litigation in *Romer v. Evans*. Oppositional forces utilized the AIDS epidemic to reshape the contours of sodomy reform litigation. And oppositional forces utilized *Baehr* to secure the passage of DOMAs in Congress and in thirty-seven states.

Didi Herman suggests that litigation is used by opposing social movements as part of their "struggle for interpretive authority" (1994, 126) over a particular set of claims. This insight accurately reflects the movement-opposition interactions seen in the struggles over sodomy reform, antigay initiatives, and same-sex marriage. The battles over each were fundamentally battles over how a given gay rights claim should be understood. In each instance, one side attempted to redefine an existing (or potential) legal condition as unjust, while the other side sought to prevent such a redefinition from occurring. Notably, this battle over the framing of gay rights claims was fought in legislatures and ballot boxes as well as in the courts.

In sum, my examination of Lambda and its gay rights litigation indicates that alliance and conflict systems have played an important role in shaping the initiation, progress, and outcomes of its legal claims. All other things being equal, it seems reasonable to posit that social movement claims will fare worst in the context of a weak alliance and strong conflict system and best in the context of a strong alliance and weak conflict system.[3] By extension, the success of movement claims made in the context of roughly equivalent alliance and conflict systems should fall somewhere in between. I do not mean to suggest here that the relationship among Lambda, its allies, and its opponents is strictly linear. There may well be a tipping point beyond which more help—or more opposition—contributes little. It may also be that the extent of the conflict system is more or less important to the outcome of a particular movement claim than the extent of the alliance system. My point here is simply that, in the context of social movements and the law, we should concern ourselves with opposing forces as much as we concern ourselves with allies.

Cultural and Legal Frames

Social movements seeking to effect change within the political system must draw on the existing cultural stock to frame their claims. I have argued that movements seeking to effect change within the legal system must draw on both the existing cultural stock and the existing legal stock to frame their claims. As Kim Scheppele (1988, 102) has noted in the context of common law, judges decide cases by reference both to social practices and to legal precedent. The legal claims that movements can successfully make are then necessarily constrained by the availability of both cultural and legal stock. I have argued in this book that shifts in legal and/or cultural stock variously opened up and closed down the spaces within which Lambda could pursue gay rights claims. The emergence of the AIDS epidemic, for instance, shifted the cultural meanings of homosexuality in ways that made it more difficult to argue that sodomy should be encompassed by the right to privacy. Conversely, the unexpected early success of *Baehr v. Lewin* prompted a radical reframing, both culturally and legally, of the meaning of same-sex marriage.

These illustrations show that legal and cultural frames change over time. It is also the case that legal and cultural frames vary across issue area. In other words, some gay rights claims fit more neatly within existing legal and cultural frames than do others. Survey data are indicative here. In 1993 a nationwide poll revealed that nearly two-thirds of those sampled believed that laws "should protect homosexuals against job discrimination" while less than one-third believed that gay and lesbian couples "should be legally permitted to adopt children."[4] Such variation in beliefs about the aspects of homosexuality that are worthy of legal protection is reflected as well in the rapidly growing body of case law devoted to gay rights claims. To take just one example, gay rights advocates such as Lambda have had quite a bit of success in litigating cases raising free speech issues, except in the context of military service, where repeated efforts to overturn the "Don't Ask; Don't Tell" policy have to date fallen flat.[5] A salient difference between the two kinds of cases is that the courts have traditionally accorded great deference to the military's assessments of its own needs. Here the positive legal weight the court traditionally attaches to free speech claims is countermanded by the court's deference to asserted national security interests. The Supreme Court's recent decision in *Lawrence v. Texas* may or may not alter the legal balancing of the interests at stake in future cases.

A key argument of this book has been that legal frames both influence and are influenced by cultural frames. A clear example of the influence of legal frames on cultural frames can be seen in the political battle over Amendment 2 in Colorado. CFV relied heavily on the distinction between "equal" and "special" rights in its campaign to get Amendment 2 passed. The organization linked both of these terms to civil rights laws and Supreme Court decisions. In fact, CFV clearly patterned its assessment of who deserved special rights on a legal test laid out by Justice Brennan in *Frontiero v. Richardson* (1973). Brennan laid out a three-pronged test for determining when legal classifications should be subject to heightened judicial scrutiny: when there has been a history of invidious discrimination against a group defined by a particular characteristic; when the characteristic that defines the group is immutable; and when the characteristic in question bears no relation to the ability of the group to perform or contribute to society.

In CFV's formulation, a group wanting "true minority rights" also had to satisfy a three-pronged test: it had to show discrimination of such severity that its members were unable to "earn an average income, get an adequate education, or enjoy a fulfilling cultural life"; the group had to be defined by an unchanging physical characteristic rather than a behavior; and it had to show that it was politically powerless.[6] While CFV's formulation was not entirely faithful to Brennan's (note especially the absence of Brennan's relevance criterion), it clearly used legal concepts to attempt to influence cultural understandings of homosexuality in relation to civil rights.

The relationship between legal and cultural frames, as I see it, is clearly interactive. Just as legal frames influence cultural ones, so do cultural frames influence legal ones. The history of litigation around same-sex marriage is illustrative here. As noted earlier in this chapter, early arguments about a "right" to same-sex marriage were all but laughed out of court for failure to state a cognizable legal claim. In *Baker v. Nelson* (1971), the Minnesota Supreme Court decreed that two men did not have a legal right to marry one another because marriage, by definition, involved one man and one woman. But by the turn of the century courts in three different states had found that the right to marriage might well extend to same-sex couples. Particularly notable here is that the specific marriage statutes being challenged were all gender neutral. That is, none of the statutes explicitly stated that marriage consisted of one man and one woman. The laws about marriage did not change in the years between *Baker v. Nelson* and *Baehr v. Lewin* (1993). What changed were the cultural frames surrounding both marriage and homosexuality. There is a romantic view that holds that even the most politically disadvantaged person in society can bring a strong legal claim to court and prevail. The lesson of same-sex marriage litigation, however, cuts against that viewpoint, suggesting instead that existing cultural biases can and do replicate themselves in legal decisions.

Despite this caution, it is clear that legal and cultural frames are not identical, and the differences between the two may present opportunities for social movement action. Once again, the battle over Amendment 2 is illustrative. Lambda and its colleagues were able to take a political defeat and translate it into a legal victory in part because the cultural and legal frames surrounding civil rights diverge. Phrases such as *special rights, protected class status, minority status,* and *quota preferences* were ubiquitous in the political campaign over Amendment 2 and clearly tapped into culturally resonant frames. But while these terms sounded as though they were legal standards, they were meaningless in a legal sense (something CFV itself recognized), and so they lost their resonance when the battle over Amendment 2 moved from the ballot box to the courtroom.

Ultimately, my examination of Lambda and its gay rights litigation shows that the existing stock of legal and cultural frames had a significant impact on Lambda's ability to mobilize the law on behalf of particular gay rights claims and that shifts in the legal and cultural stock variously opened up and closed down spaces for successful legal action. My analysis also highlights the close relationship between legal and cultural frames, showing how changes in one may stimulate changes in the other. This in turn suggests that there may be a limit to how far legal and cultural frames can diverge from one another. It may be that social movements seeking to use the legal system to counter political disadvantage will find the law to have its limits, not simply because of the court's well-known lack of enforcement power but because of the close linkage between legal and cultural frames. This hypothesis is in line with scholarship arguing that law frequently replicates social hierarchies (e.g., Galanter 1974; Scheingold 1974; Tushnet 1984).

Other Dimensions of LOS

I want to be clear that my focus on specific factors of LOS such as access and the availability of legal and cultural frames does not imply that other factors do not exist. Legal opportunity structure, like its cousin political opportunity structure, has multiple dimensions. What makes any particular aspect of LOS relevant to any given study is the nature of the question being explored; my interest in Lambda's varied ability to mobilize the law on behalf of gay rights claims within the United States led me to disregard a number of factors that might be quite relevant in a cross-national comparison of legal reform. I sketch out one such dimension here. In the aftermath of the Supreme Court's decision in *Bowers v. Hardwick,* Lambda shifted its focus away from the federal courts and to the state courts in its effort to eradicate sodomy laws. Lambda's ability to turn to the state courts was conditioned on the existence of parallel court systems with independent sources of authority. In a nation with a centralized legal system, a loss such as *Bowers* would have foreclosed all additional litigation on the legality of sodomy laws. In other words, the multiple points of access to the courts provided by the American legal system meant that litigation remained a viable alternative even after a decisive loss before the nation's highest court, a result that could not occur in a legal system in which access was controlled by one dominant court. Scholars seeking to understand the dynamics of legal change in a cross-national comparison thus might well consider the extent to which the (de)centralization of the legal system might structure reform efforts. They might likewise consider variations in the relationship of courts to other governmental institutions and variations in the capacity of the courts to resolve politicized questions, as well as the dimensions of legal opportunity utilized in the present study.

Balancing Structure and Agency

While my account has highlighted the institutions and structures shaping the litigation terrain faced by Lambda, it has also highlighted Lambda's agency. The organization has not simply waited for opportunities to arise; it has actively worked to produce them. The bulk of its actions has taken place in the context of the courtroom, obviously. To take only the most obvious examples, Lambda helped engineer the shift in legal opportunities created by *Bowers, Lawrence, Romer,* and *Baehr.*

But Lambda has also worked to shape the cultural and legal contexts surrounding gay rights claims in ways that extend beyond the courtroom. As discussed in chapter 3, the organization invests considerable resources in projects such as the Foster Care Initiative, whose emphasis is more on fostering sociopolitical change and public education than on litigation per se. Lambda's current effort to challenge the constitutionality of New Jersey's prohibition on same-sex marriage began more than a year before it actually filed *Lewis v. Harris* (in progress). Lambda spent some of that time locating appropriate plaintiffs, but it also expanded significant resources on public education during that year. It held "town meetings" across the state, designed to educate the general public and specific subgroups, such as the clergy, on the need for same-sex marriage. It sent informational packets about the upcoming lawsuits to media venues across the state and then made the seven couples available for interviews on the day the lawsuit was filed. Lambda also hired a well-known state lobbyist in an effort to deflect legislative opposition to a favorable court ruling, should one occur. These actions indicate that Lambda is well aware that the struggle for legal reform does not begin and end in the courtroom, a belief every litigator I interviewed shared with me.

Of course, the fact that actors such as Lambda can affect the LOS does not mean that the outcomes of its actions will always be desirable. The very notion of social movement agency necessarily implies that actors may make poor choices as well as smart ones.

A central finding of this study is that increases in legal opportunity do not translate automatically into litigation success. Shifts in LOS provide *opportunities* for action, not the action itself. That depends on the ability of social movement actors to recognize and respond to the opportunities presented. One implication of the importance of social movement agency to the generation of legal change is that the ability of movements to recognize and respond to shifts in the structure of legal change may wax and wane over time, depending on the availability of organizational resources. Lambda's experience is illustrative in this regard. In the 1970s, its resources were extremely limited by any estimation. Its ability to respond to opportunities for legal action was consequently also extremely limited, as its tiny docket suggests. By the late 1980s, the increased resources available to Lambda also resulted in an increase in Lambda's docket capacity. A second implication of the importance of movement agency is that shifts in the structure of legal opportunities provide only ambiguous road maps for action. Even organizations with generous resources may misinterpret the significance of an opportunity, miss it entirely, or be outmaneuvered in their attempts to exploit it.

Let me reiterate here that an LOS approach to studying movement litigation is not incompatible with the wealth of studies emphasizing the importance of resource mobilization in explaining the constituents of legal success. Indeed, my account of Lambda's varying ability to mobilize the law on behalf of gay rights claims pays careful attention to issues of resources and their mobilization. What LOS offers is a different window into the dynamics of legal change. What becomes central in an LOS-based inquiry is the interaction between actors and institutions. To borrow from Rogers Smith, an LOS approach focuses its attention on the "different types of structures or institutions that, we hypothesize, constitute and empower political actors and their environments in important ways, endowing actors with specifiable constraints or capabilities, or both" (Smith 1988, 90).

Centering the interaction between Lambda and the structure of legal opportunities has generated some important insights into the process of legal reform. Chief among them is that legal reform is not an autonomous process but is rather contingent on the interaction of a variety of institutional, legal, cultural, and strategic factors. This finding suggests that future research on the genitors of legal reform should pay careful attention to the multiple contexts within which specific reforms are situated.

Litigation and Its (Un)Intended Consequences

The LOS window into the dynamics of legal change offers insight into more than just the *process* of legal reform efforts; it also offers insight into the *value* of those reform efforts. As such, it offers new insight into a debate at the heart of much sociolegal scholarship: the value of litigation as a tool for achieving social change. My study of Lambda and its litigation reveals both the promise and the limits of legal mobilization as a tactic for achieving social reform. From an LOS perspective, litigation and legal decisions are best treated as creating moments of opportunity bounded by the specific legal and political contexts in which they occur. These opportunities may or may not be successfully exploited by activists. Litigation, in other words, can produce both intended and unintended consequences.

One clear finding from this study is that there are at least some circumstances in which reformers can be served by turning to the courts. In *Romer v. Evans,* for example, Lambda and its allies used legal mobilization to beat back a serious political attack. It is true that *Romer* was not an example of progressive reform (although the language of the Supreme Court concerning homosexuality had evolved significantly since *Bowers*); *Romer* stopped an attempt to strip lgb people of present and future rights. It restored the status quo ante. But given a sociopolitical context in which there are ongoing efforts to fence lgb people out of the political process, litigation may serve a valuable role in staunching political losses.

Lawrence v. Texas provides yet another example of a circumstance in which turning to the courts advanced movement goals. *Lawrence* was an unqualified victory for the gay rights movement. Not only did it invalidate Texas's sodomy law and by extension all other state sodomy laws, it did so in language that made it clear that lgb people deserved legal respect.

At the same time, another clear finding of this study is that litigation is no panacea for advocates of social reform. The attempts by Lambda and its compatriots to mobilize the law to eradicate sodomy laws in the 1970s and 1980s, for example, produced relatively little in the way of direct reform. The major engine of change at that time was legislative repeal, not litigation. And *Bowers* actively damaged the sociolegal position of lgb people, erecting a legal roadblock that stretched across a wide swath of gay rights claims. Even after Lambda and other gay rights litigators began turning to state courts with some success, legislative repeals accounted for a significant proportion of the laws eradicated. At the very least it seems as though legal reform and legislative reform have proceeded hand in hand. At worst, it seems as though the promise of social reform through litigation diverted energy and resources away from activities better suited to achieving the eradication of sodomy laws. To use the term Gerald Rosenberg coined in his influential book *The Hollow Hope* (1991), the lure of litigation may have acted like "fly-paper," preventing gay rights advocates from turning their talents to more fruitful forms of persuasion.

Notably though, Lambda was able to garner indirect benefits from *Bowers*, even as the case directly harmed the legal interests of lgb people. Its fund-raising soared in the aftermath of the court case, although it is impossible to determine how much of its increased funding was a product of *Bowers* and how much it was a product of Lambda's involvement in AIDS. Its stature as a force within the gay rights movement likewise grew in the aftermath of *Bowers*, although again it is impossible to determine the precise impact of *Bowers* on this process. The 1987 March on Washington, a gay rights demonstration drawing hundreds of thousands of lgb people and their supporters to Washington, DC, was also conceived in large part as a response to *Bowers*. Just as Gerald Rosenberg has suggested that favorable legal decisions on hot-button social issues tend to inspire countermobilization, it seems that *unfavorable* legal decisions can be used to generate increased mobilization on behalf of reformist aims. Ironically, then, under some conditions litigation losses may be as or more useful to social movement aims than litigation wins.

Didi Herman argues that the relationship between litigation and legal discourse on the one hand and social movement politics on the other "is something more complex than a simple 'results tally' would indicate" (1994, 120). My examination of Lambda and its litigation lends support to this contention. I have shown that litigation wins can sometimes reverse political losses (*Romer*), while litigation losses can be used to advance political ends (*Bowers*). It is equally clear that litigation wins can engender a whole host of direct and indirect consequences, both favorable and unfavorable to social movement aims. The events surrounding *Baehr v. Lewin* are only the most obvious example.

The 1993 and 1996 decisions in the case sparked massive mobilization by counter-interests. Thirty-five states and the federal government passed "defense of marriage" laws based on a preliminary legal decision that suggested that the institution of marriage *might* be opened to same-sex couples, placing significant new hurdles into the path of same-sex couples seeking the right to marry. Based largely on this series of events, Rosenberg (2001) concludes that same-sex marriage litigation, while producing localized gains for the gay rights movement (namely, reciprocal beneficiaries in Hawaii and civil unions in Vermont), has been far more harmful than helpful to the interests of lgb people.

My analysis suggests that Rosenberg's conclusion may be too bleak; litigation also seems to have produced some favorable shifts in the legal and cultural frames surrounding gay rights in general and same-sex marriage more particularly. Where we agree is in the assessment that *courts do not have the capacity to produce social change when their decisions diverge too radically from the values and expectations of the other two branches of government.* Legal and political opportunity structures, while distinct, are interdependent, and my study of same-sex marriage litigation indicates that courts too far in the vanguard of social change will find their rulings ignored, evaded, or overturned.

In the end, I would argue that Rosenberg's metaphorical use of the word *flypaper* to describe litigation is inaccurate. Instead I suggest that litigation is a match. When struck, it is unpredictable. It may fizzle out, especially in the rain. It is always dangerous. And it can, under the right circumstances, light a path out of the darkness.

Afterword: The Courts and Social Change

On November 18, 2003, the Massachusetts Supreme Judicial Court (SJC) handed down a decision that has already generated widespread legal and political consequences for lgb people. In *Goodridge v. Dept. of Public Health*, the court held that the state's refusal to marry same-sex couples violated both the Liberty and Equality Clauses of the Massachusetts constitution. On May 17, 2004, as a direct result of *Goodridge*, Massachusetts became the first state in the nation to permit same-sex couples to marry.

If litigation is a match, *Goodridge* was lit above a tinderbox. The decision and its subsequent implementation sparked a veritable explosion of political and legal activity by both proponents and opponents of extending the right to marry to same-sex couples. The battle over *Goodridge* and its meaning is already playing out in courts, legislatures, and ballot boxes across the nation and will continue to do so for some time. A complete discussion of the legal and political implications of *Goodridge* is beyond the scope of this afterword. But because the case speaks so resonantly to several of the core themes of this book—including the relationship between LOS and POS, the balance between structure and agency, and the promises and limits of legal mobilization as a tactic for achieving social reform—a short discussion of the case and its impact is in order.

Winning *Goodridge*

In 2001, seven same-sex couples sued Massachusetts for the right to marry. *Goodridge v. Dept. of Public Health* was one of several cases filed in the aftermath of the historic decision in Vermont's *Baker v. State*. In fact, Mary Bonauto of GLAD, the lead attorney in *Goodridge*, had been one of the three main attorneys in *Baker*. GLAD saw in *Goodridge* a chance to push the right-to-marry envelope further. Massachusetts shared many of the qualities that made Vermont a friendly venue for litigation. Its judiciary had shown openness to gay rights claims. The SJC's ruling in *Adoption of Tammy* (1993), for example, made Massachusetts only the second state in the nation to expressly authorize a second-parent adoption by a same-sex couple.[1] In addition, the court had a track record of reading Massachusetts's Equal Protection Clause more expansively than the federal Equal Protection Clause.

Furthermore, the state's constitution was difficult to amend, requiring approval by both the house and the senate in two successive two-year legislative sessions followed by a simple majority vote at the next regularly scheduled election. Massachusetts was also considered among the most politically tolerant of lgb people. In 1989, for example, the legislature had passed what was then the broadest gay rights law in the nation, outlawing discrimination on the basis of sexual orientation in matters of public and private employment, public accommodations, housing, and education.[2] Similarly, a 1992 executive order allowed state workers to register as domestic partners for purposes of bereavement leave and visitation rights in state prisons and hospitals. Lgb people were a core Democrat constituency in many areas of the state. In short, Massachusetts seemed one of the most promising states in the nation to pursue a right-to-marry case.

Like most of the marriage challenges preceding it, *Goodridge* lost in the early stages of litigation. The trial court dismissed the case in 2002, finding, among other things, that the state had a legitimate interest in fostering procreation and that restricting marriage to opposite-sex couples was rationally related to that interest. GLAD appealed to the SJC, which agreed to review the lower court's decision.

Bonauto made a bold tactical move during the course of the appeal: in addition to arguing that the state had no rational reason for restricting marriage to opposite-sex couples, she went on to argue that the separate-but-equal status conveyed by civil unions would not satisfy the requirements of the Massachusetts constitution. As she noted during oral argument:

> It's certainly the plaintiff's view that the Vermont approach is not the best approach for this Court to take. The reason for that is that when it comes to marriage, there really is no such thing as separating the word "marriage" from the protections it provides. The reason for that is that one of the most important protections of marriage is the word because the word is what conveys the status that everyone understands as the ultimate expression of love and

commitment and everyone understands that that spouse of yours
has an automatic right to be by your side no matter what the circumstances. I'd also say that creating a separate system just for gay
people simply perpetuates the stigma of exclusion that we now
face because it would essentially be branding gay people and our
relationships as unworthy of this civil institution of marriage.

One danger of this strategy was that it risked alienating justices on the
high court who, like many Americans, might be open to the notion of
civil unions but unreachable on the question of marriage. And, unfortunately, GLAD had little information about the attitudes of the current
SJC justices with respect to gay rights claims. While the SJC had authorized second-parent adoptions by same-sex couples in 1993, only one justice from that case remained on the court. Moreover, six of the seven justices on the *Goodridge* court had been appointed by Republican
governors; Republican-appointed judges are somewhat less open to gay
rights claims than judges appointed by Democrats (Pinello 2004).

Ultimately, the gamble paid off. By a 4–3 majority, the SJC ruled that
Massachusetts had "failed to identify any constitutionally adequate reason for denying civil marriage to same-sex couples" (*Goodridge,* 312).
Marriage, it said, could no longer be defined as "the union for life of one
man and one woman, to the exclusion of all others." The court instead
construed civil marriage to mean "the voluntary union of two persons as
spouses, to the exclusion of all others" (343). The SJC then stayed its
decision for 180 days in order "to permit the Legislature to take such
action as it may deem appropriate in light of this opinion" (344).

The legislature's initial response was to ask the SJC to clarify whether
the creation of Vermont-style civil unions would satisfy constitutional
requirements. The SJC asked both sides in *Goodridge* to respond to this
question. A wide variety of individuals and organizations, including
Lambda, filed amicus briefs arguing that civil unions were not an acceptable alternative to marriage; opponents of same-sex marriage filed a
small handful of amicus briefs as well. The SJC's reply came down some
two months later in *Opinions of the Justices to the Senate* (2004). By the
same 4–3 division, the high court made it clear that opening marriage to
same-sex couples was the only constitutionally permissible option.

The dissimilitude between the terms "civil marriage" and "civil
union" is not innocuous; it is a considered choice of language that
reflects a demonstrable assigning of same-sex, largely homosexual,

couples to second-class status. . . . The bill would have the effect of maintaining and fostering a stigma of exclusion that the [Massachusetts] Constitution prohibits. It would deny to same-sex "spouses" only a status that is specially recognized in society and has significant social and other advantages. The Massachusetts Constitution, as was explained in the *Goodridge* opinion, does not permit such invidious discrimination. (*Opinions of the Justices,* 570, quotation marks in original)

This ruling all but guaranteed that Massachusetts would begin issuing marriage licenses to same-sex couples. Short of refusing to execute the high court's order—and thereby precipitating a major constitutional crisis—the governor had no power to prevent same-sex marriages from occurring. The legislature likewise had no ability to forestall the implementation of *Goodridge.* While the legislature could begin the process of amending the state constitution to reserve marriage to opposite-sex couples if it so chose, such an amendment could not take effect until the end of 2006 at the earliest. And indeed, on May 17, 2004, when the 180-day stay imposed by the SJC expired, Massachusetts became the first state in the nation with an official public policy of recognizing marriages between members of the same sex. In the first week alone, 2,468 same-sex couples applied for marriage licenses (MacDonald and Dedman 2004).[3] As yet, Massachusetts has not released an official tally of same-sex marriages in the state, but newspaper reports indicate that license requests tapered off after the first few weeks, when most of the pent-up demand in Massachusetts had been accommodated. Rhetoric by some antigay activists notwithstanding, civilization has not collapsed.

Why Massachusetts?

Chapter 7 utilized a comparative case study of marriage litigation in Hawaii, Alaska, and Vermont to argue that similar judicial signals can create dissimilar opportunities for a particular set of disputants because of systematic differences in the political and legal opportunity structures in which those signals reverberate. *Goodridge* offers us the opportunity to revisit this subject. Massachusetts is the only state in which litigators seeking to open marriage to same-sex couples actually got what they were seeking. Why? What made postlitigation events in Massachusetts play out differently than they had in Hawaii, Alaska, and Vermont? In the following pages, I compare the legal framing of same-sex marriage, access to the formal institutional structures of the law, and the configuration of legal and political elites in Massachusetts and Vermont. Ultimately, I suggest that the central difference between the two states concerned the legal framing of the high court's decision.

Legal Framing of Same-Sex Marriage and Configuration of Judicial Elites

The legislatures in Vermont and Massachusetts were both faced with faits accompli. Massachusetts's *Goodridge* echoed Vermont's *Baker v. State* in ruling that the state-level rights and responsibilities associated with marriage must be made available equally to same- and opposite-sex couples. Where *Goodridge* differed from *Baker* is in the mandate given to the state legislature. The Vermont court explicitly declined to order the legislature to open marriage to same-sex couples and indicated that an alternative regulatory scheme such as the establishment of a domestic partnership registry for same-sex couples might well pass constitutional muster. The Massachusetts court, in contrast, appeared to indicate that the only acceptable legislative action was to open marriage to same-sex couples. When asked by the Massachusetts senate to clarify whether the institution of Vermont-style civil unions for same-sex couples would satisfy constitutional requirements, the response from the high court was unambiguous: no.

It is beyond the scope of this afterword to determine precisely why the high courts in Vermont and Massachusetts had different positions on the constitutional adequacy of the separate-but-equal institution of civil unions. It may be that differences in the availability of case law in each state partly explain the divergence in outcomes. It may also be that Bonauto's argument that civil unions were not an acceptable solution managed to capture four justices on the SJC, leading them away from a solution that they might otherwise have deemed acceptable. It may alternately be that the Vermont justices were simply more willing to temper their interpretation of what the law required based on their understanding of what political elites and popular opinion were willing to accept. It is clear, for example, that the Vermont Supreme Court was acting strategically in the way it framed its decision. Justice Amestoy's majority opinion shows that the court was cognizant of the political backlash *Baker* might cause and that it was hoping to defuse that backlash by giving Vermont's legislature the ability to choose whether to extend marriage rights to same-sex couples or develop a parallel institution (see chap. 7). No matter what the impetus for the SJC's ruling, it clearly constrained the alternatives available to the legislature in a way *Baker* did not.

Configuration of Political Elites and Access to the Formal Institutional Structure of the Law

It is difficult to know whether Massachusetts legislators were less open to the possibility of same-sex marriage than Vermont legislators were. It is clear, however, that they were not more open than their Vermont counterparts. Legislative reaction in Massachusetts initially mirrored the reaction in Vermont. Although the wording of *Goodridge* seemed unambiguous, a number of legislators expressed the belief that the 180-day stay imposed by the SJC was in fact a signal to the legislature that, in the words of Governor Mitt Romney (R), "a provision which provided benefits, obligation, rights, and responsibilities, which are consistent with marriage but perhaps could be called by a different name, would be in conformity with their decision" (Phillips and Lewis 2003). The senate moved rapidly to pursue the possibility of civil unions. Within a few weeks, it had crafted a bill and sent it up to the SJC for an advisory opinion clarifying whether the institution of civil unions for same-sex couples would in fact satisfy constitutional requirements. Further legislative consideration of *Goodridge* was tabled pending the high court's decision.

When the SJC quashed the civil union option, however, the legislature actively took up the question of amending the state's constitution to circumvent the high court's ruling. By happenstance, *Opinions of the Justices to the Senate* came down on February 4, 2004, just one week before a constitutional convention was scheduled to begin. (Constitutional conventions in Massachusetts are simply joint meetings of the house and senate in which potential constitutional amendments are discussed.) Although a dozen or so possible constitutional amendments were slated for discussion, the subject of same-sex marriage leapfrogged to the top of the agenda, ultimately becoming the sole focus of the gathering.

The convention was deeply divided, with legislators falling into three main blocs. House Speaker Finneran (D), an opponent of same-sex marriage, backed an amendment that limited marriage to opposite-sex couples but did not prevent the legislature from providing some statutory benefits to same-sex couples. This bloc was numerically the largest, falling just shy of the votes needed to ensure the amendment's passage. The second largest bloc favored implementing *Goodridge*. The final bloc supported senate president Travaglini's preferred amendment, which would ban same-sex marriage while at the same time creating civil unions (Lewis 2004). Neither Finneran nor Travaglini was able to forge a majority coalition within the two-day time period allotted for the convention. Another daylong convention was scheduled for mid-March.

Intense politicking for votes on all sides occurred during that month. Finneran and Travaglini eventually joined together to back an amendment that would ban same-sex marriages but create civil unions that functioned like marriages for all purposes of state law. This amendment ultimately passed but not without impassioned debate and several revisions and not until the end of March, after yet a third constitutional convention had been convened. If the house and senate pass the amendment again during the next legislative session, it will go before voters in November 2006.

Political opposition to *Goodridge* was not limited to the legislature. Within hours of the decision's announcement, Governor Romney held a press conference denouncing the ruling and calling for a constitutional amendment to reserve marriage to opposite-sex couples. He fought against implementation of the ruling every step of the way. Immediately after the legislature okayed a proposed constitutional amendment, Romney announced that he would ask the SJC to stay the implementation of *Goodridge* until the November 2006 vote, arguing that too much confusion would result if same-sex couples married and then voters banned such marriages. His intention was stymied, though, when the state's attorney general, whose responsibilities include representing the executive branch in all court matters, refused to transmit Romney's request, saying that the governor lacked valid legal grounds for requesting a stay (Phillips and Burge 2004).

In an attempt to at least limit the number of same-sex couples who could marry, Romney then turned to a 1913 law that prohibited out-of-state couples from marrying in Massachusetts if such a marriage was against the public policy of their home state.[4] He ordered municipal clerks not to issue licenses to same-sex couples who resided outside of Massachusetts, since no other state in the nation permitted them to marry. He likewise ordered the state's Registry of Vital Records and Statistics to refuse to record such marriage licenses.[5]

In sum, the different outcomes in Massachusetts and Vermont cannot be attributed to a more favorable configuration of political elites in the former state. The governor of Massachusetts fought actively against implementing the high court's ruling, using the power of his office to limit the scope of the decision whenever possible. Legislators in both states initially plunked for civil unions, but when that option was foreclosed in Massachusetts, the legislature began the cumbersome process of amending the state's constitution in order to prevent same-sex couples from marrying. Vermont legislators might well have chosen the same route, of course, had the decision in *Baker* not given them the freedom to craft an alternative to marriage for same-sex couples. We will never know.

Marriage vs. Civil Unions

In July 2004, as I write this afterword, lgb people in Massachusetts find themselves in an unusual position. They live in the only state in the nation that recognizes the right of same-sex couples to marry as a matter of public policy. In many ways, their legal status is analogous to the status of lgb people in Vermont. As with civil unions in Vermont, marriages in Massachusetts entitle same-sex couples to all the state-level benefits and responsibilities accorded to married opposite-sex couples. And like civil unions, those marriages do not currently entitle same-sex couples to any of the myriad of federal benefits and responsibilities allotted as a matter of course to opposite-sex couples. Nor is it clear that same-sex marriages performed in Massachusetts will be recognized by other states.

   Given the extent of the legal similarities between civil unions in Vermont and same-sex marriages in Massachusetts, one might wonder why Bonauto and others were so intent on pursuing marriage. The answer is that the institutions differ in two important respects—one involving legal frames and one involving cultural frames. There is a crucial legal difference between same-sex couples married in Massachusetts and couples with a civil union. The former, but not the latter, have standing to challenge federal and state laws that fence lgb people out of marriage. Indeed, even as I write the first legal challenge to the constitutionality of the Defense of Marriage Act has been filed (Brink 2004).

   It is likewise clear that the cultural frames surrounding marriage and civil unions differ significantly. Civil unions are, after all, nothing more than attempts to give same-sex couples the legal status that attaches to marriage *without* giving them the cultural status that attaches to marriage. That the Vermont and Massachusetts legislatures both preferred to design a new, separate-but-equal legal status for same-sex couples rather than allow them to marry is testament to this fact. That people attach different cultural meanings to marriage and civil unions is also evidenced in public opinion surveys. A January 2004 Gallup poll, for example, showed that 24 percent of respondents supported legal marriage for same-sex couples while 34 percent supported the establishment of civil unions.[6]

The decision by GLAD to pursue marriage instead of civil unions reflected its awareness of the differences between the two institutions, and the organization pursued its goal despite its awareness that winning the right to marry would be more likely to stir a political backlash than winning the right to civil union. In part, it wanted to win the right to marry in Massachusetts because being married would give same-sex couples access to federal courts to challenge the constitutionality of DOMA as well as the constitutionality of statewide antimarriage laws. As noted in chapter 5, all things being equal, organized litigators generally prefer to bring cases in federal rather than state courts, because litigating state by state is more time consuming and expensive than litigating in the federal system. A well-executed federal challenge has the potential to disable all state antimarriage laws in one fell swoop.

That said, GLAD, Lambda, and the other members of the Litigators' Roundtable would prefer to avoid a federal DOMA challenge for the next several years at least. Their preference is instead to continue filing cases in states perceived to be relatively open to gay rights claims. In Bonauto's words, "I would like the opportunity for states to wrestle with this before we have to go into federal court" (Garrow 2004, 57). In part they are concerned that a hastily brought federal challenge would result in a legal loss, creating an additional hurdle for future litigation. They are equally—if not more—concerned that precipitous federal litigation would provoke a massive political backlash. The state-by-state approach, as they see it, would give judges, legislators, and the general public time to get comfortable with the notion of same-sex couples marrying; to realize that, again in Bonauto's words, "the sky doesn't fall" (57). The preferred litigation strategy of Roundtable members reflects their keen awareness of the overlap between legal and cultural frames.

The second reason GLAD chose to pursue marriage rather than civil unions had less to do with the legal differences between the two institutions and more to do with the cultural differences. Bonauto and many of her fellow litigators were frankly upset that the Vermont Supreme Court had stopped short of requiring marriage in *Baker v. State*, instead allowing the legislature to create a separate-but-equal institution for lgb people. Indeed, Beth Robinson, one of the three cocounsel in *Baker*, referred to the day she received news of the Vermont high court's decision as one of the worst days in her life.[7] The decision, as she saw it, recognized the legal impermissibility of discrimination against same-sex couples but facilitated the continued imposition of social distinctions between same-sex and opposite-sex couples. For all that civil unions inarguably advanced the legal interests of same-sex couples, the different labeling was a symbolic slap in the face—and one that gay rights litigators were determined to address.

Goodridge was not the only case brought with the specific intent to secure marriage rather than civil unions or some equivalent separate-but-equal legal status. Lambda, for example, filed *Lewis v. Harris* in New Jersey in 2002. It too seeks to convince the courts that marriage—and only marriage—is required under the state's constitution.[8] *Goodridge* was simply the first case to win. Its success in turn shifted the LOS surrounding same-sex marriage in a far-reaching fashion.

The Consequences of Winning *Goodridge*

A core premise of the LOS approach is that legal decisions—whether wins or losses—should be understood as creating moments of opportunity for a wide range of legal and political actors operating within their own specific legal and political contexts. These opportunities may or may not be exploited successfully, depending on the actors' particular constraints and capabilities as well as their strategic choices. Courtroom victories, in other words, do not translate inexorably into legal reform; legal reform is contingent on the interaction of a variety of institutional, cultural, and strategic factors.

I have already discussed the translation of *Goodridge* into public policy within Massachusetts. But as with *Baehr v. Lewin* and *Baker v. State* before it, the opportunities provided by *Goodridge* range far beyond the borders of its home state. The dominoes set into motion by *Goodridge* are still falling, and it is not yet possible to assess the case's full effect on the larger struggle for gay rights. Even at this early stage, however, it is obvious that *Goodridge* has been the catalyst for widespread mobilization across the nation as supporters and opponents of the decision have struggled to reframe the cultural and legal meaning of marriage. I suggested in chapter 8 that social movement litigation is a metaphorical match: always dangerous, occasionally prone to fizzle out when struck, but also a potentially useful tool. An examination of a few of the most prominent early responses to *Goodridge* reveals both the danger and potential utility of litigation as a tool to achieve social reform.

Among the costs of winning *Goodridge*, the most consequential to date has been this: legislators, governors, and citizens across the nation have sought to insulate their states from the Full Faith and Credit implications of legalizing same-sex marriage in Massachusetts. While *Baehr*-inspired concerns about same-sex marriage led states to pass mini-DOMA statutes in the 1990s, this time around the focus has largely been on constitutional amendments. As of August 4, 2004, legislatures in nine states had passed amendments to restrict marriage to opposite-sex couples. Voters in Missouri have already ratified that state's proposed amendment; six of the other amendments will be decided by voters before the end of the year.[9] Citizen petition drives have placed marriage amendments on the ballot in an additional six states.[10] History suggests that opponents of same-sex marriage will probably win the lion's share of these votes; no statewide ballot measure designed to prevent same-sex couples from marrying has ever failed (Peterson 2004). It should be noted that none of the proposed marriage amendments provides for civil unions as an alternative legal institution for same-sex couples. Utah's proposed amendment, in fact, expressly bars state recognition of any sort of same-sex "domestic partnership."

The spate of constitutional amendments proposed in *Goodridge*'s shadow illustrates the interdependence of legal and political opportunity structures and lends additional support to the claim that courts issuing decisions too far in the vanguard of social change will find their rulings ignored, evaded, or overturned. One way to construe the impact of *Goodridge* is to say that advances in the legal rights of lgb people in one state have engendered significant damage to the legal interests of lgb people in another state (Missouri) as well as the very real potential for similar damage in an additional twelve states.

Another cost of *Goodridge* has been the revitalization of the Federal Marriage Amendment (FMA). Originally introduced into the House of Representatives in 2002, the FMA had garnered a hundred cosponsors in the House by the fall of 2003 but none in the Senate. One week after *Goodridge* was handed down, five senators joined together to introduce the FMA into the Senate, where it quickly gained five additional sponsors.[11] President George W. Bush expressed conditional support for a constitutional amendment banning same-sex marriage in his January 21, 2004, State of the Union address. Then, shortly after the Massachusetts Supreme Judicial Court clarified its ruling by stating that civil unions were not a constitutionally permissible alternative to marriage, Bush threw his full support behind the FMA. *Goodridge* figured prominently in Bush's announced rationale for supporting the FMA.

> In recent months, however, some activist judges and local officials have made an aggressive attempt to redefine marriage. In Massachusetts, four judges on the highest court have indicated they will order the issuance of marriage licenses to applicants of the same gender in May of this year. . . .
>
> On a matter of such importance, the voice of the people must be heard. Activist courts have left the people with one recourse. If we are to prevent the meaning of marriage from being changed forever, our nation must enact a constitutional amendment to protect marriage in America.[12]

Were the FMA to take effect, it would constitute an all-but-insurmountable defeat for the gay rights movement, erecting a hurdle that could only be dismantled by the passage of another constitutional amendment specifically repealing the first. The difficulty of amending the U.S. Constitution, however, makes it highly unlikely that the FMA will ever pass. Constitutional amendments require a two-thirds majority vote in both houses of Congress and ratification by thirty-eight state legislatures to take effect. A recent attempt by Senate majority leader Bill Frist to invoke cloture and force a vote on the measure (S.J.Res.40) garnered only forty-eight votes, well short of the sixty needed and shorter still of the sixty-seven votes needed to pass the FMA. But as John Feehery, spokesman for Republican House Speaker Dennis Hastert, has said, "Sometimes you win for losing" (Barrett 2004). A number of Republicans seeking election in 2004—including President Bush—have emphasized their support for the FMA, seeking to paint Democrats who have expressed opposition to it as out of touch with American values (see, e.g., Dewar and Cooperman 2004; Nagourney and Kirkpatrick 2004).

This electoral strategy is not without its risks. Surveys attempting to ascertain public support for same-sex marriage are open to interpretation. When asked flatly whether they support or oppose opening marriage to same-sex couples, Americans indicate opposition to it by a margin of two to one, a ratio that has remained reasonably constant for some five years.[13] However, when asked to choose between marriage, civil unions, or no legal recognition at all for same-sex couples, a solid majority of respondents indicate their support for either marriage or civil unions. Only about two-fifths are unwilling to accord any legal recognition to same-sex couples.[14] The American public has become significantly more willing to give legal recognition to same-sex couples over the years (see fig. 6 in chap. 5). Much of this movement has undoubtedly come about in response to the litigation of cases such as *Baehr* and *Baker*. Conservative Republicans are gambling that same-sex marriages in Massachusetts will bring social conservatives out to the polls (e.g., Klein 2004). Gay rights litigators are gambling that those same marriages will allay fears and increase public support for legal recognition as same-sex marriage becomes normalized.

Of all the early responses to *Goodridge,* the most unexpected was this: in early 2004, San Francisco; Portland, Oregon; and a handful of other localities began issuing marriage licenses to same-sex couples until ordered to desist by courts, state attorneys general, and other authoritative interpreters of state law. San Francisco and Portland were by far the most consequential actors. Together they issued over seven thousand licenses while the other localities issued fewer than a hundred licenses altogether. A full examination of the reasons why these localities took the actions they did when they did is beyond the scope of this afterword. For the moment, I simply note that these actions were influenced by *Goodridge.* To take just one example, San Francisco mayor Gavin Newsom (D) had been in the audience when President Bush opined the need to protect the sanctity of marriage in his 2004 State of the Union address. Newsom released a press statement decrying Bush's statement within a few days of the address and began consulting with his staff, the NCLR, the ACLU, and others involved in the movement for gay rights about whether it was possible for San Francisco County to begin issuing marriage licenses to same-sex couples.[15] Under his direction, San Francisco began issuing licenses on February 12, 2004, and continued to do so for four weeks, until the state's supreme court ordered it to desist.

The SJC's decision in *Goodridge* together with the decisions by various localities to issue marriage licenses has, predictably, engendered a spurt of new right-to-marry litigation. Lambda promptly took on several new marriage cases. Together with the ACLU and the NCLR, Lambda successfully derailed an attempt by an antimarriage group to enjoin San Francisco from marrying same-sex couples (*Proposition 22 Legal Defense and Education Fund v. Martin et. al.* 2004). Working again with the ACLU and the NCLR, Lambda subsequently sued the state of California, arguing that its refusal to allow same-sex couples to marry violated state constitutional guarantees of liberty, privacy, and equality (*Woo v. Lockyer,* in progress). Lambda also brought suit in New York, making substantially the same argument as it had in *Woo* (*Hernandez v. Robles*, in progress).

Andersen v. Sims has been the most consequential of Lambda's new cases to date. In March 2004 Lambda and the Northwest Women's Law Center filed suit in Washington, arguing, among other things, that denying same-sex couples the ability to marry impermissibly infringed upon the fundamental right to marry under the state's constitution. On August 4, 2004, the trial court judge agreed, striking down part of the state's marriage laws but staying his decision pending review by the state's supreme court.

Other suits have been filed as well. The ACLU has initiated new right-to-marry cases in Maryland, New York, Oregon, and Washington, while the NCLR is pursuing a marriage challenge in Florida.[16] Private litigators have also filed a handful of cases. It is quite clear at this point that right-to-marry cases will be at the center of gay rights litigation for the foreseeable future.

This quick review of some prominent early responses to *Goodridge* is, necessarily, an incomplete analysis of the case's impact on the fight for gay rights. Yet it nicely illustrates both the promise and the danger of turning to litigation as a tool to fight for sociolegal reform. Litigators accomplished something extraordinary in *Goodridge*. By turning to the courts they changed the legal landscape surrounding marriage in Massachusetts, and they did so despite the objections of the legislative and executive branches. Their victory in turn inspired Mayor Newsom of San Francisco to grant marriage licenses to same-sex couples, and his actions in turn inspired Multnomah County and scattered other localities to begin issuing licenses as well. As I write, the California Supreme Court has just ruled the San Francisco licenses invalid. An Oregon trial court, conversely, has commanded the state to recognize the licenses issued in Multnomah County and given the state legislature ninety days after the start of its next regular session to "produce legislation that would balance the substantive rights of same-sex domestic partners with those of opposite-sex married couples."[17] Courts in other states are now grappling with *Goodridge*-inspired litigation as well, and a Washington trial court has already ruled that same-sex couples have a constitutional right to marry under that state's constitution.

But by turning to the courts—and by arguing that the civil unions were not an acceptable alternative to marriage for same-sex couples—litigators also fomented a political backlash. It seems clear that the Massachusetts legislature would have passed a civil unions bill without feeling

the need to resort to the constitutional amendment process, had only the
SJC—and by extension GLAD and other gay rights advocates—been
amenable to it. Should the constitutional amendment pass, lgb people in
Massachusetts will still have the option to enter into civil unions but at
the cost of a constitutional prohibition on same-sex marriage. This is a
much bigger barrier than they faced prior to the litigation of *Goodridge*.
The backlash has also extended far beyond Massachusetts's borders.
Missouri has already passed a constitutional amendment banning same-
sex marriage; twelve more states will vote on similar measures by the end
of 2004. It is not surprising that some of those states—including Missouri—have reacted as they have. Oklahoma, Mississippi, and Utah, for
instance, are widely considered to be generally hostile to gay rights
claims. Michigan, Ohio, and Wisconsin, conversely, have moderately
good records on gay rights issues. Wisconsin, for example, was the first
state in the nation to pass a statewide gay rights law. That these states
may well pass antimarriage amendments is more troubling.

The specter of an amendment to the U.S. Constitution also cannot be
completely dismissed. The odds against it are certainly high; the Constitution is notoriously difficult to amend, and there is no consensus among
political elites about the desirability of the FMA. Organized gay rights
advocates are also pursuing a strategy they believe is likely to minimize
antagonism toward the concept of same-sex marriage. But it should be
noted that the Litigators' Roundtable holds no veto power over marriage
litigation. As I write, a private litigator in Florida is pursuing several
cases challenging the constitutionality of Florida's ban on same-sex marriage as well as one case challenging the constitutionality of DOMA. The
latter case employs litigants who were married in Massachusetts. The
cases have been loudly decried by the universe of organized gay rights litigators (see, e.g., Rostow 2004). The Florida courts are widely considered
to be unfriendly to gay rights claims, and the Florida constitution is
exceptionally easy to amend. The DOMA challenge enters the federal
court system years before organized litigators think is wise and does so
under the Eleventh Circuit, widely considered to be one of the worst cir-
cuits in which to bring gay rights claims. The cases are, in short, disasters
waiting to happen. It is possible that one of these cases, or others equally
foolish, might shift the structure of legal and/or political opportunities in
such a fashion that an amendment to the U.S. Constitution might become
more likely.

Alternately, the hope of organized gay rights litigators that the marriage beachhead established in Massachusetts will promote greater legal,

political, and cultural tolerance of same-sex couples may come true. An LOS approach cannot forecast outcomes, but it can help us conceptualize the relationship between legal decisions and public policy. A legal decision such as *Goodridge* is neither a win nor a loss; it does however, reshape the landscape for political debate.

Notes

CHAPTER ONE

1. The Stonewall Riot of 1969 is commonly considered to mark the beginning of the modern-day civil rights movement. See chapter 2 for an extended discussion of Stonewall and its impact on gay rights.

2. Because the terminology used to signify sexual orientation is so hotly debated, a discussion of my choice of terms is in order here. For the sake of brevity, I use *gay rights movement* as shorthand for the movement for lesbian, gay, and bisexual rights. While I use *gay rights* to describe the social movement, the word *gay* is not adequate to refer to lesbian, gay, and bisexual individuals. Some aspects of gay rights have historically concerned lesbians more than gay men and vice versa, while others have implicated both equally. Our terminology must take this into account. I therefore speak of gay men, lesbian women, and bisexual people as appropriate.

3. New York State Judiciary Law § 495(5).

4. *United Transportation Union v. State Bar of Michigan* (1971).

5. For in-depth analyses of the impact of sodomy laws on gay rights, see Cain 1993, 2000; Rivera 1985, 1986.

6. This term comes from March and Olson 1994.

7. As such, new institutionalism stands in contrast to what might be termed single-agent accounts of legal change, most prominently the attitudinal model. Several scholars have already addressed the limitations of the attitudinal model and laid out the rationale for new institutionalism (see especially Smith 1988; Clayton and Gillman 1999; Maltzman, Spriggs, and Wahlbeck 1999). I will not revisit that subject here.

8. I do not mean to imply here that earlier work on organized litigation never contemplated the larger world within which litigation took place. The importance of the law, the judges, and the wider political environment has commonly been noted—usually in discussions about the importance of controlling which cases to bring and when and where to bring them (Cortner 1968; Kluger 1975; Sorauf 1976; Tushnet 1987; Vose 1959; Wasby 1983). However, these other aspects have rarely been explored systematically (cf. Kobylka 1987; Lawrence 1990).

9. Michael Lipsky (1970, 14), however, is generally credited with the insight at the heart of political opportunity structure:

> We are accustomed to describing communist political systems as "experiencing a thaw" or "going through a process of retrenchment." Should it

not at least be an open question as to whether the American political system experiences such stages and fluctuations? Similarly, is it not sensible to assume that the system will be more or less open to specific groups at different times and at different places?

10. For an excellent treatment of underlying political culture as a factor influencing social movement options, see Whittier 1995. For the argument that such factors should not be considered political, see McAdam 1996.

11. It should be noted that international tribunals have heard claims brought by peace activists hailing from the United States as well as other nations. For the purpose at hand, I simply wish to point out that the U.S. courts are generally closed to peace activists. For most American movements, access to the courts is not an all-or-nothing thing, because the majority of them make multiple sets of claims. For example, the women's movement has encompassed issues as varied as abortion, domestic violence, sexual harassment, pay equity, child care, employment discrimination, health care, racism, poverty, and school athletics, not to mention suffrage. Inability to get access to the courts in one area does not preclude access in others.

12. See, for example, Lawrence 1990; Rubin 1987. But see Epstein 1985 for an examination of groups who turned to the courts in order to retain legal rights.

13. Judges, however, are not the only legal elites. The Office of the Solicitor General of the United States, for example, is sometimes referred to as the "tenth justice" because of its influence in Supreme Court decision making; its success rate in seeking Supreme Court review varies between 75 to 90 percent (Perry 1991). Other studies have shown that the solicitor general's support of a legal claim increases the likelihood that the Court will treat that claim favorably (Segal and Spaeth 1993). That is precisely why amicus support from the solicitor general is so desirable. Although little empirical work has been done on this point, the presence of state attorneys general in a case may influence its outcome as well.

14. There is mixed evidence about the impact of amicus briefs on judicial decisions. Compare McGuire 1990 with Songer and Sheehan 1992. However, the presence of amicus briefs does increase the likelihood that the Supreme Court will decide to review a case (Epstein and Knight 1998).

15. Providing, of course, that the user was not warned of the risk.

16. Attitudinalists largely dispute this claim as it applies to the U.S. Supreme Court but agree that lower courts are constrained by precedent, at least to some extent. See Segal and Spaeth 1993.

17. See *Planned Parenthood of Missouri v. Danforth* (1976); *Thornburgh v. American College of Obstetricians and Gynecologists* (1986); *Webster v. Reproductive Health Services* (1989); *Planned Parenthood v. Casey* (1992).

18. For a discussion of alternative legal categories within which abortion rights could have been grounded, see Koppelman 1990; Regan 1979.

CHAPTER TWO

1. Official harassment of gay bars and their patrons may seem to be a relatively frivolous problem. It is important to understand, however, that gay bars

were central to the formation of lesbian and gay communities. Faderman (1991, 80) contends that lesbian bars were "the single most important public manifestation of the [working-class lesbian] subculture for many decades" (see also Kennedy and Davis 1993). From the emergence of the first recognizable lesbian and gay subcultures in the first decades of the twentieth century through the 1960s, bars served as the primary route for gay people to find each other. The role of bars in the gay community has been somewhat similar to the role of churches in the black community, providing a haven from a hostile society and a place to meet and talk with like-minded others. Harassment of gay bars in the 1950s and 1960s, then, struck at the very heart of lesbian and gay communal life.

2. Immigration and Nationality Act of 1952, 8 U.S.C. § 212(a)(4).

3. A notable exception to this trend occurred in 1952 when Dale Jennings was entrapped by a plainclothes policeman and charged with lewd and dissolute behavior. Jennings was one of the founders of the Mattachine Society, a group founded in 1951 with the purpose of transforming homosexuality from a stigma to a source of pride and communal identity (D'Emilio 1983, 58). After some internal debate, Mattachine decided to fight the charges against Jennings and to use the trial and its attendant publicity to publicize the police practice of entrapping gay men. It wrote letters and press releases and used the "informal communications network of the gay male subculture" (70) to advertise the trial and to defray legal expenses. At the trial, Jennings took the then-unheard of route of admitting his homosexuality but denying the charges. After deliberating for thirty-six hours, the jury deadlocked, an outcome the Mattachine Society viewed as a great victory.

4. *Clackum v. United States* (1960). Under Air Force regulations a person could be administratively discharged if a conviction by general court martial seemed unlikely.

5. Ultimately, she won her case, establishing the principle that service members accused of misconduct are entitled to procedural due process in discharge proceedings. The case secured a minimal level of protection for service members accused of homosexuality. See Cain 1993 for a thoughtful discussion of this and other early legal challenges.

6. "ACLU Statement on Homosexuality," quoted in D'Emilio (1983, 156). Ironically, 1957 is also the year that the first substantive legal challenge to governmental policy was filed (*Kameny v. Bruckner,* 1960). Frank Kameny, an astronomer for the U.S. Army Map Service, was dismissed in 1957 solely on the basis of his homosexuality. Although he lost at every level, Kameny appealed his firing all the way to the Supreme Court (which denied his writ of certiorari in 1961). He took the then-unusual route of arguing for the morality of homosexuality, as well as disputing the authority of the government to police the moral beliefs of its employees. For Kameny's own take on his litigation, see his interview in Marcus 1992 (93–103).

7. Records of homosexuality as a precipitating factor in divorce go back as far as 1908. See Rivera 1979 (879–83), as well as 78 A.L.R.2d 807 (1961).

8. *Commonwealth v. Bradley* (1952), *Immerman v. Immerman* (1959), and *Nadler v. Superior Court* (1967). What probably occurred is that many lesbian and gay parents facing custody battles gave up their children without a fight,

either through fear that their sexual orientation would become public knowledge or through the fear that their homosexuality by its very nature would be considered sufficient reason to deny them custody in any courtroom. In addition, the cases that did occur were often deliberately left unpublished (see Hunter and Polikoff 1976; Rivera 1979).

9. In further explaining its reasoning, the ALI made a discursive move that would subsequently be replicated by many others: it framed sexual activity and the interest of the state in regulating it differently based on the sexual orientation and marital status of the participants. As the institute explained in an extended comment on the subject (ALI 1962), the case for continuing to criminalize "untraditional" sexual practices between husbands and wives was the weakest. Such conduct was "anything but uncommon" and could be part of a "healthy and normal marital relationship." Moreover, criminal sanctions were "inconsistent with the social goal of protecting the marital relationship against outside interference." With respect to unmarried heterosexual couples, "[t]he wrong, if one exists, arises from the fact of sexual intimacy out of wedlock and not from the kind of conduct with which gratification is achieved." Such conduct was really "only a variant of adultery and fornication," which the ALI also believed should be decriminalized. For the state to distinguish between "styles of sexual intimacy" served no legitimate purpose.

The case for retaining criminal sanctions on "deviate sexual intercourse" between same-sex couples was stronger than for either married or unmarried heterosexual couples. Continued sanctions, said the institute, might be advocated "on the ground that such conduct threatens the moral fabric of society by undermining the viability of the family or on the supposition that permitting such behavior between consenting adults leads inevitably to the corruption of youth." The ALI noted the lack of evidence or "reasoned analysis" indicating that homosexual conduct corrupted youth but found the moral question to be more problematic. Even if homosexual conduct was "a moral default for which the actor may justifiably be condemned"—a question on which the organization expressed no opinion—practical considerations warranted eliminating criminal penalties for it. The action was victimless, enforcement tactics were often unseemly, and the threat of enforcement probably deterred some people from seeking "assistance for their emotional problems."

10. For the International Congress on Penal Law's endorsement, see *New York Times*, August 30, 1964, 36, cited in D'Emilio 1983 (144). For a sampling of supportive law journal articles, see Gallo et al. 1966; Hughes 1962; Johnsen 1968; Lamb 1969; Schwartz 1963.

11. *Griswold*, 485–86. *Griswold*'s articulation of a fundamental right to marital privacy sparked immediate opposition within the Court itself. The 6–3 decision produced three concurrences and two dissents. Both dissenters disagreed with the wisdom of the statute ("an uncommonly silly law" in Justice Stewart's words) but did not find it to violate any provision of the federal Constitution. Two of the concurrences found the constitutional failing of Connecticut's statute to lie entirely within the Fourteenth Amendment rather than an amorphous privacy right located in the "penumbras" of the First, Fourth, Fifth, Ninth, and Fourteenth Amendments.

12. Although the case implicated the right to privacy, *Stanley* was brought as a First Amendment challenge. Justice Marshall's opinion for the Court goes on to state: "If the First Amendment means anything, it means that the State has no business telling a man, sitting alone in his own house, what books he may read or what films he may watch. Our whole constitutional heritage rebels at the thought of giving government the power to control men's minds" (565).

13. *Eisenstadt* achieved this outcome through equal protection analysis.

14. *Griswold,* 498–99, citations omitted. *Poe v. Ullman* (1961) was another challenge to the constitutionality of Connecticut's ban on the use of contraceptives. The appeal in *Poe* was dismissed on jurisdictional grounds, when the Court held that the five challengers (two married couples and a physician) had failed to establish their standing to challenge the law. Justice Harlan's lengthy dissent took the Court to task for its refusal to decide the case on its merits. *Poe* shows that the parameters of access to the legal system was an important constraint on the actions of birth-control advocates (see Garrow 1994).

15. Not surprising is the fact that all three affiliates were located in places that had active lgb communities. For more on the position of the ACLU with respect to the civil liberties implications of homosexuality, see Bullough 1986.

16. See letter from then–ACLU associate director Alan Reitman to gay rights activist Frank Kameny (of *Kameny v. Bruckner* fame), May 28, 1962, General Correspondence, vol. 59, 1962, *ACLU Papers,* quoted in D'Emilio 1983 (212).

17. Letter from Reitman to E. A. Dioguardi, May 10, 1962, General Correspondence, vol. 59, 1962, *ACLU Papers,* quoted in D'Emilio 1983 (212).

18. The notion of a repertoire of litigation draws on Tilly's (1978) notion of a repertoire of contention.

19. Quoted in Bragg 1994 (13).

20. For case studies of movements that have turned to the courts to achieve their social aims, see Burstein 1991; Epstein 1985; Handler 1978; and O'Connor 1980.

21. For in-depth accounts of NAACP litigation in these areas, see Greenberg 1977; Hahn 1973; Kellogg 1967; Kluger 1975; Tushnet 1987; Vose 1959; Wasby 1983.

22. For discussions of these other groups, see especially Epstein, George, and Kobylka 1992; Scheppele and Walker 1991.

23. For sodomy, see chapter 4. For employment, see, for example, *McConnell v. Anderson* (1971). For military service, see, for example, *Matlovich v. Secretary of the Air Force* (1974).

24. For example, *Gay Students Organization of the University of New Hampshire v. Bonner* (1974).

25. See chapter 7 for a discussion of these and other same-sex marriage cases.

CHAPTER THREE

1. Rhonda Rivera's 1979 survey of "the legal position of homosexual persons in the United States today" was a pioneering effort to uncover cases involving homosexuality. She discussed the problems she encountered in her research,

including the fact that legal digests often did not list homosexuality under a separate topical heading (as they do now) and that cases involving homosexuality were relatively unlikely to be published in law reporters (Rivera 1979).

2. Under the law, private citizens can legally engage in many forms of discrimination that are illegal when committed by state actors. It makes sense, then, for organizations seeking to eradicate discrimination to focus their initial efforts on state actors.

3. Lambda's records for this period are extremely fragmented, probably because it relied exclusively on volunteer attorneys and lacked a location (and staff support) to maintain a centralized set of records. As a result, there is uncertainty about the exact number of cases in which the organization officially played a role. By formal role, I mean that Lambda either litigated the case or filed an amicus curiae (friend of the court) brief. I have been able to document Lambda's formal involvement in forty-two cases. There are a handful of other cases, however, in which Lambda's early records suggest that it *might* have played a role, although I have not found any briefs or other official court documents. If I could not be certain of Lambda's involvement in a case, I did not include it.

It may seem odd not to know for sure, but using other sources to confirm Lambda's participation is more complicated than it might appear. Legal briefs are not easily available for most non–Supreme Court cases. In addition, legal decisions (which generally are available) are inconsistent with respect to whether they report the organizational affiliation of counsel and any amicus participation. Computerized databases such as LEXIS/NEXIS are quite good at noting the affiliation of counsel and any amici, but their records are much less complete for litigation in the 1970s than they are for litigation today. *Lesbian/Gay Law Notes*—the premier legal newsletter—did not begin publishing until 1981.

4. Two cases in which sodomy laws were *not* expressly invoked were *People v. Hammel* (1978), an unpublished case involving allegations of police brutality, and *Lambda Legal Defense and Education Fund v. Con Edison* (1978), a case involving the inclusion of advertisements in a pamphlet an electric company sent out to its customers.

5. New York Penal Law § 240.35(3) was challenged in *New York v. Uplinger*. New York's highest court found the statute unconstitutional in 1983.

6. The ex-spouse custody cases were *Mueller v. Mueller* (1980) and *Matter of Clifford* (1978). The other dispute was *Matter of Brown* (1977).

7. Judges look to many "relevant circumstances" in determining a child's best interests. For example, the wishes of both the child and the (prospective) parent(s) are commonly considered, as is the relationship of the child with her (prospective) parents and any other people who might significantly affect her best interests, the child's adjustment to her living arrangements, and the mental and physical health of all involved.

8. The Gay Rights Advocates subsequently changed its name to the National Gay Rights Advocates. The Lesbian Rights Project was a product of the Equal Rights Advocates. In 1987, it severed ties with its parent group and changed its name to the National Center for Lesbian Rights.

9. While the Gay Rights Advocates collapsed in 1991, all the other organi-

zations continue to exist. In 1993 the five extant gay legal groups were joined by a sixth: the Servicemembers Legal Defense Network.

10. For example, when Abby Rubenfeld came on board as Lambda's first managing attorney in 1983, her office was located next to that of the ACLU's Nan Hunter. (Hunter, who has become one of the foremost legal theorists of gay rights, was then working on the ACLU's Reproductive Rights Project.) Rubenfeld and Hunter talked frequently about litigation strategies in ongoing cases.

11. Nan Hunter went on to head this new project.

12. These laws varied widely in their scope. Generally they provided at least a minimal amount of protection from discrimination based on sexual orientation in public employment. Several also prohibited such discrimination in public accommodations. Note that I use the word *law* loosely here, including not only legislative acts but also executive orders and other formal tools of public policy. See generally Button, Rienzo, and Wald 1997.

13. They failed, however, to repeal Seattle's ordinance, garnering only 37 percent of the vote. See Adam 1995 (113).

14. For extended discussions of the rise of the New Right movement and its impact on gay rights, see Clendinen and Nagourney 1999; Herman 1997.

15. The Democrats took the opposite tack in their platform, suggesting that legislative and administrative steps be taken to discourage state-sanctioned discrimination on the basis of sexual orientation. Although it was the first time the Democratic platform had ever alluded to homosexuality, gay rights activists widely viewed the statement as disappointing because it failed to list any concrete steps to fight antigay discrimination. See Clendinen and Nagourney 1999.

16. For more on the tensions between gay men and lesbians in early gay liberation groups, see Adam 1995; Faderman 1991.

17. The case was *LaBreque v. Bradner Smith and Company* (1989).

18. Its cosponsors were the New York City Department of Health's Office of Gay and Lesbian Concerns, New York University's Womyn's Center, and the San Francisco–based Lesbian Rights Project.

19. Although the Gay Rights Advocates and the Lesbian Rights Project were both located in San Francisco, they appear to have avoided such power struggles, largely, I think, because they divided their "turf" along gender lines.

20. Author's interview with Kevin Cathcart, July 3, 1997.

21. For example, in 1980, then–Lambda executive director Roz Richter attended a meeting coordinated by the National Gay Task Force to discuss the implication of several judicial decisions involving gays in the military and to consider future litigation strategies. See *Lambda Update* 1980 (fall–winter).

22. For discussions of membership in the movement see Altman 1971; Halley 1989; Phelan 1989; Stychin 1998; and Taylor and Whittier 1992. For discussions of movement goals, see Ettelbrick 1989; Stoddard 1989; Sullivan 1995; and Vaid 1995. For discussions of the proper vehicles for attaining those goals, see Kramer 1989; Signorile 1994; and Sullivan 1995.

23. For in-depth discussions of the emergence of AIDS in the United States, see Altman 1986; Shilts 1987.

24. The hotline reported receiving some two hundred calls a day after Hud-

son's announcement, which works out to over four thousand calls a month. Although New York City had about 33 percent of the AIDS cases in the nation in 1985, heterosexual panic was not limited to AIDS epicenters. An AIDS hotline in Boston, for example, reported receiving thirty-four hundred phone calls in the month of August.

25. The archetypal example of this contagion fear was the book by Masters, Johnson, and Kolodny (1988) titled *Crisis: Heterosexual Behavior in the Age of AIDS*. The book received widespread media coverage (including a *Newsweek* cover article by the same name) but was also widely discredited by other experts. As Fumento (1990) shows, media emphasis on contagion fear decreased markedly after this point.

26. For AIDS arguments in the context of gay rights organizations, see, for example, *Gay Student Services v. Texas A&M University* (1984). For such arguments in the context of parenting, see, for example, *North v. North* (1994) and *In re Charles B.* (1990). In the context of employment, see, for example, *Leckelt v. Board of Commissioners* (1990).

27. The case involved a coop building's attempt to evict Dr. Joseph Sonnabend from his office space in the building, because he treated people with AIDS (*People of the State of New York, Joseph Sonnabend, M.D., et al. v. 49 West 12 Street Tenants Corporation*, 1993).

28. Then–executive director Tom Stoddard made this connection explicit in a 1987 *New York Times* article, when he noted that, "Without AIDS, Lambda would not be getting grants from mainstream foundations" (Shipp 1987).

29. The legal impact of *Bowers* is discussed in chapter 4.

30. Author's interview with Evan Wolfson, June 27, 1997.

31. Ibid.

32. For more on the immediate political response to *Bowers*, see Barker and Wheeler 1987; Dunlap 1994; Finder 1986.

33. *Bowers*, in fact, continued to figure in Lambda's solicitation materials until the Supreme Court finally struck down the decision in *Lawrence v. Texas* (2003).

34. The firms were Skadden, Arps, Wathcell Lipton, and Nizer, Benjamin. See Shipp 1987.

35. The midwest office was directly the product of a bequest. While most bequests had no strings attached, some were dedicated to specific ends. One such bequest was conditioned on the opening of an office in Chicago by the close of 1992.

36. These numbers exclude the value of donated legal services. In 2002, donated services were valued at approximately $1.5 million.

37. For examples of second-parent adoption cases, see *In re Adopt of BLVB & ELVB* (1993) and *Matter of Dana/Matter of Jacob* (1995). For same-sex coparent custody disputes, see *Alison D. v. Virginia M.* (1991) and *V.C. v. M.J.B.* (2000). For donor insemination disputes, see *Thomas S. v. Robin Y* (1994) and *Leckie v. Voorhies* (1994).

38. These cases and their aftermath are discussed in chapter 7.

39. This phrase comes from the 1993 Colorado Supreme Court decision in *Romer v. Evans*.

40. *Romer* and other cases arising from antigay measures are discussed in chapter 6.

41. One assault was so vicious that the boy required surgery to repair the damage. The school eventually settled the case for nearly $1 million after Lambda procured a ruling in the Seventh Circuit Court that held that the school had deliberately denied the boy protection from years of vicious abuse because he was gay.

42. See, for example, *East High Gay/Straight Alliance v. Salt Lake City Board of Education* (1999) and *Colín v. Orange Unified School District* (2000).

43. *Brandon v. Richardson County* (2002). The film *Boys Don't Cry* recounted Teena's story.

44. *In Matter of Estate of Marshall G. Gardiner* (2002). The validity of the Gardiner marriage was challenged by Marshall Gardiner's son after Gardiner died. (J'Noel had undergone sex reassignment years before the marriage and had successfully changed all her legal documentation to reflect her status as a postoperative female; her husband knew all about it.) The Kansas Supreme Court ultimately set aside the marriage, ruling that J'Noel remained a man for marriage purposes and that two men could not marry.

45. The report is titled "Youth in the Margins" and is available from Lambda.

46. For more information on the gay rights positions of presidential candidates, see Egan 1992; Schmalz 1992.

47. This is not to say that Clinton was an ideal ally. To the contrary, he quickly proved inconstant. Immediately after his election, Clinton used the agenda-setting capacity of his position to open a political debate about homosexuality and military service. He announced his intention to follow through on a campaign promise to rescind the ban on military service. However, this announcement sparked opposition among many members of the public, opposition that received a boost when the joint chiefs of staff announced that they opposed Clinton's plan and Senator Sam Nunn, chairman of the Senate Armed Services, commenced hearings on the issue.

Gays in the military blossomed into the first crisis of Clinton's young presidency, and by May of 1993 he was trying to distance himself from his promise to overturn the ban and to lay the groundwork for a political compromise. In July 1993, this compromise was announced. The new policy was dubbed "Don't Ask; Don't Tell." Under it, lgb people would be allowed to serve in the military, so long as they did not reveal their sexual orientation publicly and did not otherwise violate military law (which, among other things, prohibited sodomy without respect to the gender of the participants).

48. This is discussed in greater detail in chapter 7.

49. Lambda had previously filed an amicus brief in the case.

50. This ruling was based on the 1998 passage of a constitutional amendment giving the Hawaii legislature the authority to restrict marriage to opposite-sex couples. See chapter 7 for more details.

51. *Goodridge* succeeded where earlier litigation had fallen short. In November 2003, Massachusetts's Supreme Judicial Court ruled that same-sex couples

had the right to marry under the state's constitution; on May 17, 2004, the first such marriages took place. As *Baehr* had earlier, *Goodridge* set a number of wheels into motion. Within a few months of the decision, state legislatures across the nation began to consider constitutional amendments refusing recognition to same-sex marriages validly performed in other jurisdictions. President George W. Bush endorsed a proposed amendment to the U.S. Constitution that would restrict marriage to opposite-sex couples. San Francisco, Oregon's Multnomah County, and other localities scattered around the nation began issuing marriage licenses to same-sex couples until ordered to desist by courts, state attorneys general, and other authoritative interpreters of state law. And Lambda began litigating marriage challenges in three additional states: California (*Proposition 22 Legal Defense and Education Fund v. Martin et al.* in progress), New York (*Hernandez v. Robles,* in progress), and Washington (*Andersen v. Sims,* in progress). It is quite clear that the shift in legal frames surrounding marriage that began with *Baehr* is still in progress and will occupy the center of the battle over gay rights for the foreseeable future.

52. These states were California (1992), Connecticut (1991), Hawaii, (1991), Maryland (2001), Massachusetts (1989), Minnesota (1993), Nevada (1999), New Hampshire (1997), New Jersey (1992), New York (passed in 2002, took effect in 2003), Rhode Island (1995), Vermont (1992), and Wisconsin (1982). Maine passed a comprehensive law in 1997, but it was repealed by a ballot measure in 1998.

53. These states were Colorado (1990), Delaware (2001), Illinois (1996), Indiana (2001), Montana (2000), New Mexico (1985), Pennsylvania (1988), and Washington (1985). An Ohio executive order issued in 1983 was rewritten in 1999 to exclude lgb employees. Executive orders issued in Ohio and Iowa in 1999 were repealed in 2000. For more information on states with gay rights laws, see van der Meide 2000.

54. In 1998, for example, the Alabama Supreme Court upheld a trial court's change of custody from a lesbian mother to a heterosexual father, despite undisputed evidence that the child was happy and well adjusted living in her mother's care. The court was greatly disturbed that the women had "established a two-parent home environment where their homosexual relationship is openly practiced and presented to the child as the social and moral equivalent of a heterosexual marriage" (*Ex parte J.M.F.,* 14–15).

55. These states were Iowa, Maryland, Massachusetts, Minnesota, Nevada, Oregon, and Washington.

56. These cities were Atlanta, Baltimore, Boston, Chicago, Los Angeles, Madison, New York, Portland, San Francisco, and Seattle.

57. A small sampling of religious figures and organizations includes the Rt. Rev. John Shelby Spong, Bishop Walter Righter, the American Friends Service Committee (Quakers), the Association of American Hebrew Congregations, and the Unitarian Universalist Association. For a more complete listing of prominent individuals and groups supporting the Marriage Project, see the Lambda Legal Defense and Education Fund web site at www.lambdalegal.org.

58. The three cities were Ithaca, New York; and Los Angeles and West Hollywood, California. Politicians included Rep. John Lewis (D-GA) and Mayor Willie Brown (D) of San Francisco.

59. These states were Alabama, California, Idaho, Nebraska, South Carolina, South Dakota, and Virginia.

60. These states were Alabama, California, Colorado, Georgia, Idaho, Michigan, Mississippi, Missouri, Nebraska, South Carolina, and South Dakota.

CHAPTER FOUR

1. This occurred despite the fact that the great majority of sodomy statutes were gender neutral on their face, prohibiting particular acts without respect to the gender of the actors. As Janet Halley has noted (1993, 1737) sodomy has come to constitute a "rhetorical proxy" for homosexuality.

2. *Lawrence* raised an equal protection claim in addition to the privacy claim. It also asked the Supreme Court to overturn its ruling in *Bowers*.

3. Illinois repealed its sodomy statute in 1961.

4. In 1990, an entry-level court in Michigan ruled the state's sodomy law unconstitutional (*Michigan Organization for Human Rights [MOHR] v. Kelly*). By refusing to appeal the lower court's decision, the state's attorney general limited the holding of the court to one county and threw the enforceability of the statute into a sort of legal limbo. In figure 1, I treat Michigan as maintaining its sodomy law. Justice Kennedy's majority opinion in *Lawrence*, conversely, treats Michigan as a "reformed" state. *MOHR* is discussed in more detail in chapter 5.

5. The other four were treason, murder, witchcraft, and "willful and proposed burning of ships houses" (Katz 1983, 74).

6. The two remaining states may have had prohibitions against sodomy and/or buggery; the record is unclear. (Ironically, one of the states in which the record is unclear is Georgia, the state that would give birth to *Bowers*.) See Goldstein 1988.

7. For example, *Glover v. State* (1913) and *State v. Stuart* (1913).

8. The states were Colorado (1972), Oregon (1972), Delaware (1973), Hawaii (1973), and Ohio (1974).

9. The states were Montana (1973), Texas (1973), Kentucky (1974), Arkansas (1977), Missouri (1977), and Kansas (1983).

10. The great majority of sodomy charges are brought in cases where there are also allegations of rape or aggravated assault. (Because consent is not a defense to sodomy, it is often easier to prove than rape or assault.) For a discussion of the criminal enforcement of sodomy statutes, see *Harvard Law Review* 1989 (vol. 102).

11. See *Virginia v. American Booksellers Ass'n* (1988, 392–93).

12. For more details about the circumstances surrounding Hardwick's arrest, see Harris 1986; Irons 1988.

13. Author's interview with Kathleen Wilde, who served as lead counsel for Hardwick until the case was accepted by the Supreme Court.

14. For a fascinating study of the Court's agenda-setting process, see Perry 1991.

15. Justice Douglas had retired from the Court shortly before *Doe* arrived. He was replaced by Stevens.

16. For an extensive analysis of the precedential value of summary affirmances and reversals, see Phillips 1978.

17. See *Kelly v. State* (1980) and *People v. Masten* (1980).

18. For example, *Petition of Nemetz* (1980), involving immigration, and *Childers v. Dallas Police Department* (1981), involving public employment.

19. *People v. Onofre* (1980), *Commonwealth v. Bonadio* (1980), and *Baker v. Wade* (1982). *Baker* was subsequently reversed by the Fifth Circuit (1985).

20. *People v. Onofre* (1978). The trial court's decision is not reported but is included in the petition for a writ of certiorari filed by the state of New York in the case.

21. For example, *State v. Pilcher* (1976) and *State v. Saunders* (1977).

22. The quotations in this paragraph are all drawn from the 1982 federal district court opinion.

23. Baker's suit was financed primarily by the Texas Human Rights Foundation, a gay rights group that had organized primarily to support his suit. Lambda was not involved with *Baker* during its initial phase of litigation, although, as I detail later, it became very involved in later phases of the case.

24. The testimony of Dr. James Grigson, reported in *Baker,* 1132–34.

25. Several cases were in the litigation pipeline when *Bowers* came down. For example, *State v. Walsh* (1986), a challenge to Missouri's sodomy law, was awaiting decision by the state's high court when *Bowers* was announced. Two weeks after the announcement, the Missouri Supreme Court upheld the statute, relying largely on *Bowers*. Lambda subsequently withdrew a sodomy challenge it had in progress in Louisiana. Other gay rights litigators did the same with their pending challenges.

26. Recall that the right to privacy articulated in *Griswold* and elaborated in *Stanley, Eisenstadt,* and *Roe* served as a legal linchpin for the decisions in *Onofre* and *Baker*.

27. The exception is Antonin Scalia. Technically, he filled Rehnquist's seat when Rehnquist became chief justice in Burger's stead. Although a vocal conservative voice on the Court, Scalia's voting record in civil liberties cases has been somewhat more liberal than Rehnquist's—roughly equivalent to Burger's record.

28. It is interesting that her nomination raised the ire of pro-lifers, because as an Arizona state legislator she had cast several votes in opposition to pro-life bills. In 1974, for example, she voted against a proposal urging Congress to pass a constitutional amendment overturning *Roe v. Wade* (Witt 1986). However, Reagan's advisors assured pro-life leaders that O'Connor "was personally opposed to abortion" and she "believe[d] abortion to be a legitimate matter for legislative regulation" (Abraham 1985, 332).

29. For example, she dissented in *Akron v. Akron Center for Reproductive Health* (1983), the first abortion-related case to come before the Court during her tenure, attacking the trimester framework of *Roe v. Wade* and arguing that the nature of the fundamental right recognized in *Roe* was limited rather than absolute. O'Connor's harsh attack on the trimester framework of *Roe v. Wade* in *Akron* in turn sparked a renewed emphasis by pro-life groups on attacking the legal grounding of the right to abortion (Epstein and Kobylka 1992, 248).

30. *Baker* offers a wonderful example of the impact of elections on the process of litigation. The federal civil rights complaint Baker filed in 1979 named Dallas district attorney Henry Wade (of *Roe v. Wade* fame) and Dallas city attorney Lee Holt as defendants. (The state of Texas intervened in the case via its attorney general.) To ensure that the district court ruling would be binding on every jurisdiction in Texas, Baker also named "all district, county and city attorneys in the State of Texas" as defendants in the case (*Baker,* 1982, 1125). The ninety-five-odd attorneys were all notified of the suit and of their right to intervene in the case. None chose to do so. Wade and Holt were then certified by the district court as representatives of the entire class of defendants. All the defendants were duly notified when Baker prevailed in U.S. District Court.

Between Baker's initial filing in 1979 and his court victory in 1982, however, Danny Hill had been elected as Potter County's district attorney. When he was notified of the outcome of the case, he promptly filed an appeal to the Fifth Circuit. Texas's attorney general also filed a Fifth Circuit appeal, but a few days later he lost his bid for reelection. His successor, Jim Mattox, took office in January 1983 and after reviewing the particulars of *Baker* chose to withdraw the appeal. When Hill learned of Mattox's action, he petitioned the Texas Supreme Court to *compel* the attorney general to continue the appeal. When the Texas high court refused even to hear the petition, Hill filed concurrent motions in both the U.S. District Court and the Fifth Circuit to set aside the judgment and substitute himself as the class representative.

Much of the appeals litigation concerned whether Hill had standing to pursue an appeal (either in his official or private capacity), even though his predecessor had chosen not to intervene in the case and Texas's attorney general had chosen as a matter of public policy not to pursue the case further. The question of Hill's standing bounced up and down the federal court ladder for several years. See *Baker* (5th Cir. 1985, 291–92) for a further discussion of Hill's involvement with the case.

31. The existing statute (Tex. Pen. Code. Ann. § 21.06) prohibited *most* same-sex sexual intimacy, but not all: lesbians and gay men were not prohibited from "kissing, hugging, or sexually stimulating their partners with hands or fingers" (*Baker,* 1982, 1151). The current statute classified sodomy as a Class C misdemeanor bringing a $200 fine. Under HB 2138, a first offense would be classified as a third-degree felony, bringing imprisonment of two to ten years and a $5,000 fine. Subsequent offenses would be second-degree felonies, warranting imprisonment of two to twenty years and a $10,000 fine.

32. Ceverha and Hill were also connected directly: Ceverha joined Hill's petition to compel the attorney general to appeal *Baker.*

33. Cameron has been a key champion of the argument that lgb people pose threats to children, family stability, and public health. His suggested policies toward gay men in the face of AIDS have included quarantine, facial tattooing, and extermination (Pietrzyk 1994), though he has noted that the last is "not politically or socially acceptable at this time" (Pietrzyk 1994, 10–11). Cameron's credibility as a scientist has been roundly attacked by gay rights advocates, who point to the fact that Cameron resigned from the American Psychological Association to avoid investigation into charges of his unethical conduct as a psychologist.

These charges included Cameron's continuing misrepresentation of research on the origins and nature of homosexuality.

34. Lambda became involved in *Baker* and *Texas A&M* when DDAA did. Lambda's primary role in both cases was to counter DDAA's "AIDS-threat" arguments. It did so through a multipronged strategy. It arranged for medical experts to file amicus briefs exploring the public health implications of AIDS. It relied on those experts to argue that sodomy statutes impaired public health rather than promoting it, because they caused individuals to conceal or distort relevant information about their sexual practices and inhibited effective public education efforts. Lambda also argued that the rapid state of evolution in scientific understandings about AIDS made it unwise for courts to rush to judgment on the constitutional questions raised by the epidemic.

35. The quote comes from Lambda's *Onofre* brief and cites Richards 1979 (1003–4).

36. Okla. Stat. Tit. 70, § 6–103.15 (A) (2).

37. Dicta are expressions in a court's opinion that are not essential to deciding the specific case at hand. They are not legally binding but can be useful indicators of how a court might approach future cases.

38. Letter to William B. Rogers (ACLU of Oklahoma), Leonard Graff (GRA), and Lucia Valeska (NGTF), dated August 3, 1982.

39. Faced with the inevitability of a Tenth Circuit ruling, Lambda and the national ACLU both filed amicus briefs in the case. Lambda's records offer no explanation for the organization's decision to file an amicus brief, but two likely reasons present themselves. The first highlights a common problem facing social movement litigators: their inability to always control the initiation and progress of cases. Given Lambda's inability to convince the GRA to halt *NGTF*, Lambda was faced with two real options: do nothing or add its voice to the case and hope, by doing so, to sway the Tenth Circuit by its presence and its arguments. Lambda's decision to join *NGTF* may alternately have reflected its desire to protect its position as a litigator within the gay rights movement. By joining the case as an amicus, Lambda would be able to "claim" the case as its own and point to it as evidence of the important work done by the organization.

40. Justice Powell, the tie-breaking vote in *Bowers,* did not participate in *NGTF* because he was recovering from surgery.

41. Hardwick's sex partner, in contrast, chose not to join the case, apparently because of concerns over his job (he was a teacher) and his marriage. See Harris 1986.

42. The ACLU, like Lambda, farms out much of its day-to-day litigation to a network of cooperating attorneys who volunteer their services pro bono.

43. Wilde, interview.

44. The groups were GRA, GLAD, the Lesbian Rights Project, the Texas Human Rights Foundation, and a Pennsylvania group called Custody Action for Lesbian Mothers (CALM). As one participant at this gathering said to me, "it was the first time gay legal activists got together in one room to talk and plan."

45. A critic might suggest that building two cases was more than the task force could handle and that by dividing its energies in this fashion the task force diminished its ability to litigate either one of the cases effectively. This criticism is misguided. First, while the task force played an important role as a mechanism of

intracommunity communication and coordination, the ACLU actually sponsored *Bowers,* while the Texas Human Rights Foundation sponsored *Baker.* The ACLU's pockets were more than deep enough to adequately fund its case, and it commonly handled multiple suits at the same time.

Second, the task force did an excellent job of mobilizing allied support in support of Michael Hardwick. It coordinated the submission of seven amicus briefs on behalf of twenty-three organizations and two states. Three came from members of the task force and also had other signatories. Lambda's brief was cosigned by GLAD, two lgb bar associations, and a national lgb political group. The Lesbian Rights Project submitted a brief joined by a host of women's rights groups. The National Gay Rights Advocates contributed a brief that was cosigned by four California-based legal advocacy groups. The task force also coordinated the submission of an amicus brief from a consortium of religious groups that argued that the criminalization of private consensual sodomy had no legitimate basis in contemporary morality. A brief submitted by the American Psychological Association and the American Public Health Association argued that sodomy statutes furthered neither personal nor public health. Impressively, the state of New York also submitted a brief on Hardwick's behalf, drawing on *Onofre;* the state of California signed the brief as well.

46. Hardwick's litigation team changed for the Supreme Court phase of the case. Up until the Supreme Court granted Georgia's petition for a writ of certiorari, Wilde served as Hardwick's lead counsel. At this point, constitutional scholars Laurence Tribe and Kathleen Sullivan entered the case, and Tribe became Hardwick's lead counsel. (Wilde continued on as one of the team of attorneys working on the case.) Although memories are no longer clear on the subject, it appears that the notion to bring in Tribe and Sullivan was initially voiced by members of the task force.

47. Quoted in Garrow 1994, 660–61. *Robinson v. California* is a 1962 case in which the Supreme Court held that the Eighth Amendment barred convicting a defendant due to his "status" as a narcotics addict, since that condition was "apparently an illness which may be contracted innocently or involuntarily" (*Robinson,* 667).

48. See *Bowers,* 1985, Brief of Appellants on Appeal, 33 (on file with Lambda).

49. About 73 percent of the respondents knew about the Supreme Court decision. Of this group, 47 percent disapproved and 41 percent approved.

50. Author's interview with Evan Wolfson, June 27, 1997.

51. Stoddard and then–legal director Abby Rubenfeld supplemented written appeals for mobilization with a bevy of interviews and speaking engagements; both also wrote law review articles attacking *Bowers.* See Rubenfeld 1986 and Stoddard 1987.

52. The Eleventh Circuit issued its decision on May 21, 1985. Rock Hudson's illness became public knowledge on June 24, 1985. The Supreme Court granted certiorari on November 4, 1985.

CHAPTER FIVE

1. Letter to Abby Rubenfeld, July 7, 1986 (on file with author).
2. Ky. Rev. State. Ann. § 510.100. "Deviate sexual intercourse" was defined

as "any act of sexual gratification involving the sex organs of one person and the mouth or anus of another" (Ky. Rev. State. Ann. § 510.010).

3. See especially *People v. Lino* (1994). If *MOHR* is understood to mean that Michigan effectively eradicated its sodomy statutes in 1990, then the beginning of stage 4 should move up from 1992 to 1990. The ambiguity of this temporal boundary highlights the fact that shifts in the structure of legal opportunities do not always occur at discrete points in time.

4. Amici included the American Friends Service Committee, the American Public Health Association, the Presbyterian Church (USA), the Union of American Hebrew Congregations, the Unitarian Universalist Association, and the United Methodist Church.

5. These were not the only constitutional challenges to sodomy laws to occur. Scattered individuals arrested and/or convicted of sodomy also challenged the law. Of those cases, only *Miller v. State of Mississippi* (1994) made it as far as a state court of last resort. Miller was convicted of committing "unnatural intercourse" with a seventeen-year-old male employee of the restaurant he managed, after first getting him drunk; he was sentenced to ten years in jail. He appealed, challenging his conviction on a number of grounds, including that Mississippi's law (Miss. Code Ann. § 97-29-59 [1972]) violated state and federal guarantees of privacy. The Mississippi Supreme Court relied on *Bowers* to dismiss Miller's federal privacy claim. It declined to address Miller's state claim, because the case did not involve consenting adults. Said the court, "Clearly, no right of privacy attaches to sexual acts committed with children, who have been illegally supplied with alcohol" (*Miller*, 394).

I do not address *Miller* and similar sodomy law challenges because they were not part of any concerted effort to eradicate sodomy laws. Moreover, they were often poorly argued. (Miller's attorneys, for example, cited only one earlier Mississippi case in support of their state privacy argument, and that case was only tangentially related to their claim.)

6. See, for example, *Campbell v. Sundquist* (1996), *Gryczan v. State* (1997), and *State v. Powell* (1998).

7. The ACLU also argued that the solicitation statute violated Christensen's free expression rights to the extent that it criminalized discussions about engaging in private, consensual, noncommercial sodomy.

8. Arrests for private, consensual opposite-sex sodomy were likewise rare. As in *Powell*, virtually all arrests and convictions came in cases where sodomy was a lesser included charge to a sexual assault of some kind.

9. There are some limitations to this claim. The state can impose time, place, and manner restrictions, for instance, so long as those restrictions advance a legitimate governmental purpose.

10. These cases were *State of Louisiana v. Baxley* (1994), *Sawatzky v. Oklahoma City* (1995), *Christensen v. Georgia* (1996), and *City of Topeka v. Movsovitz* (1998).

11. The exceptions were *State of Texas v. Morales* and *Louisiana Electorate of Gays and Lesbians v. Louisiana* (2002).

12. The exception to this trend was *Sanchez v. Puerto Rico* (2002).

13. *Doe v. Ventura* (2002), citing *Lefler v. Lefler* (1999, 422).

14. The amicus brief submitted by Concerned Women for America advanced

the argument that sodomy laws were necessary to prevent the spread of AIDS by promiscuous gay men, some of whom actively sought to catch and/or transmit the disease (27–28).

15. Poll results from Gallup and Princeton Survey Research Associates (PSRA) differ significantly from the ANES. According to Gallup and PSRA data, more than eight out of ten respondents favored equal employment rights for lesbians and gay men by the mid-1990s (see Yang 2000, 6–9). Differences in the Gallup/PSRA and ANES findings are probably a product of question wording. The ANES asked respondents whether they favored or opposed *laws* to protect homosexuals against job discrimination. Both Gallup and PSRA phrased their questions as one of "equal rights . . . in terms of job opportunities." There is a difference between favoring the abstract notion of equal rights and supporting laws designed to protect members of specific groups against job discrimination, and it is not surprising to find more support for the former than the latter.

16. The question wording was as follows: "Do you think homosexuals should be allowed to serve in the United States Armed Forces or don't you think so?" Data provided for analysis by the Inter-University Consortium for Social Research.

17. The question wording was as follows: "Do you think gay or lesbian couples, in other words homosexual couples, should be legally permitted to adopt children?" Data provided for analysis by the Inter-University Consortium for Social Research.

18. It is intriguing that all of these issues seeped into the public consciousness as a result of Lambda-backed court cases.

19. The Defense of Marriage Act is discussed further in chapter 7.

20. The ACLU raised federal equal protection and establishment of religion claims in *Sawatzky;* it raised federal privacy and equal protection claims in *Movsovitz*. GLAD and the ACLU of Rhode Island filed amici briefs in *State v. Lopes,* which involved a heterosexual man, and raised federal privacy and equal protection claims.

21. These states were Arkansas, Kansas, Maryland, Missouri, Oklahoma, and Texas.

22. As noted in chapter 3, this sort of lawyer swapping occurs commonly.

23. The factual underpinnings of *Sanchez* were in many ways as compelling as sodomy reform litigators could hope for, given that none of the plaintiffs in the case had been arrested. Rev. Margarita Sanchez had been threatened by a government official with prosecution under Puerto Rico's sodomy law as a consequence of her exercise of the right to free speech. In 1997, Sanchez had testified before a committee of the Puerto Rico House of Representatives in opposition to a bill banning same-sex marriage. She was the only witness to testify against the bill. During her testimony she was questioned about her sexual activity, unlike any of the other witnesses. A legislator then threatened her with criminal prosecution as a result of her sexual orientation and sexual activity. The Puerto Rico Department of Justice subsequently announced that it intended to enforce the sodomy law if police brought them evidence of violations.

24. Michael Hardwick and his unidentified companion were held for over twelve hours. John Lawrence and Tyrone Garner were held for over a day.

25. That Kennedy authored the majority opinion in *Lawrence* had a touch of poetic justice to it: Kennedy had been tapped to fill Powell's seat.

26. This number includes Michigan for reasons discussed earlier in this chapter.

27. *United States v. Marcum* was before the U.S. Court of Appeals for the Armed Forces. Article 125 of the Code of Conduct prohibits consensual sodomy, regardless of the gender of the participants. Sodomy is defined to include oral and anal sex.

28. The subject of same-sex marriage will be discussed at length in chapter 7. It should be noted here, however, that GLAD (the organization behind the case) never expressly raised *Lawrence* as a rationale for its argument that the Massachusetts constitution required the recognition of same-sex marriages. *Lawrence* is a federal constitutional case. *Goodridge* was based entirely on state constitutional arguments.

29. Justice Kennedy's opinion in *Lawrence* had specifically noted that the case did not involve minors.

30. This is ironic in that Justice Kennedy declined to rule on the equal protection claim in *Lawrence* because he felt that the privacy claim was the more fundamental of the two and that a ruling on the merits of the latter would inevitably implicate the former. He wrote:

> As an alternative argument in this case, counsel for the petitioners and some *amici* contend that *Romer* provides the basis for declaring the Texas statute invalid under the Equal Protection Clause. That is a tenable argument, but we conclude the instant case requires us to address whether *Bowers* itself has continuing validity. Were we to hold the statute invalid under the Equal Protection Clause some might question whether a prohibition would be valid if drawn differently, say, to prohibit the conduct both between same-sex and different-sex participants. Equality of treatment and the due process right to demand respect for conduct protected by the substantive guarantee of liberty are linked in important respects, and a decision on the latter point advances both interests. (*Lawrence*, 2482)

31. The Republican leadership in the Senate has used *Lawrence* to argue the need for a federal constitutional amendment to ban same-sex marriage. See United States Senate Republican Policy Committee 2003.

CHAPTER SIX

1. The laws targeted by these measures varied widely in their scope. Most commonly, they provided at least a minimal amount of protection from discrimination based on sexual orientation in public employment. Many also prohibited discrimination in public accommodations. A few addressed other gay rights concerns, such as family and medical leave, health benefits, and domestic partnership. (Note that I use the word *law* loosely here to include not only legislative acts but also executive orders and other formal tools of public policy.)

2. This table excludes measures designed to prevent same-sex couples from legally marrying each other. See chapter 7 for a discussion of ballot measures in this context.

3. This success rate stands in stark contrast to the larger universe of popularly generated ballot measures, which succeed about 33 percent of the time (see Gamble 1997). However, it parallels the success of ballot measures concerned more specifically with civil rights. Gamble (1997) examined ballot measures in five different areas: housing and accommodations, school desegregation, English-language laws, AIDS, and gay rights. She found that civil rights protections were rolled back at the ballot box about three-quarters of the time.

4. *Citizens for Responsible Behavior v. Superior Court* (1991); *Romer v. Evans; In re Advisory Opinion to the Attorney General* (1994); *Morris v. Hill* (1996); *Equality Foundation of Greater Cincinnati. v. City of Cincinnati* (1997); *Lowe v. Keisling* (1994); *Rose v. Keisling* (1996). The notable exception to this trend is *Equality,* which will be discussed subsequently.

5. For in-depth examinations of the electoral strategies of antigay rights activists, see Adams 1994; Lewin 1993; McCorkle and Most 1997.

6. See Schattschneider 1960 for further discussion of the impact of expanding the scope of conflict.

7. This is not to say that twenty-six states never utilize the initiative/referendum process. Most states, for example, require that proposed constitutional amendments be voted on by the electorate. *Legislatively* generated ballot measures, however, are different from *popularly* generated ballot measures. For an extended conversation about the use of referenda and initiatives, see Butler and Ranney 1978.

8. During this time, state legislatures enacted gay rights laws in seven states: Wisconsin, Massachusetts, Connecticut, Hawaii, New Jersey, Vermont, and California. Executives in ten states issued executive orders: Pennsylvania, California, New York, Ohio, New Mexico, Rhode Island, Washington, Minnesota, Oregon, and Louisiana. California is the only state to have both a legislatively originated and an executively originated gay rights policy.

9. It should be noted here that most states permit popularly initiated ballot measures in *local* elections (Eule 1990). Whether local gay rights laws generally face repeal efforts is a question beyond the scope of this study. Information is scattered and more difficult to obtain. Unlike statewide repeals, local repeal efforts rarely generate much nationwide publicity. Lambda keeps records of most measures that *qualify* for the ballot but rarely notes repeal *attempts.*

10. For more on the requirements for putting proposed measures onto the ballot, see Kehler and Stern 1994; Magleby 1984; Witt and McCorkle 1997.

11. California, Florida, and Oregon all have single-subject requirements for ballot initiatives.

12. Alaska, Florida, Idaho, Michigan, and Idaho all have title and/or summary requirements for proposed ballot measures.

13. *In re Advisory Opinion to the Attorney General* (1994). For other examples of successful preelection challenges to antigay measures, see *Collins v. Commonwealth* (1990), blocking a referendum to repeal Massachusetts's newly enacted gay rights law on subject-matter grounds; *Faipeas v. Anchorage* (1993),

blocking a referendum to repeal the sexual orientation clause of Anchorage's public employment and municipal contractor law because of its misleading title; and *Iorio v. Citizens for a Fair Tampa* (1995), blocking a referendum to repeal a Tampa, Florida, ordinance barring discrimination based on sexual orientation, based on postsignature changes in the wording of the ballot measure.

14. For other examples of courts rejecting preelection challenges, see *Privacy Right Education Project v. Moriarty* (1993), ruling that a challenge to a Missouri antigay initiative still in the signature-gathering phase was premature; *Lowe v. Keisling* (1994), ruling that a proposed statewide initiative did not violate Oregon's single-subject rule; and *Wagner v. Secretary of State* (1995), ruling that a proposed statewide measure in Maine was a permissible statutory initiative rather than an impermissible constitutional initiative and that the language of the measure was not misleading.

15. Executive Summary, Human Rights Ordinance, part 3, article 5, chapter 1, part 3, sections 1-5-301 through 1-5-321.

16. One wonders, in fact, *why* the Human Rights Commission of Colorado Springs proposed to include sexual orientation in the first place.

17. The membership of CFV shook itself out a bit as the group got rolling. Marco, for example, left the group after a few months, although he remained an important advisor. See Herman 1997 (143–44) for an fuller discussion of the membership of CFV.

18. Quoted in *Romer*, 1996, Brief for the NAACP Legal Defense and Educational Fund, Inc., the Mexican American Legal Defense and Educational Fund, and Women's Legal Defense Fund as *Amici Curiae* in Support of Respondents, 13, 18. One of these "facts" was that "Lesbians are now having babies conceived by homosexual semen."

19. The source for this and all other campaign materials is Gerstmann 1999 unless specifically stated otherwise.

20. Quoted in *Romer*, 1993, Plaintiffs-Appellees' Answer Brief, 11.

21. Ibid., 11–12.

22. For extended discussions of attitudes toward civil rights laws in the context of gay rights, see Button, Rienzo, and Wald 1997; Schacter 1994.

23. For more on the use of symbols in politics, see Sears 1993.

24. The lineup changed a bit over the course of litigation. The plaintiff with AIDS died. A few individual plaintiffs dropped out, citing fear of adverse consequences in their personal lives. Two individual plaintiffs joined the case, as did the Boulder Valley School District.

25. There was significant dissension among the legal team over the timing of the legal challenge. Both Lambda and the ACLU thought the best legal strategy was to seek to prevent Amendment 2 from ever going into effect. Dubofsky thought the better strategy was to wait and gather evidence of the harmful effects of the law and then bring suit to declare it unconstitutional. Lambda and the ACLU ultimately prevailed. For a recounting of intralitigator tensions in *Romer v. Evans* see Keen and Goldberg 1998 (17–22).

26. For more on the impact of member turnover, see Schwartz 1988; Epstein and Kobylka 1992.

27. For restrictions on the franchise, see *Kramer v. Union Free Sch. Dist. No.*

15 (1969) and *Cipriano v. City of Houma* (1969). For reapportionment, see *Reynolds v. Sims* (1964) and *Davis v. Bandemer* (1986). For minority party rights, see *Illinois State Board of Elections v. Socialist Workers Party* (1979) and *Norman v. Reed* (1992).

28. *Romer*, 1996, Brief for Respondents, 17.

29. *Romer*, 1996, Brief for Amici Curiae Asian American Legal Defense and Education Fund et al., 18–19.

30. Ibid., 21.

31. *Romer*, 1996, Brief for Respondents, 41.

32. *Romer*, 1993, State of Colorado Trial Brief, 69.

33. In the context of owner-occupied rental housing, such an exception is sometimes referred to as the "Mrs. Murphy's Boarding House" exception. See Anderson 1997.

34. *Romer*, 1993, State of Colorado Trial Brief, 72, citing *Pierce v. Society of Sisters* (1925) and also referencing Aldous Huxley's *Brave New World* (1932).

35. Ibid., 75.

36. *Romer*, 1996, Brief for Respondents, 45.

37. Of course, nothing prevents them from *becoming* legal standards in the future, should a court or legislature choose to invest them with legal meaning.

38. There are myriad examples of the legal system operating as an obstacle to, rather than a facilitator of, social reform in the context of other movements (e.g., Forbath 1991; Haines 1996). The movement to outlaw child labor is one classic example. Here, Congress was far more receptive to the claims of movement activists than were the courts. In fact, the Supreme Court twice overturned congressional legislation designed to end child labor, effectively blocking social reform in the area for several decades (Paul 1960).

39. For a more in-depth examination of the use of litigation to advance gay rights claims in the context of employment, see Achtenberg 1996; Leonard 1993.

40. Cf. Olson 1990.

CHAPTER SEVEN

1. For accounts of such "secret" same-sex marriages, see Eskridge 1996; Faderman 1991.

2. See, for example, *Jones v. Hallahan* (1973); *Singer v. Hara* (1974); *Jennings v. Jennings* (1974); *Slayton v. State* (1982); *Adams v. Howerton* (1982); *De Santo v. Barnsely* (1984); *In re Succession of Bacot* (1987); *Gajovski v. Gajovski* (1991).

3. Compare Eskridge 1996; Mohr 1995; Sullivan 1995; and Wolfson 1994— arguing for same-sex marriage—with Duclos 1991; Foster 1998; Hunter 1991; and Polikoff 1993—arguing against the pursuit of same-sex marriage.

4. As Ettelbrick saw it, seeking marriage ran contrary to the goals of gay liberation. These goals, she said,

must simply be broader than the right to marry. Gay and lesbian marriages may minimally transform the institution of marriage by diluting its traditional patriarchal dynamic, but they will not transform society. They will not demolish the two-tier system of the "haves" and the "have-nots." We must not fool ourselves into believing that marriage will make it acceptable to be gay or lesbian. We will be liberated only when we are respected and accepted for our differences and the diversity we provide to this society. (Ettelbrick 1989, 8)

5. Hawaii, like many other states, has an equal rights amendment in its constitution, making discrimination on the basis of gender subject to strict scrutiny.

6. Hawaii Revised Statute 572–1.

7. Article IV, section 1, of the U.S. Constitution states that "Full faith and credit shall be given in each state to the public acts, records, and judicial proceedings of every other state. And the Congress may by general laws prescribe the manner in which such acts, records and proceedings shall be proved, and the effect thereof."

8. See generally the Restatement (Second) of Conflict of Laws § 283 (1988).

9. See chapter 3 for a small sample of supporters. For a more complete listing of prominent individuals and groups supporting the Marriage Project, see the Lambda Legal Defense and Education Fund web site at www.lambdalegal.org.

10. Utah passed its legislation in 1995. Alaska, Arizona, Delaware, Georgia, Idaho, Illinois, Kansas, Michigan, Missouri (struck down in 1998 by the Missouri Supreme Court), North Carolina, Oklahoma, Pennsylvania, South Carolina, South Dakota, and Tennessee passed legislation in 1996.

11. Defense of Marriage Act (DOMA) 2(a), 28 U.S.C.A. 1738C (West Supp. 1998). DOMA is particularly notable because Congress rarely regulates domestic relationships, which are generally viewed as falling within the sphere of the states. For a fuller discussion of DOMA, see Butler 1998.

12. Senator Richard Lugar did not endorse the rally. Patrick Buchanan appeared in person, while Senator Bob Dole, former governor Lamar Alexander, and Steve Forbes sent written letters of support. See Dunlap 1996.

13. The name of the case had become *Baehr v. Miike* by this point. It took over three years to work its way to trial because the trial court judge (Judge Chang) postponed the proceedings in order to give the Commission on Sexual Orientation and the Law time to study and report on the legal inequities facing same-sex couples.

14. 1997 Haw. Sess. Laws 2786, Act 383.

15. Opinion of the Attorney General, No. 97–05 (1997).

16. 1997 Haw. Sess. Laws 2883, H.B. 117.

17. Approximately $1.5 million was spent by each side during the campaign. The Mormon Church was the largest donor to the proamendment side. The Human Rights Campaign was the largest donor to the antiamendment forces. See Eskridge 2002 for a more in-depth discussion of the subject.

18. The case at this point was known as *Baehr v. Anderson*.

19. These states were Arkansas, Florida, Indiana, Maine, Minnesota, Mississippi, Montana, North Dakota, and Virginia.

20. Alabama, Iowa, Kentucky, Washington, and, of course, Hawaii passed mini-DOMAs in 1998. In addition, Alaska passed a second mini-DOMA.

21. These states were California, Colorado, Nebraska, and West Virginia.

For a more extended exploration of the introduction, progress, and outcomes of anti-same-sex marriage bills, see the Lambda Legal Defense and Education Fund web site at www.lambdalegal.org.

22. 1996 Alaska Stat. § 25.011(a) and 25.05.013(e).

23. S.J. Res. 42, 20th Leg., 2d Legis. Sess. (Alaska 1998).

24. Although the campaign in Alaska received far less national media attention than the campaign in Hawaii, organized interests spent a lot of time and money attempting to influence the outcome. See Clarkson, Coolidge, and Duncan 1999.

25. For more on the origin of *Baker* see Eskridge 2002.

26. In this way, *Baker v. State* had a very different relationship to the universe of organized gay rights litigators than did *Storrs v. Holcomb* (1996). *Storrs* was a same-sex marriage suit brought in Ithaca, New York, by a gay male couple without the involvement of any gay rights organizations. The case raised numerous claims, including ones based on the U.S. Constitution. This frightened Lambda and the other litigators fighting for same-sex marriage because they had worked to *avoid* raising federal constitutional claims in order to ensure that the presumptively unfriendly U.S. Supreme Court would not be able to overturn a state court decision upholding the right to same-sex marriage. In the American system, state cases that do not raise federal claims cannot be heard by the U.S. Supreme Court. *Storrs* was ultimately dismissed by the New York courts, because the plaintiffs had made a procedural error by failing to include a necessary party (the New York State Department of Health). Robinson and Murray did not wish to seem like "renegades" (Robinson's word, spoken in a telephone interview with me on May 19, 2002) and so worked assiduously with Mary Bonauto of GLAD to ensure that the major groups were consulted and involved in decision-making processes.

27. *In re Adopt of B L V B* (1993). Second-parent adoptions allow both parents in a dual-adult household to establish legal relationships with the children of the household.

28. The Common Benefits Clause reads as follows: "That government is, or ought to be, instituted for the common benefit, protection and security of the people, nation or community; and not for the particular emolument or advantage of any single man, family, or set of persons who are a part only of that community" (VT Constitution, Ch. 1, Art. 7).

29. The state actually laid out seven rationales for banning same-sex marriage, but the court found all but one to be "absurd." See Eskridge 2002.

30. It is not uncommon to dispense with trials in civil cases when the court determines that there are no significant matters of factual dispute.

31. Amicus briefs for the plaintiffs were filed by more than fifteen organizations, including Lambda, the ACLU, and the National Organization for Women. The state's position also drew a number of supporting briefs, including ones from the Christian Legal Society, Agudath Israel of America, and the Roman Catholic Diocese of Burlington, Vermont.

32. This part of the ruling commanded a 4–1 majority. The lone dissenter, Denise Johnson, argued that the court's own logic compelled it to order marriage licenses to same-sex couples.

33. Fifteen Vermont Statutes Annotated § 1204 (2000).

34. It is intriguing that statistics from the Vermont Department of Vital Statistics show that the majority of civil unions have been performed for couples who do not reside in Vermont. In 2000, nearly 80 percent of the 1,702 civil unions joined together non-Vermont couples. This statistic suggests that the majority of couples seeking civil unions are interested in its symbolic and/or political value rather than its monetary and personal benefits.

35. Lambda has already litigated cases involving interstate recognition of civil unions, with mixed results. For example, a Georgia court refused to recognize a woman's civil union to her partner as the equivalent of a marriage for purposes of determining custody (*Burns v. Burns*, 2002). Susan Burns and her ex-husband had entered into a consent decree prohibiting either parent from having their child in the home when an unrelated adult was staying overnight. Burns had argued that her civil union made her legally related to her same-sex partner and that the consent decree was therefore not applicable. The court disagreed, finding that it was not authorized to consider a civil union the equivalent of marriage, and that the state's prohibition of same-sex marriage would render the question moot in any respect. A New York court, in contrast, recently recognized a civil union as the legal equivalent of marriage for purposes of New York's wrongful death statute, allowing a gay man to sue a hospital for malpractice in the death of his partner (*Langan v. St. Vincent's Hospital,* 2003). Said the court, "in Vermont, John Langan is the spouse of Neal Spicehandler and is entitled to recover for his wrongful death. The issue remains, whether under full faith and credit, or principles of comity, he will be recognized as a spouse in New York, as would a spouse in a sister state common law marriage. . . . New York will recognize a marriage sanctioned and contracted in a sister state and there appears to be no valid legal basis to distinguish one between a same-sex couple" (*Langan,* 418).

36. "A Historic Victory: Civil Unions for Same-Sex Couples—What's Next!" was published on July 6, 2000. It can be accessed at www.lambdalegal.org.

37. Nebraska Constitution Art. 1, § 29 (2001).

38. In Hawaii, proposed constitutional amendments may also be placed on the ballot by a majority vote of each house at each of two successive sessions.

39. Alaska Constitution Art. XIII, § 1.

40. Hawaii Constitution Art. XVII, § 3.

41. Vermont Constitution § 72.

42. Although without direct influence on the legislative process in Vermont, both of its senators (then–Republican James Jeffords and Democrat Patrick Leahy) also praised the decision for its fairness and flexibility.

43. Robinson, Murray, and the other gay rights activists lobbying the legislature were also unhappy with the committee's decision to support civil unions rather than same-sex marriage. However, they quickly decided to throw their support behind the civil union legislation because they came to believe that marriage was not politically feasible and that dissent within the lgb activist community might well torpedo the civil unions proposal. In effect, they decided that half a loaf was better than none. Robinson (2001) discussed this decision-making process in a speech to law students reprinted in the *Seton Hall Constitutional Law Journal.*

44. The vote in the senate was 19–11.

45. Personal interview with Beth Robinson, May 19, 2002.

46. It is worth noting here as well that although this chapter has focused on the effect of legal "wins" on the real lives of lgb people, a legal opportunity perspective is equally useful in helping to understand the effect of legal "losses."

47. For example, the television shows *Roseanne* (1995), *Friends* (1996), and *Mad About You* (1998) have all featured same-sex weddings.

48. Lambda keeps a running tally of religious organizations supporting same-sex marriage. See the Marriage Project at www.lambdalegal.org.

CHAPTER EIGHT

1. These states were Arizona, Indiana, Massachusetts, and New Jersey.

2. For more information about judicial perceptions of homosexuality in the context of custody cases, see Benkov 1994; Katz 1988; Rivera 1986.

3. The latter formulation should occur rarely, if at all. As Meyer and Staggenborg (1996) have noted, social movements almost always generate opposition because they create political openness on their issues of concern.

4. See chapter 5.

5. See especially the Lambda case *Able v. United States* (1998).

6. See chapter 5. See also Gerstmann 1999.

AFTERWORD

1. As noted in chapter 7, second-parent adoptions allow both parents in a dual-adult household to establish a legal relationship with the children of the household. Massachusetts's decision came down less than three months after Vermont's parallel determination in *In re BLVB*.

2. Gen. L., Ch. 151B, § 3(6) (11/89).

3. This number comes from a survey done by the *Boston Globe*. Official statistics about the number of same-sex couples seeking licenses were unavailable at the time of writing.

4. Massachusetts Laws, Ch. 207 § 11.

5. Not surprisingly, GLAD has already set its sights on the 1913 law. *Cote-Whitacre v. Dept of Public Health* was filed in July 2004 and argues that the law's application violates equal protection rights under the state constitution as well as the Privileges and Immunities Clause of the U.S. Constitution (*Cote-Whitacre*, Verified Complaint seeking Declaratory and Injunctive Relief and Mandamus, 18).

6. The marriage question was worded as follows: "Would you favor or oppose a law that would allow homosexual couples to legally get married, or do you not have an opinion either way?" Twenty-four percent favored the law, 53 percent opposed it, and 23 percent had no opinion. The civil union question was: "Would you favor or oppose a law that would allow homosexual couples to legally form civil unions, giving them some of the legal rights of married couples, or do you not have an opinion either way?" Thirty-four percent favored the law, 41 percent opposed it, and 25 percent had no opinion.

7. Beth Robinson, personal interview, May 19, 2002.

8. The trial court ruled against Lambda's claim just a few weeks before the SJC handed down *Goodridge*. The case is currently on appeal.

9. Legislatively generated amendments are on the ballot in Georgia, Kentucky, Louisiana, Mississippi, Oklahoma, and Utah. Tennessee and Wisconsin both require that proposed constitutional amendments be passed by the legislature in two consecutive sessions before going to the voters.

10. Citizen-generated amendments are on the ballot in Arkansas, Michigan, Montana, North Dakota, Ohio, and Oregon. In each instance, organizers were able to gather far more signatures than necessary to place the initiatives on the ballot. Organizers in Michigan, for example, submitted 475,000 signatures, far more than the 317,000 needed by law.

11. Updated lists of the sponsors of the FMA can be found at http://thomas.loc.gov.

12. The full transcript of President Bush's February 24, 2004, remarks on the Federal Marriage Amendment can be found on the White House web site, http://www.whitehouse.gov/news/releases/2004/02/20040224-2.html (accessed July 22, 2004).

13. For example, a Gallup poll taken in July 2004 asked: "Do you think marriages between homosexuals should or should not be recognized by the law as valid, with the same rights as traditional marriages?" Thirty-two percent of respondents indicated that such marriages should be recognized as valid. This response differs only slightly from responses to the same question or similar questions asked in Gallup polls as far back as 1999.

14. For example, a CBS News/New York Times poll conducted in July 2004 asked the following question: "Which comes closest to your view? Gay couples should be allowed to legally marry. OR, Gay couples should be allowed to form civil unions but not legally marry. OR, There should be no legal recognition of a gay couple's relationship." Twenty-eight percent of respondents favored marriage, 31 percent preferred civil unions, and 38 percent felt that no legal recognition should occur.

15. Newsom's chief stumbling block was that California's Proposition 22 expressly limited marriage to opposite-sex couples. Newsom eventually claimed that California's equal protection clause gave him the right to disregard the plain meaning of Proposition 22. The law unconstitutionally discriminated against same-sex couples, he argued; by disregarding it, he was actually following the constitution.

16. The ACLU cases are *Deane and Polyak v. Conaway* (MD), *Gallagher v. New York*, *Li v. Multnomah County* (OR), and *Castle v. State of Washington*. The NCLR case is *Higgs v. State of Florida*.

17. *Li v. Multnomah County*, Opinion and Order, 16.

References

Abraham, Henry J. 1985. *Justices and Presidents*. 2d ed. New York: Oxford University Press.

Achtenberg, Roberta, ed. 1996. *Sexual Orientation and the Law*. Rev. ed. New York: Clark Boardman Callaghan.

Adam, Barry D. 1995. *The Rise of a Gay and Lesbian Movement*. Rev. ed. New York: Twayne.

Adams, William E., Jr. 1994. "Pre-Election Anti-Gay Ballot Initiative Challenges: Issues of Electoral Fairness, Majoritarian Tyranny, and Direct Democracy." *Ohio State Law Journal* 55:583–635.

Altman, Dennis. 1971. *Homosexual Oppression and Liberation*. New York: Avon Books.

Altman, Dennis. 1986. *AIDS in the Mind of America: The Social, Political, and Psychological Impact of a New Epidemic*. New York: Doubleday.

Alumbaugh, Steven, and C. K. Rowland. 1990. "The Links between Platform-Based Appointment Criteria and Trial Judges' Abortion Judgments." *Judicature* 74:153–62.

American Civil Liberties Union. 2000. *Lesbian and Gay Rights 2000: An ACLU Report*. http://archive.aclu.org/issues/gay/2000report/index.html. Accessed May 17, 2004.

American Law Institute (ALI). 1962. "Model Penal Code § 213.2 Comment 2." Philadelphia: American Law Institute.

Anderson, Keirsten. 1997. "Note: Protecting Unmarried Cohabitants from the Religious Freedom Restoration Act." *Valparaiso University Law Review* 31:1017–78.

Banaszak, Lee Ann. 1996. *Why Movements Succeed or Fail: Opportunity, Culture, and the Struggle for Woman Suffrage*. Princeton: Princeton University Press.

Barker, Karlyn, and Linda Wheeler. 1987. "Gay Activists Arrested at High Court; Peaceful Civil Disobedience by 572 Culminates Week's Events." *Washington Post*, October 14.

Barrett, Ted. 2004. "Amendment Might Lack Congressional Support." *CNN.com*, February 24. www.cnn.com/2004/ALLPOLITICS/02/24/elec04 .congress.marriage/index.html. Accessed July 24, 2004.

Baum, Lawrence. 1989. "Comparing the Policy Positions of Supreme Court Justices from Different Periods." *Western Political Quarterly* 42 (December): 510–21.

Benkov, Laura. 1994. *Reinventing the Family: The Emerging Story of Lesbian and Gay Parents.* New York: Crown.

Bragg, Rick. 1994. "From Night of Rage, Seeds of Liberation." *New York Times,* June 23.

Brink, Graham. 2004. "Couple Sues to Uphold Gay Marriage." *St. Petersburg Times,* July 21.

Bullough, Vern. 1986. "Lesbianism, Homosexuality, and the American Civil Liberties Union." *Journal of Homosexuality* 13:23–32.

Burstein, Paul. 1991. "Legal Mobilization as a Social Movement Tactic: The Struggle for Equal Employment Opportunity." *American Journal of Sociology* 96:1201–25.

Butler, Charles J. 1998. "Note: The Defense of Marriage Act: Congress' Use of Narrative in the Debate over Same-Sex Marriage." *New York University Law Review* 73:841–79.

Button, James W., Barbara Ann Rienzo, and Kenneth D. Wald. 1997. *Private Lives, Public Conflicts: Battles over Gay Rights in American Communities.* Washington, DC: CQ Press.

Cain, Patricia. 1993. "Litigating for Lesbian and Gay Rights: A Legal History." *Virginia Law Review* 79:1551–641.

Cain, Patricia. 2000. *Rainbow Rights: The Role of Lawyers and Courts in the Lesbian and Gay Civil Rights Movement.* Boulder: Westview Press.

Canon, Bradley C., and Charles A. Johnson. 1999. *Judicial Policies: Implementation and Impact.* 2d ed. Washington, DC: CQ Press.

Cathcart, Kevin. 1993. "Executive Director's Update." *Lambda Update* 10 (summer): 31.

Cathcart, Kevin. 2003. "Landmark Supreme Court Victory Effectively Strikes Down All Remaining Sodomy Laws." www.lambdalegal.org, June 26.

Clarkson, Kevin G., David Orgon Coolidge, and William C. Duncan. 1999. "The Alaska Marriage Amendment: The People's Choice on the Last Frontier." *Alaska Law Review* 16:213–68.

Clayton, Cornell W., and Howard Gillman. 1999. *Supreme Court Decision-Making: New Institutionalist Approaches.* Chicago: University of Chicago Press.

Clendinen, Dudley, and Adam Nagourney. 1999. *Out for Good: The Struggle to Build a Gay Rights Movement in America.* New York: Simon & Schuster.

Cortner, Richard C. 1968. "Strategies and Tactics of Litigants in Constitutional Cases." *Journal of Public Law* 17:287–307.

Costain, Anne N. 1992. *Inviting Women's Rebellion: A Political Process Interpretation of the Women's Movement.* Baltimore: Johns Hopkins University Press.

Cowan, Ruth. 1977. "Women's Rights through Litigation: An Examination of the ACLU Women's Rights Project, 1971–1976." *Columbia Human Rights Law Review* 8:373–412.

Coyle, Marcia. 2002. "Marriage, Military Might Wait Their Turn in Court." *National Law Journal,* July 7.

Coyle, Marcia. 2003. "Buoyed by Recent Supreme Court Ruling, Advocates for Gay Rights Form a Sweeping Litigation Plan." *Broward Daily Business Review,* July 18.

D'Emilio, John. 1983. *Sexual Politics, Sexual Communities.* Chicago: University of Chicago Press.

D'Emilio, John. 1986. "Making and Unmaking Minorities: The Tensions between Gay History and Politics." *Review of Law and Social Change* 14:915–22.

"Developments in the Law: Sexual Orientation and the Law." *Harvard Law Review* 102:1508–1671.

Dewar, Helen, and Alan Cooperman. 2004. "Senate Scuttles Amendment Banning Same-Sex Marriage." *Washington Post,* July 14.

"Docket Update: LaBrecque v. Bradner Smith & Company." 1988. *Lambda Update* (summer): 10.

Douglass, David. 1997. "Taking the Initiative: Anti-Homosexual Propaganda of the Oregon's Citizen's Alliance." In *Anti-Gay Rights: Assessing Voter Initiatives,* edited by Stephanie L. Witt and Suzanne McCorkle. Westport, CT: Praeger.

Duberman, Martin. 1993. *Stonewall.* New York: Dutton.

Duclos, Nitya. 1991. "Some Complicating Thoughts on Same-Sex Marriage." *Law & Sexuality* 1:31–61.

Dunlap, David P. 1996. "Fearing a Toehold for Gay Marriages, Conservatives Rush to Bar the Door." *New York Times,* March 6, 13.

Dunlap, Mary. 1994. "Gay Men and Lesbians Down by Law in the 1990's USA: The Continuing Toll of *Bowers v. Hardwick.*" *Golden Gate University Law Review* 24:1–39.

Egan, Timothy. 1992. "Anti-Gay Backlashes Are on 3 States' Ballots." *New York Times,* October 4.

Eisenger, Peter K. 1973. "The Conditions of Protest Behavior in American Cities." *American Political Science Review* 67:11–28.

Epp, Charles R. 1998. *The Rights Revolution: Lawyers, Activists, and Supreme Courts in Comparative Perspective.* Chicago: University of Chicago Press.

Epstein, Lee. 1985. *Conservatives in Court.* Knoxville: University of Tennessee Press.

Epstein, Lee, and Jack Knight. 1998. *The Choices Justices Make.* Washington, DC: CQ Press.

Epstein, Lee, and Joseph Fiske Kobylka. 1992. *The Supreme Court and Legal Change: Abortion and the Death Penalty.* Thornton H. Brooks Series in American Law and Society. Chapel Hill: University of North Carolina Press.

Epstein, Lee, Tracey E. George, and Joseph Fiske Kobylka. 1992. *Public Interest Law: An Annotated Bibliography and Research Guide.* New York: Garland.

Eskridge, William N. 1996. *The Case for Same-Sex Marriage: From Sexual Liberty to Civilized Commitment.* New York: Free Press.

Eskridge, William N. 1999. *Gaylaw: Challenging the Apartheid of the Closet.* Cambridge, MA: Harvard University Press.

Eskridge, William N. 2002. *Equality Practice: Civil Unions and the Future of Gay Rights.* New York: Routledge.

Eskridge, William N., Jr., and Philip P. Frickey. 1994. "Foreword: Law as Equilibrium." *Harvard Law Review* 108:27–108.

Essoyan, Susan. 1994. "Social Issues; Hawaii Tries to Take a Stand against Same-Sex Marriages." *Los Angeles Times,* April 26.

Ettelbrick, Paula. 1989. "Since When Is Marriage a Path to Liberation?" *OUT/LOOK: National Lesbian and Gay Quarterly* 6 (fall): 8. Reprinted in *Lesbians, Gay Men, and the Law*, edited by William B. Rubenstein. New York: New Press, 1993.

Eule, Julian N. 1990. "Judicial Review of Direct Democracy." *Yale Law Journal* 99:1503–89.

Faderman, Lillian. 1991. *Odd Girls and Twilight Lovers: A History of Lesbian Life in Twentieth-Century America*. New York: Penguin Books.

Finder, Alan. 1986. "Police Halt Rights Marchers at Wall St." *New York Times*, July 5.

Forbath, William E. 1991. "Would European Models of Government Make America More Democratic? A Skeptical View." *Law & Social Inquiry* 16:717–23.

Foster, Sheila Rose. 1998. "The Symbolism of Rights and the Costs of Symbolism: Some Thoughts on the Campaign for Same-Sex Marriage." *Temple Political & Civil Rights Law Review* 7:319–28.

Freiberg, Peter. 1997. "Courting Gay Civil Rights." *Washington Blade*, January 3.

Fumento, Michael. 1990. *The Myth of Heterosexual AIDS*. New York: Basic Books.

Galanter, Marc. 1974. "Why the 'Haves' Come out Ahead: Speculations on the Limits of Legal Change." *Law & Society Review* 9 (1): 95–160.

Galanter, Marc. 1983. "The Radiating Effects of Courts." In *Emprirical Theories About Courts*, edited by Keith O. Boyum and Lynn Mather. New York: Longman.

Gallo, Jon J., Stefan M. Mason, Louis M. Meisinger, Kenneth D. Robin, Gary D. Stabile, and Robert J. Wynne. 1966. "The Consenting Adult Homosexual and the Law: An Empirical Study of Enforcement and Administration in Los Angeles County." *UCLA Law Review* 13:644–832.

Gamble, Barbara. 1997. "Putting Civil Rights to a Popular Vote." *American Journal of Political Science* 41:245–69.

Gamson, William A. 1975. *The Strategy of Social Protest*. Homewood, IL: Dorsey Press.

Gamson, William, and David S. Meyer. 1996. "Framing Political Opportunity." In *Comparative Perspectives on Social Movements*, edited by Doug McAdam, John D. McCarthy, and Mayer N. Zald. Cambridge: Cambridge University Press.

Garrow, David J. 1994. *Liberty and Sexuality: The Right to Privacy and the Making of Roe v. Wade*. New York: MacMillan.

Garrow, David J. 2004. "Toward a More Perfect Union." *New York Times*, May 9.

Gerstmann, Evan. 1999. *The Constitutional Underclass: Gays, Lesbians, and the Failure of Class-Based Equal Protection*. Chicago: University of Chicago Press.

Goffman, Erving. 1974. *Frame Analysis*. Boston: Northeastern University Press.

Goldberg-Hiller, Jonathan. 2002. *The Limits to Union: Same-Sex Marriage and the Politics of Civil Rights*. Ann Arbor: University of Michigan Press.

Goldstein, Anne B. 1988. "History, Homosexuality, and Political Values: Searching for Hidden Determinants of *Bowers v. Hardwick*." *Yale Law Journal* 97:1073–103.

Goldstein, Anne B. 1993. "Reasoning about Homosexuality: A Commentary on Janet Halley's 'Reasoning About Sodomy: Act and Identity in and after Bowers v. Hardwick'." *Virginia Law Review* 79:1781–1804.

Gostin, Lawrence. 1990. "AIDS Litigation Project: A National Review of Court and Human Rights Commission Decisions." *Journal of the American Medical Association* 263:1961–70.

Graff, Christopher. 2000. "A Poll of Vermonters Shows a Majority Disagrees with December's Supreme Court Ruling on Same-Sex Marriages." *Associated Press State and Local Wire*, January 25.

Greenberg, Jack. 1977. *Judicial Process and Social Change: Constitutional Litigation*. St. Paul, MN: West.

Hahn, Jeanne. 1973. "The NAACP Legal Defense and Educational Fund: Its Judicial Strategy and Tactics." In *American Government and Politics*, edited by Stephen L. Wasby. New York: Scribner.

Haider-Markel, Donald P., and Kenneth J. Meier. 1996. "The Politics of Gay and Lesbian Rights: Expanding the Scope of the Conflict." *Journal of Politics* 58:332–49.

Haines, Herbert H. 1996. *Against Capital Punishment: The Anti-Death Penalty Movement in America, 1972–1994*. New York: Oxford University Press.

Halley, Janet. 1989. "The Politics of the Closet: Towards Equal Protection for Gay, Lesbian, and Bisexual Identity." *UCLA Law Review* 36:915–76.

Halley, Janet. 1993. "Reasoning about Sodomy: Act and Identity in and after *Bowers v. Hardwick*." *Virginia Law Review* 79:1721–80.

Handler, Joel F. 1978. *Social Movements and the Legal System: A Theory of Law Reform and Social Change*. New York: Academic Press.

Harkavy, Ward. 1993. "Original Sin." *Westword*, September 8–14.

Harris, Art. 1986. "The Unintended Battle of Michael Hardwick." *Washington Post*, August 21.

Herman, Didi. 1994. *Rights of Passage: Struggles for Lesbian and Gay Legal Equality*. Toronto: University of Toronto Press.

Herman, Didi. 1997. *The Antigay Agenda: Orthodox Vision and the Christian Right*. Chicago: University of Chicago Press.

Hertzog, Mark. 1996. *The Lavender Vote: Lesbians, Gay Men, and Bisexuals in American Electoral Politics*. New York: New York University Press.

Hitchens, Donna J., and Barbara Price. 1978–79. "Trial Strategy in Lesbian Mother Custody Cases: The Use of Expert Testimony." *Golden Gate Law Review* 9:451–79.

Horowitz, Donald L. 1977. *The Courts and Social Policy*. Washington, DC: Brookings Institution.

Hughes, Graham. 1962. "Morals and the Criminal Law." *Yale Law Review* 71:662–83.

Hunter, Nan D. 1991. "Marriage, Law, and Gender: A Feminist Inquiry." *Law & Sexuality* 1:9–30.

Hunter, Nan D. 1993. "Identity, Speech, and Equality." *Virginia Law Review* 79:1695–719.

Hunter, Nan D., and Nancy D. Polikoff. 1976. "Custody Rights of Lesbian Mothers: Legal Theory and Litigation Strategy." *Buffalo Law Review* 25:691–723.

Hunter, Nan D., Sherryl E. Michaelson, and Thomas Stoddard. 1992. *The Rights of Lesbians and Gay Men.* 3d. ed. Carbondale: Southern Illinois University Press.

Huxley, Aldous. 1932. *Brave New World.* New York: Bantam Books.

Irons, Peter. 1988. *The Courage of Their Convictions.* New York: Free Press.

Jenkins, J. Craig, and Charles Perrow. 1977. "Insurgency of the Powerless: Farm Workers' Movements, 1946–1972." *American Sociological Review* 51:812–29.

Johnsen, Ronald P. 1968. "Sodomy Statutes—A Need for Change." *South Dakota Law Review* 13:384–97.

Kahn, Ronald. 1996. "Social Science, Social Facts, and the Rights of Subordinated Groups." Paper presented at the Joint International Conference of the Law and Society Association and the Research Committee on the Sociology of Law of the International Sociological Association, Glasgow, Scotland.

Kahn, Ronald. 1999. "Institutional Norms and Supreme Court Decision-Making: The Rehnquist Court on Privacy and Religion." In *Supreme Court Decision-Making,* edited by Cornell Clayton and Howard Gillman. Chicago: University of Chicago Press.

Kairys, David, ed. 1982. *The Politics of Law: A Progressive Critique.* New York: Pantheon.

Katz, Jonathan. 1983. *Gay/Lesbian Almanac.* New York: Carroll and Graf.

Katz, Katheryn. 1988. "Majoritarian Morality and Parental Rights." *Albany Law Review* 52:405–69.

Keen, Lisa, and Suzanne B. Goldberg. 1998. *Strangers to the Law: Gay People on Trial.* Ann Arbor: University of Michigan Press.

Kehler, D., and R. M. Stern. 1994. "Initiatives in the 1980s and 1990s." In *The Book of the States 1994–95.* Lexington, KY: Council of State Governments.

Kellogg, Charles. 1967. *NAACP.* Baltimore: Johns Hopkins.

Kennedy, Elizabeth Lapovsky, and Madeline D. Davis. 1993. *Boots of Leather, Slippers of Gold.* New York: Routledge.

Kitschelt, Herbert. 1986. "Political Opportunity Structures and Political Protest: Anti-Nuclear Movements in Four Democracies." *British Journal of Political Science* 16:57–85.

Klein, Rick. 2004. "Groups Hold Out for Public Furor before Acting." *Boston Globe,* May 18.

Kluger, Richard. 1975. *Simple Justice.* New York: Alfred A. Knopf.

Kobylka, Joseph F. 1987. "A Court-Created Context for Group Litigation: Libertarian Groups and Obscenity." *Journal of Politics* 49:1061–78.

Koppelman, Andrew. 1990. "Forced Labor: A Thirteenth Amendment Defense of Abortion." *Northwestern University Law Review* 84:480–535.

Kramer, Larry. 1989. *Reports from the Holocaust.* New York: St. Martin's Press.

Kriesi, Hanspeter, Ruud Koopmans, Willem Duyvendak, and Marco G. Giugni. 1992. "New Social Movements and Political Opportunities in Western Europe." *European Journal of Political Research* 22:219–44.

Krislov, Samuel. 1963. "The Amicus Curiae Brief: From Friendship to Advocacy." *Yale Law Journal* 72:694–721.

Lamb, Paul L. 1969. "Criminal Law—Consensual Homosexual Behavior—the Need for Legislative Reform." *Kentucky Law Journal* 57:591–98.

Lambda Legal Defense and Education Fund (LLDEF). 1998. *Snapshots from a Civil Rights Movement*. New York: Lambda Legal Defense and Education Fund.

Lambda Legal Defense and Education Fund. 2004. "Vision: A New Day for LGBT Americans." www.lambdalegal.org/cgi-bin/iowa/static.htm.?page =forging_vision. Accessed on May 3, 2004.

Lambda News. 1976. "Money."

Lambda News. 1977. "Money," 2, no. 1 (April).

Lambda Update. 1984. "Lambda fights for lesbian teachers rights." February.

Lambda Update. 1985. "Ad Hoc Task Force." Winter.

Lawrence, Susan. 1990. *The Poor in Court: The Legal Services Program and Supreme Court Decision Making*. Princeton: Princeton University Press.

Leonard, Arthur. 1993. "Sexual Orientation and the Workplace: A Rapidly Developing Field." *Labor Law Journal* 44:574–83.

Leonard, Arthur. 1997. "Marriage Pot Boils in Hawaii." *Lesbian/Gay Law Notes,* February. On-line edition, www.qrd.org/qrd/usa/legal/lgln/1997/07 .and.08.

Lewin, Tamar. 1993. "Sights Are Set on Other Anti-Gay Measures." *New York Times,* December 15.

Lewis, Raphael. 2004. "Three Viewpoints Produced Gridlock." *Boston Globe,* February 14.

Lipsky, Michael. 1970. *Protest in City Politics*. Chicago: Rand McNally.

Lisberg, Adam, and Nancy Remsen. 1999. "Legislators Embrace Idea of 'Domestic Partnership'." *Burlington Free Press,* December 21.

Los Angeles Times. 1986. "A Far Greater Threat," July 2.

MacDonald, Christine, and Bill Dedman. 2004. "About 2,500 Gay Couples Sought Licenses in 1st Week." *Boston Globe,* June 17.

Magleby, David B. 1984. *Direct Legislation: Voting on Ballot Propositions in the United States*. Baltimore: Johns Hopkins University Press.

Maltzman, Forrest, James F. Spriggs, and Paul J. Wahlbeck. 1999. "Strategy and Judicial Choice: New Institutionalist Approaches to Supreme Court Decision-Making." In *Supreme Court Decision-Making,* edited by Cornell Clayton and Howard Gillman. Chicago: University of Chicago Press.

Maltzman, Forrest, James F. Spriggs, and Paul J. Wahlbeck. 2000. *Crafting Law on the Supreme Court: The Collegial Game*. New York: Cambridge University Press.

Manwaring, David Roger. 1962. *Render unto Caesar: The Flag-Salute Controversy*. Chicago: University of Chicago Press.

March, James G., and Johan P. Olson. 1994. "The New Institutionalism: Organizational Factors in Political Life." *American Political Science Review* 78:734–49.

Marcus, Eric. 1992. *Making History: The Struggle for Gay and Lesbian Equal Rights, 1945–1990*. New York: HarperPerennial.

Marcus, Ruth. 1990. "Powell Regrets Backing Sodomy Law." *Washington Post,* October 26.

Masters, William H., Virginia E. Johnson, and Robert C. Kolodny. 1988. *Crisis: Heterosexual Behavior in the Age of AIDS.* New York: Grove.

McAdam, Doug. 1982. *Political Process and the Development of Black Insurgency, 1930–1970.* Chicago: University of Chicago Press.

McAdam, Doug. 1996. "Conceptual Origins, Current Problems, Future Directions." In *Comparative Perspectives on Social Movements,* edited by Doug McAdam, John D. McCarthy, and Mayer N. Zald. New York: Cambridge University Press.

McAdam, Doug, Sidney Tarrow, and Charles Tilly. 1996. "To Map Contentious Politics." *Mobilization* 1 (1): 17–34.

McCann, Michael W. 1986. *Taking Reform Seriously: Perspectives on Public Interest Liberalism.* Ithaca: Cornell University Press.

McCann, Michael W. 1994. *Rights at Work: Pay Equity Reform and the Politics of Legal Mobilization, Language, and Legal Discourse.* Chicago: University of Chicago Press.

McCarthy, John D. 1996. "Constraints and Opportunities in Adopting, Adapting, and Inventing." In *Comparative Perspectives on Social Movements,* edited by Doug McAdam, John D. McCarthy, and Mayer N. Zald. New York: Cambridge University Press.

McCarthy, John D., and Mark Wolfson. 1992. "Consensus Movements: The Dynamics of Mobilization and Growth." In *Frontiers of Social Movement Theory,* edited by Carol Mueller and Aldon Morris. New Haven: Yale University Press.

McCorkle, Suzanne, and Marshall G. Most. 1997. "Fear and Loathing on the Editorial Page: An Analysis of Idaho's Anti-Gay Initiative." In *Anti-Gay Rights: Assessing Voter Initiatives,* edited by Stephanie L. Witt and Suzanne McCorkle. Westport, CT: Praeger.

McGuire, Kevin T. 1990. "Obscenity, Libertarian Values, and Decision-Making in the Supreme Court." *American Politics Quarterly* 18:47–67.

Meltsner, Michael. 1973. *Cruel and Unusual: The Supreme Court and Capital Punishment.* New York: Random House.

Merry, Sally Engle. 1985. "Concepts of Law and Justice among Working-Class Americans: Ideology as Culture." *Legal Studies Forum* 9:59–70.

Meyer, David S. 1993. "Protest Cycles and Political Process: American Peace Movements in the Nuclear Age." *Political Research Quarterly* 47:451–79.

Meyer, David S., and Suzanne Staggenborg. 1996. "Movements, Countermovements, and the Structure of Political Opportunity." *American Journal of Sociology* 101 (6): 1628–60.

Mohr, Richard D. 1986. "Mr. Justice Douglas at Sodom: Gays and Privacy." *Columbia Human Rights Law Review* 18:43–110.

Mohr, Richard D. 1995. "The Case for Gay Marriage." *Notre Dame Journal of Law, Ethics, & Public Policy* 9:215–39.

Nagourney, Adam. 1996. "Christian Coalition Pushes for Showdown on Same-Sex Marriage." *New York Times,* May 30.

Nagourney, Adam, and David D. Kirkpatrick. 2004. "Urged by Right, Bush Takes On Gay Marriages." *New York Times,* July 12.

Newsweek. 1986. "A Newsweek Poll: Sex Laws," July 14.

New York Times. 1986. "Crime in the Bedroom," July 2.

O'Connor, Karen. 1980. *Women's Organizations' Use of the Courts.* Lexington, MA: Lexington Books.

Olson, Susan M. 1984. *Clients and Lawyers: Securing the Rights of Disabled Persons.* Westport, CT: Greenwood Press.

Olson, Susan M. 1990. "Interest-Group Litigation in Federal District Court: Beyond the Political Disadvantage Theory." *Journal of Politics* 52:855–82.

Patton, Cindy. 1997. "Queer Space/God's Space: Counting Down to the Apocalypse." *Rethinking Marxism* 9 (2): 1–23.

Paul, Arnold M. 1960. *Conservative Crisis and the Rule of Law: Attitudes of Bar and Bench 1887–95.* Ithaca: Cornell University Press.

Perkins, Will. 1992. "Views on Gay Rights." *Denver Post,* October 11.

Perry, H. W., Jr. 1991. *Deciding to Decide: Agenda Setting in the United States Supreme Court.* Cambridge: Harvard University Press.

Peterson, Kavan. 2004. "Battle over Gay Marriage Goes to Voters." *Stateline.org,* April 22. www.stateline.org/stateline/?pa=story&sa=ShowStoryInfo&id= 366573 (accessed July 24, 2004).

Phelan, Shane. 1989. *Identity Politics: Lesbian-Feminism and the Limits of Community.* Philadelphia: Temple University Press.

Phillips, Frank, and Kathleen Burge. 2004. "Reilly Gives Governor a Hurdle." *Boston Globe,* March 30.

Phillips, Frank, and Raphael Lewis. 2003. "Civil Union Law Sought: Romney Says Move Would Satisfy the SJC." *Boston Globe,* November 20.

Phillips, Thomas L., Jr. 1978. "Note: The Precedential Effect of Summary Affirmances and Dismissals for Want of a Substantial Federal Question by the Supreme Court after *Hicks v. Miranda* and *Mandel v. Bradley.*" *Virginia Law Review* 64:117–43.

Pietrzyk, Mark E. 1994. "Queer Science: Paul Cameron, Professional Sham." *New Republic,* October 3, 10–12.

Pinello, Daniel R. 2003. *Gay Rights and American Law.* Cambridge: Cambridge University Press.

Polikoff, Nancy. 1993. "We Will Get What We Ask For: Why Legalizing Gay and Lesbian Marriage Will Not 'Dismantle the Legal Structure of Gender in Every Marriage.'" *Virginia Law Review* 79:1535–50.

Regan, Donald. 1979. "Rewriting Roe v. Wade." *Michigan Law Review* 77:1569–646.

Richards, David A. J. 1979. "Sexual Autonomy and the Constitutional Rights to Privacy: A Case Study in Human Rights and the Unwritten Constitution." *Hastings Law Journal* 30:957–1018.

Riggle, Ellen D. B., and Barry L. Tadlock. 1999. *Gays and Lesbians in the Democratic Process: Public Policy, Public Opinion, and Political Representation, Power, Conflict, and Democracy.* New York: Columbia University Press.

Rimer, Sara. 1985. "Fear of AIDS Grows among Heterosexuals." *New York Times,* August 30.

Rinehart, Steve. 1998. "Gay Marriage Haunts Campaign." *Anchorage Daily News,* September 13.

Rivera, Rhonda. 1979. "Our Straight-Laced Judges: The Legal Position of Homo-sexual Persons in the United States." *Hastings Law Journal* 30:799–955.

Rivera, Rhonda. 1985. "Queer Law: Sexual Orientation in the Mid-Eighties: Part I." *University of Dayton Law Review* 10:459–540.

Rivera, Rhonda. 1986. "Queer Law: Sexual Orientation in the Mid-Eighties: Part II." *University of Dayton Law Review* 11:327–71.

Robinson, Beth. 2001. "The Road to Inclusion for Same-Sex Couples: Lessons from Vermont." *Seton Hall Constitutional Law Journal* 11 (2): 237–57.

Rosenberg, Gerald N. 1991. *The Hollow Hope: Can Courts Bring about Social Change?* Chicago: University of Chicago Press.

Rosenberg, Gerald N. 2001. "Same-Sex Marriage, Gay Rights and the (Counter?) Mobilization of Law." Paper presented at the 2001 Annual Meeting of the Law & Society Association, July 4–7, Budapest, Hungary.

Rostow, Ann. 2004. "Florida Suit Challenges Federal Marriage Law." *Gay.com*, July 21. www.gay.com/news/article.html?2004/07/21/1. Accessed August 12, 2004.

Rubenfeld, Abby. 1986. "Lessons Learned: A Reflection upon Bowers v. Hardwick." *Nova Law Review* 11:59–70.

Rubenstein, William B. 1997. "Divided We Litigate: Addressing Disputes among Group Members and Lawyers in Civil Rights Campaigns." *Yale Law Journal* 106:1623–80.

Rubin, Eva R. 1987. *Abortion, Politics, and the Courts.* Rev. ed. Westport, CT: Greenwood Press.

Rucht, Dieter. 1996. "The Impact of National Contexts on Social Movement Structures: A Cross-Movement and Cross-National Comparison." In *Comparative Perspectives on Social Movements,* edited by Doug McAdam, John D. McCarthy, and Mayer N. Zald. New York: Cambridge University Press.

Ruggie, Mary. 1987. "Workers' Movements and Women's Interests." In *The Women's Movements of the United States and Europe,* edited by Mary Feinsod Katzenstein and Carol McClurg Mueller. Philadelphia: Temple University Press.

Sawyers, Traci M., and David S. Meyer. 1999. "Missed Opportunities: Social Movement Abeyance and Public Policy." *Social Problems* 46 (2): 187–206.

Schacter, Jane S. 1994. "The Gay Civil Rights Debate in the States: Decoding the Discourse of Equivalents." *Harvard Civil Rights-Civil Liberties Law Review* 29:283–317.

Schattschneider, E. E. 1960. *The Semi-Sovereign People: A Realist's View of Democracy in America.* New York: Holt Reinhart and Winston.

Scheingold, Stuart A. 1974. *The Politics of Rights: Lawyers, Public Policy, and Political Change.* New Haven: Yale University Press. Reprint, Ann Arbor: University of Michigan Press, 2004.

Scheppele, Kim Lane. 1988. *Legal Secrets: Equality and Efficiency in the Common Law.* Chicago: University of Chicago Press.

Scheppele, Kim Lane, and Jack L. Walker. 1991. "The Litigation Strategies of Interest Groups." In *Mobilizing Interest Groups in America: Patrons, Professions, and Social Movements.* Ann Arbor: University of Michigan Press.

Schmalz, Jeffrey. 1992. "Gay Politics Goes Mainstream." *New York Times,* October 11.

Schmalz, Jeffrey. 1993. "Poll Finds an Even Split on Homosexuality's Cause." *New York Times*, March 3.

Schultz, David, ed. 1998. *Leveraging the Law: Using the Courts to Achieve Social Change*. New York: Peter Lang.

Schwartz, Herman. 1988. *Packing the Courts: The Conservative Campaign to Rewrite the Constitution*. New York: Scribner's.

Schwartz, Louis B. 1963. "Morals Offenses and the Model Penal Code." *Columbia Law Review* 63:669–86.

Sears, David. 1993. "Symbolic Politics: A Socio-Psychological Theory." In *Explorations in Political Psychology*, edited by Shanto Iyengar and W. J. McGuire. Durham, NC: Duke University Press.

Segal, Jeffrey A., and Harold J. Spaeth. 1989. "Decisional Trends on the Warren and Burger Courts: Results from the Supreme Court Data Base Project." *Judicature* 73 (June–July): 103–7.

Segal, Jeffrey, and Harold J. Spaeth. 1993. *The Supreme Court and the Attitudinal Model*. New York: Cambridge University Press.

Shapiro, Joseph P., Gareth G. Cook, and Andrew Krackov. 1993. "Straight Talk about Gays." *U.S. News & World Report*, July 5.

Shilts, Randy. 1982. *The Mayor of Castro Street*. New York: St. Martin's Press.

Shilts, Randy. 1987. *And the Band Played On*. Updated ed. New York: St. Martin's Press.

Shilts, Randy. 1993. *Conduct Unbecoming: Lesbians and Gays in the U.S. Military*. New York: St. Martin's Press.

Shipp, E. R. 1987. "Concern over AIDS Helps Rights Unit." *New York Times*, May 3.

Signorile, Michelangelo. 1994. *Queer in America: Sex, the Media, and the Closets of Power*. Updated ed. New York: Doubleday.

Skocpol, Theda. 1984. "Sociology's Historical Imagination." In *Vision and Method in Historical Sociology*, edited by Theda Skocpol. New York: Cambridge University Press.

Smart, Carol. 1989. *Feminism and the Power of Law*. London: Routledge.

Smith, Rogers M. 1988. "Political Jurisprudence, the 'New Institutionalism,' and the Future of Public Law." *American Political Science Review* 82:89–108.

Smith, Rogers M. 1995. "Ideas, Institutions, and Strategic Choices." *Polity* 28:135–40.

Snow, David E., E. Burke Rochford Jr., Steven K. Worden, and Robert D. Benford. 1986. "Frame Alignment Processes, Micromobilization, and Movement Participation." *American Sociological Review* 51 (4): 464–81.

Songer, Donald R., and Reginald S. Sheehan. 1992. "Who Wins on Appeal? Upperdogs and Underdogs in the United States Courts of Appeals." *American Journal of Political Science* 36:235–58.

Sorauf, Frank J. 1976. *The Wall of Separation: Constitutional Politics of Church and State*. Princeton: Princeton University Press.

Specter, Michael. 1985. "Disease Brings Fear, Bias against AIDS Victims." *Washington Post*, August 2.

Stein, Theodore. 1996. "Child Custody and Visitation: The Rights of Lesbian and Gay Parents." *Social Service Review* 70:435–50.

Stoddard, Thomas B. 1987. "Bowers v. Hardwick: Precedent by Personal Predilection." *University of Chicago Law Review* 54:648–56.

Stoddard, Thomas B. 1989. "Why Gay People Should Seek the Right to Marry." *OUTLOOK, National Lesbian and Gay Quarterly* 6 (fall): 8. Reprinted in *Lesbians, Gay Men, and the Law,* edited by William B. Rubenstein. New York: New Press, 1993.

Stychin, Carl F. 1998. *A Nation by Rights: National Cultures, Sexual Identity Politics, and the Discourse of Rights.* Philadelphia: Temple University Press.

Sullivan, Andrew. 1995. *Virtually Normal: An Argument about Homosexuality.* New York: Alfred A. Knopf.

Tarrow, Sidney. 1988. "National Politics and Collective Action: Recent Theory and Research in Western Europe and the United States." *Annual Review of Sociology* 14:421–40.

Tarrow, Sidney. 1994. *Power in Movement: Social Movements, Collective Action, and Politics.* Cambridge: Cambridge University Press.

Taylor, Verta, and Nancy E. Whittier. 1992. "Collective Identity in Social Movement Communities: Lesbian Feminist Mobilization." In *Frontiers in Social Movement Theory,* edited by Aldon Morris and Carol McClurg Mueller. New Haven: Yale University Press.

Teal, Donn. 1971. *The Gay Militants.* New York: Stein and Day.

Thomas, Kendall. 1993. "The Eclipse of Reason: A Rhetorical Reading of Bowers v. Hardwick." *Virginia Law Review* 79:1805–32.

Tilly, Charles. 1978. *From Mobilization to Revolution.* Reading, MA: Addison-Wesley.

Tushnet, Mark. 1987. *The NAACP'S Legal Strategy against Segregated Education, 1925–1950.* Chapel Hill: University of North Carolina Press.

Tushnet, Mark. 1984. "An Essay on Rights." *Texas Law Review* 62:1363–403.

Tymkovich, Timothy M., John Daniel Dailey, and Paul Farley. 1997. "A Tale of Three Theories: Reason and Prejudice in the Battle over Amendment 2." *University of Colorado Law Review* 68:287–347.

United States Senate Republican Policy Committee. 2003. "The Threat to Marriage from the Courts," July 29.

Vaid, Urvashi. 1995. *Virtual Equality: The Mainstreaming of Gay and Lesbian Liberation.* New York: Anchor Books.

van der Meide, Wayne. 2000. "Legislating Equality: A Review of Laws Affecting Gay, Lesbian, Bisexual, and Transgendered People in the United States." New York City: Policy Institute of the National Gay and Lesbian Task Force.

Vose, Clement E. 1959. *Caucasians Only.* Berkeley: University of California Press.

Wasby, Stephen L. 1983. "Interest Groups and Litigation." *Policy Studies Journal* 11 (4): 657–70.

Whittier, Nancy. 1995. *Feminist Generations: The Persistence of the Radical Women's Movement.* Philadelphia: Temple University Press.

Witt, Elder. 1986. *A Different Justice.* Washington, DC: CQ Press.

Witt, Stephanie L., and Suzanne McCorkle. 1997. *Anti-Gay Rights: Assessing Voter Initiatives.* Westport, CT: Praeger.

Wolfson, Evan. 1994. "Crossing the Threshold: Equal Marriage Rights for Lesbian and Gay Men and the Intra-Community Critique." *New York University Review of Law and Social Change* 21:567–615.

Yang, Alan. 2000. *From Wrongs to Rights, 1973–1999: Public Opinion on Gay and Lesbian Americans Moves Towards Equality.* New York City: Policy Institute of the National Gay and Lesbian Task Force.

Zald, Mayer N. 1996. "Culture, Ideology, and Strategic Framing." In *Comparative Perspectives on Social Movements: Political Opportunities, Mobilizing Structures, and Cultural Framings,* edited by Doug McAdam, John D. McCarthy, and Mayer N. Zald. New York: Cambridge University Press.

Table of Cases

Note: Cases marked with an asterisk are those in which Lambda participated.

Index

Achtenberg, Roberta, 58
ACLU v. Echohawk, 152
Adam, Barry D., 17
Adams, William E., Jr., 147–48
Ad-Hoc Task Force to Challenge
  Sodomy Laws, 40, 41–42, 85–87, 96,
  99, 106, 137, 248n. 45. *See also*
  Lambda Legal Defense and Education Fund
AIDS: cases and case law concerning,
  12–13, 37–38, 43; history of, 42, 112;
  as justification for discrimination
  against lgb people, 43, 78–81, 242n.
  26, 248n. 34; legislative response to,
  40, 150–52; relationship between
  AIDS and gay rights, 3, 43–44, 46,
  51, 142, 150–51
Alaska, 191–94, 197–99; cases and case
  law concerning gay rights, 12, 175,
  183–84; initiatives and referenda
  concerning gay rights, 144; laws and
  legislation concerning gay rights,
  183–84, 198. *See also Brause and
  Dugan v. Bureau of Vital Statistics*
Altman, Dennis, 24
Alumbaugh, Steve, 75
Amendment 2. *See* Colorado, Amendment 2
American Civil Liberties Union
  (ACLU), 47, 83, 85, 111, 178,
  186–87; gay rights cases, 4, 52, 62,
  81, 87, 96, 104, 107, 137–38, 150–52;
  Lesbian and Gay Rights Project, 40,
  41, 47, 85, 122, 125–31, 160; New
  York Civil Liberties Union, 28, 34,

36, 37, 41; other regional affiliates,
  22, 41, 47, 65, 82–83, 84–85, 96, 101,
  110, 160; position on homosexuality, 18, 22; relationship with
  Lambda, 28, 34, 36, 41, 52, 56–57
American Law Institute (ALI), 19–20,
  62, 238n. 9
American National Election Study
  (ANES), 114–17, 251n. 15
American Psychiatric Association, 55,
  71
American Psychological Association,
  55, 103
Americans with Disabilities Act
  (ADA), 112
Antigay initiatives and referenda, 3,
  52, 124, 143–49; political campaigns
  to enact, 152–59; state ballot
  requirements, 149–50, 154; types of,
  147–49. See also *Citizens for
  Responsible Behavior v. Superior
  Court*; Colorado, Amendment 2;
  Romer v. Evans
*Appeal in Pima County Juvenile
  Action B-10489*, 93
Arizona, 54, 93, 98, 144–45, 147
Arkansas, 98, 105, 111, 129–30

*Baehr v. Anderson. See Baehr v.
  Lewin*
Baehr v. Lewin: decision, 52–53,
  180–81; facts, 178; impact of, 53,
  178–83, 187–88, 194–96, 199–200,
  217–18; litigation of, 178
Baehr v. Miike. See Baehr v. Lewin